PKI Security Solutions for the Enterprise:

Solving HIPAA, E-Paper Act, and Other Compliance Issues

PKI Security Solutions for the Enterprise:

Solving HIPAA, E-Paper Act, and Other Compliance Issues

Kapil Raina

WILEY

Wiley Publishing, Inc.

Publisher: Robert Ipsen
Executive Editor: Carol Long
Assistant Developmental Editor: Adaobi Obi Tulton
Editorial Manager: Kathryn Malm
Managing Editor: Angela Smith
Text Design & Composition: Wiley Composition Services

This book is printed on acid-free paper. ∞

Published by Wiley Publishing, Inc., Indianapolis, Indiana
Published simultaneously in Canada

Wiley also publishes its books in a variety of electronic formats. Some content that appears in print may not be available in electronic books.

Library of Congress Cataloging-in-Publication Data:

ISBN: 0-471-31529-X

Printed in the United States of America

10 9 8 7 6 5 4 3 2 1

To Amrita,
For all of her love and understanding
in helping me reach my dreams.

Contents

Acknowledgments

As with any complex work such as this book, quite a number of people have helped contribute to the knowledge and wisdom found in this book. I have listed those who have directly contributed to this work through their guidance or direct contribution to some of the material. I can never thank all of these people enough, as their respective expertise truly helped make this book a realistic, real-world project.

Adaobi Obi Tulton, Assistant Developmental Editor, for her untiring efforts to help develop and produce this book. I want to thank her for going above and beyond to help keep this project on time and with a high degree of quality and content. Her expertise has greatly enhanced the quality of this book.

Bikram Bakshi, Director, Business Development, Bionetrix, Inc. Thanks to Bikram for his contribution to the Chapter 5 case study about biometrics and PKI and personal support for this project. His extraordinary effort has added an invaluable element to the book.

Carol Long, Executive Acquisitions Editor, Wiley Technology Publishing, for her guidance in content, scope, flexibility, and vision on this project.

David Ramon, CEO, USA.net, for his ongoing support for this and some of my other security book projects.

Doug Jones, Executive Chief Architect, YAS Broadband Venture, for his contribution and guidance to the DOCSIS and broadband material in Chapter 9.

Geoff Kahler, VP Marketing, Identrus, LLC for his guidance in the financial solutions including Identrus for Chapter 6.

Greg Worch, formerly with Identrus, LLC, for his guidance in developing material and case studies for Chapter 6.

Gregory Alan Bolcer, CTO, Endeavors Technology, Inc, for his and the whole Endeavors team's help in developing material in Chapter 8 for the IM case study.

Jennifer Angle, Director Product Marketing, USA.net, for her and the USA.net team's guidance in some of the secure email solutions coverage.

Julian Waits, VP of Sales and Business Development, Bionetrix, Inc. Julian's contribution and guidance on biometrics and PKI is very much appreciated.

Karla Friede, who in addition to working as a Marketing Consultant for Flatrock, has a depth of industry experience including VP of Marketing for Geotrust, The Ascent Group, and Mentor Graphics. Thanks for her efforts in her contribution to the material for Chapter 9's case study, "Case Study: Flatrock Levels the IPSec VPN Space."

Kim Novak, Technical Project Manager, VeriSign, Inc., for her help and guidance in developing the resources needed for the DOCSIS-related discussions in Chapter 9.

Louisa Hebden and Sharon McMaw, Royal Bank of Scotland, for their assistance and guidance in developing material for Chapter 6.

Minna Tao, for her guidance in development and coverage of financial topics related to PKI for Chapter 6.

Nancy Davoust, Executive Security consultant, YAS Broadband Venture, for her contribution and guidance to the DOCSIS and broadband material in Chapter 9.

Rick Triola, Chairman & CEO, ezEscrow, Inc. Thanks to Rick and his team for contributions to the Chapter 6 case study for electronic signatures for mortgages.

Roger Wood, Senior Product Manager, Flatrock, Inc. Roger has seventeen years of networking experience including more than nine years with Cisco Systems. His contribution and guidance on the material for Chapter 9's case study, "Case Study: Flatrock Levels the IPSec VPN Space," has been invaluable.

Rouzbeh Yassini, Founder and CEO, YAS broadband Venture, for his contribution and guidance to the DOCSIS and broadband material in Chapter 9.

Sarah Granger, Technical Editor for this book. An *enormous* thanks to Sarah for working with crazy deadlines and intensely complex material. Her input has been instrumental in producing a work that is clear and comprehensive. Her past experience in technical writing has been invaluable in developing a high-quality book in such a short time frame.

Introduction

Increasingly as the world relies on electronic commerce, the need for security becomes critical. The Internet provides an excellent vehicle for increasing transaction efficiencies and extending the scope of communication and business. Perhaps the most critical element of security is the ability to provide trust and confidence to transactions over the Internet.

Some may argue that we already have tools for affording trust to Internet transactions and communications. The Internet, though, can still be viewed only as an ancient settlement that has point solutions for affording security for its residents. For example, solutions like anti-virus software or firewalls do not help in establishing the identity of the parties during transactions. Nor can such solutions guarantee an understanding of the level of trust when dealing with a merchant or another individual.

So how can we provide trust and confidence to the Internet? To accommodate the scale of transactions across the Internet, some of the few technologies that can accomplish this include Public Key Infrastructure (PKI). For many, PKI induces fear of complex and long deployments. Perhaps this may have been the case several years ago when PKI was not considered essential nor were pre-integrated PKI applications ready for use.

Today, PKI has been viewed as critical not only to the commercial sector but also to the government sector. As a result, many aspects required for successful PKI, such as insurance and legal aspects, have been greatly improved. For example, most countries within the last few years have passed laws that make digital signatures legally equivalent to physically drafted signatures. In addition, many countries also have regulatory elements to the Certificate Authorities (CAs) to ensure the quality of their operations and in some cases their viability to support national projects based on PKI.

Have PKI deployments become easier? Yes, to a large degree. Part of the offset of the complexity of PKI has been in the increased education of IT professionals, improved skill sets, and simplification by PKI vendors in the deployment complexity.

Overview of the Book and Technology

When the idea for this book came to me, I was interested in focusing primarily on showing how PKI is being used in various segments of business and government. During this research I was very surprised by how extensive the use of PKI is and how much it has penetrated all aspects of ecommerce. Even more surprising was the number of governments around the world that now have digital signature laws and regulatory requirements for CAs and other organizations related to PKI.

This book covers the essential basics of PKI. My intent, though, was not to cover the theoretical aspects, but rather show specific examples and provide models for PKI development and deployment. There are already many fine books on PKI design and architecture. In many ways, both technologists and business people can use this book as it provides an understanding of how the technology can be used and how it can be financially justified.

Wherever possible, each section of the book includes a case study or a reference to an actual implementation of that aspect of the PKI technology. This realism highlights how PKI is already being used and can serve as a model for making decisions about if and how to use PKI to provide trust and confidence on the Internet.

How This Book Is Organized

The book is divided into three main parts:

Part One: Trust Basics: Ins and Outs of PKI.   In this section, information is given to provide a base knowledge of PKI. The concepts of PKI and how the technology works are discussed. Furthermore, basic concepts on how to understand PKI from a business aspect are also discussed. Because the business justification of PKI is as important as the technology itself, both aspects are discussed in the same section. Although this section gives a very brief glimpse of the technology, it does provide a sufficient, independent basis for understanding later elements of the book.

Part Two: Solutions for Trust.   With the understanding of the basics of PKI, this section describes how PKI is implemented and used in various segments. The breakdown by vertical applications was designed to show

how PKI varies from segment to segment. In addition, this structure allows for discussion of specific industry consortia and standards bodies that guide PKI development to address specific, unique needs of that vertical. Some of the most popular vertical applications were chosen. Nonetheless, there are many more not discussed in this book that may be found through the additional resources referenced in the Appendix.

Part Three: Trust Solutions Guide.   This section aims to provide concrete vendor and solution examples. Think of this section as a high-level overview of specific companies and products that can help achieve the aims discussed in Part II, "Solutions for Trust." The aim here is to provide a starting point so that you can choose the right combination of vendors and products for your PKI deployment. For those of you already using PKI, this section can show the other areas in which PKI can be leveraged, either through existing products you may already have or new products that can enhance your existing PKI infrastructure.

Although the book has been structured for an audience with very little knowledge of PKI and related topics, for readers who already have an advanced understanding of the technology, Parts Two and Three, "Solutions for Trust" and the "Trust Solutions Guide," will serve as an excellent reference. In fact, the book has been designed to be used as a reference tool as much as a tutorial. The book does contain information that is of a time-sensitive nature, and thus the Appendix becomes useful in helping you keep up to date on events in this area of security.

Note that although some applications are covered in a particular vertical, that does not mean that it is the only vertical that has utility for that security application. The intent has been to emphasize some of the more popular uses of a particular application within the most commonly used vertical.

Chapter 1: What Is Trust?

This chapter explains the fundamental requirement for leveraging the Internet for ecommerce and trust. It explains how trust can be defined, how it is currently managed, and some key elements required to ensure a lasting trust relationship between two parties.

Chapter 2: Complexities of PKI

With the goal of achieving trust, as established in Chapter 1, this chapter focuses on the most efficient solution for establishing this trust, PKI. The chapter reviews the basic concepts and introduces tips and techniques to guide in successful implementation. This chapter is important for beginners to the technology and was designed to be an introductory text to this security technology.

Chapter 3: Best Practices of PKI

In order to avoid the pitfalls of implementing PKI, this chapter reviews best practices in designing and implementing PKI solutions. Design, implementation, vendor selection, and choosing insource or outsource models are all discussed. Although it is very difficult to capture the breadth of knowledge in this area in a single chapter, the text takes an overview approach that highlights the main points to consider in PKI deployment.

Chapter 4: Selling PKI

Realizing that designing and implementing PKI is only part of the security battle, learning how to justify PKI to customers, partners, and internal decision makers is critical for a successful security deployment of PKI. This chapter provides tools, including quantitative metrics, to help rationalize and guide decision-making processes in how and when PKI provides cost-efficient solutions for security problems.

Chapter 5: Healthcare Solutions

Focused on the healthcare vertical, this chapter covers those topics directly relevant to the healthcare industry. Laws and unique attributes to this vertical are discussed, and those key drivers for the technology are covered in detail. Many examples are given to show the reader actual implementations in healthcare for PKI. Consortiums and standard bodies are highlighted to indicate the progress and important developments that PKI brings to the healthcare community.

Chapter 6: Financial Solutions

Security is never more important than when dealing with money. The financial vertical has specific legal and business drivers, which make PKI ideal as a security solution for that space. Examples, in the form of case studies and sidebars, are given to provide reference models for readers' own implementations and development projects. Although only a few specific legal aspects are covered, all of the material can be used as a basis for developing models for other PKIs, including models for financial organizations in all parts of the world.

Chapter 7: Government Solutions

Government deployment of PKI solutions truly shows the scalability of PKI technology, given the large numbers of users involved in such deployments.

This chapter shows examples of legal drivers and applications that governments around the world are using to deploy PKI. One of the most important aspects of this chapter is the emphasis on how governments treat PKI as a national infrastructure and provide regulatory guidance to ensure the quality and sustainability of CAs.

Chapter 8: Communications Solutions

It has been long said that one of the killer applications for the Internet has been communications applications such as email. As a result of the impact of communications on our daily personal and professional lives, this chapter covers security communications strategies. The chapter covers the range of applications from email to instant messaging. A key emphasis is to describe a variety of methods, spanning the user experience from very secure solutions to easy-to-use, mobile solutions.

Chapter 9: Other Solutions

Of course, it is impossible to cover all the applications that use PKI to create trust and confidence in electronic transactions. An attempt is made, though, to capture solutions here not discussed thus far. Much of this chapter focuses on device certificate applications. Device certificates are digital credentials that identify a device (rather than a person). Device certificates are quickly becoming the most popular and prevalent use of digital certificates.

Chapter 10: Overview of Trust Solutions

One of the challenges with discussing models and applications of a technology is that information alone does not help in choosing and understanding specific products and companies in the market. This chapter is dedicated to helping users relate specific products on the market to the various categories discussed throughout this book. Although this material will change as products and companies change, this serves as a good base to learn about actual product examples.

Chapter 11: The Future of PKI

This chapter addresses future trends and emerging technologies in the PKI space. It is important to keep aware of trends in this space to plan appropriately and take advantage of changes. As the security market consolidates, companies should see big benefits in consolidated functionality.

Appendix

The appendix presents a variety of resources and guides to additional information. Security is a never-ending game of improving the level of confidence of people and machines in conducting safe, secure transactions. The appendix also has more international material, to ensure that the reader is aware, regardless of where he or she may be in the world, that PKI is directly relevant globally.

Who Should Read This Book

The audience for this book can be quite varied, ranging from novices in PKI technology to security experts looking to gain specific knowledge. In general, the first part of the book has been designed to give an overview of the PKI technology along with the challenges and advantages the technology offers. The next part of the book would be common for any reader as it highlights current, realistic examples of how PKI has been used. This will serve as an ideal model for all readers. The final part of the book is meant as a reference guide to help readers understand specific companies and products.

Business Decision Makers

One interesting aspect of this book is that, while it does focus heavily on the technology, a fair amount of effort has been made to ensure that the business aspects of this technology have been discussed. All too many times, technologists create wonderful solutions, only to be left unable to justify their expense to the decision makers. Specific chapters, such as Chapters 3, 4, and 10, include elements that highlight resource and time discussions to help guide decision makers in making appropriate resource allocations for successful security deployment. As a decision maker, you are looking for the risk-to-reward ratio as well as business justification strategies. For this purpose Chapter 4 has been designed specifically for you.

Project Managers/Consultants

Chapters 2 and 3 are most relevant to project managers as specific examples of project timelines are discussed. Techniques and tips (as well as challenges) for successful deployment are discussed. One key aspect that all project managers need to understand is how to parallelize PKI task deployments.

Absolute Beginners

If you are new to PKI and related security technologies, then you must read the book from cover to cover. The book progresses in its depth of the topics covered, leading to the final chapter, which discusses future trends of the technology. It is recommended, if more detail on theoretical design and architecture of PKI-related technologies is required, that other books on PKI be explored. The Appendix will also prove useful as pointers to other resources that can explain various topic areas.

Tools You Will Need

No specific software is associated with this book. As a side note, it is important to understand that many of the products and technologies mentioned in this book are usually available in some type of trial or test modes. It is recommended that the reader evaluate any software related to PKI technology in some type of pilot program. The advantages of PKI security solutions can far outweigh the effort of deployment; however, it is important to proceed with care in deploying enterprise-wide applications of any type.

You can refer to my website, www.securitypundit.com for further resources and guides beyond what this book covers.

Summary

This book was designed to impart tools and techniques for leveraging PKI as a method to create trust and confidence in electronic transactions and communications. Although this book is only a starting point, that it focuses on solutions and real-life applications should be a good base for understanding in this area. Try not to think of PKI as having to "arrive" as a mainstream application but rather as an application that is already in widespread use across many countries and vertical applications. The "Year of PKI" has already come and gone. We are now in the "Decade of PKI."

Trust Basics: Ins and Outs of PKI

CHAPTER 1

What Is Trust?

The hot new buzzword for the twenty-first century is *trust*. We are asked to trust that Web site purchases are safe, we are asked to trust that the car dealer is making us a good deal, and we are even asked to trust in our local politicians! This move into trust instead of security has been positive for the computer security field. We cannot avoid security issues, but we can create an umbrella solution that may include risk mitigation in addition to security techniques, also known as "trust." Trust consists of more than just secure computer systems. After all, the security of a computer system extends far beyond just a well-protected operating system. We have to consider the reliability of inside employees, physical security, and so on in a more holistic view.

Trust in the Digital World

Trust must be applied in the context of the business or use of the trust application. For example, in financial applications, the consequences from loss of use of systems are extremely high. As a result, the level of trust between two transacting parties must be much higher than that of, for example, consumer applications, where an individual loss is relatively small. As we will see in the rest of this book, the application of trust varies from industry to industry. Therefore, we provide, in these initial chapters, a generic platform and set of guidelines. Each industry, and to some degree each specific company, must examine this platform and customize and apply it accordingly. We can safely make some assumptions, though, that will be used as a basis for comparing levels of trust among peer merchants or companies.

Defining Trust

Trust consists of three key elements:

Predictability. The ability to consistently produce an expected (positive) result will allow the consumer of these services to waive the need to constantly keep a high state of vigilance. The more predictable the security, service, and quality of an online merchant, the easier it will be for a consumer to purchase those services.

Assets. Generally we are not concerned with trust unless there are significant assets (whether physical or logical) that risk being damaged or lost. The greater the value, the more trust becomes a requirement. Web sites like eBay, an online auction site, use partners for escrow services for higher-value trades (usually over U.S. $500) as a method of increasing trust in transactions between two unknown parties.

Uncertainty. Trust is required when there is an amount of uncertainty in the ability to verify an operation or result. Generally, if all information is known about the parties and the transaction, then the need for trust is greatly reduced. Most transactions, however, occur with a level of uncertainty, including unknown history with buyer or seller, unknown quality of service or goods, and so on.

To better understand the concepts of trust, let's take the example of a merchant Web site. A merchant must accomplish two main business goals: new sales (selling to new customers) and renewal sales (selling to repeat customers). New sales without renewals create very high costs of customer acquisitions. One way to increase renewals is to create a higher level of predictability of service and security through the initial transaction experience. Predictability can be achieved by using common security protection methods, such as setting up the systems to produce the comforting "lock" symbol (which indicates a secure connection via the Secure Sockets Layer (SSL) protocol in the browser. In addition, a certification logo or privacy statement can provide information that a trusted third party has also objectively reviewed this site.

In our example of the merchant site, the merchant's assets can be measured in two ways: hard assets (the goods or services that are being sold) and goodwill (the branding and positioning of the merchant and/or the goods being sold). For most companies, the goods and the branding (that is, the reputation) are equally important. Losing goods to fraud results in a direct material loss. Tarnished branding or reputation can result in a decrease of future sales (for example, Andersen Consulting after its involvement with the Enron scandal in 2002).

Finally, the merchant's consumer must believe that the data, such as credit card information, is being transmitted to a place where it will be handled with good security practices. Not being able to see the transaction take place, as would be possible in a physical store, for example, means the user must make a leap of faith. Too much of a leap (for example, dealing with an unknown merchant) may prevent the user from proceeding. An example of this as a key marketing tool can be found in a campaign launched by Hotwire, an online travel booking company, back in May 2002. Hotwire positioned itself against Priceline by claiming a user could get airline fares before having to submit credit card information. On the surface, this appears to ease consumer fears that credit card information will be needed only once the flight is selected. Priceline, however, does not necessarily use the credit card information provided unless a transaction takes place. The leap of faith that Priceline will not use the credit card information until the end user is ready creates the need for trust.

The interesting aspect about trust is that it takes a long time to build, but it can disappear virtually overnight. One key example includes Arthur Andersen's downfall as a result of its affiliation with the Enron scandal. The flip side of this is that once a user provides trust, the user tends to be loyal. The less trust that is required, the easier it is for the end user to flip to another merchant. In essence, for a merchant to retain consumers and increase renewal sales, *it is essential to create such a value in being trusted that it would be more difficult for the consumer to reestablish that level of trust with another merchant.*

Implementing Trust

How do we implement these concepts of trust in an Internet infrastructure? In terms of our focus, computer security, we can see that several technologies have been developed to support each of the three main pillars of trust (see Table 1.1).

Table 1.1 Sample Technologies Mapping to Trust Pillars

TECHNOLOGY	HOW TRUST PILLARS ARE SUPPORTED
Vulnerability analysis	Mitigates attacks on assets to increase predictability and reduce uncertainty of service quality.
Online escrow services	Provide for protection of assets when dealing with uncertainty with unknown parties. Predictability is achieved through a history of escrow transactions.
Audit trails	Allow for analysis and screening of issues that reduce predictability of service.
Firewalls	Protect assets from online attacks.

Smart cards increase predictability through standard methods of authentication and storage of security credentials. Implementation of trust turns out to be, as expected, much more difficult than simply understanding the meaning of trust. Establishing trust in our everyday lives can take months, years, or even decades. In the world of digital commerce, trust must be achieved more quickly and sustained more effectively.

Trust Policies

One of the simplest, yet most effective, methods of establishing trust for a digital commerce scenario is to establish well-thought-out, transparent policies of trust. These policies would cover (at a minimum) the following concepts:

- Privacy
- Proper use of information
- Recourse in the event of a breach of trust
- Internal mechanisms to ensure continuity of trust
- User consent

Privacy

Privacy policies are designed to ensure that the user understands the impact of sharing personal information with a business. Given that the Internet can accelerate the dissemination of information, it is important to help users understand how personal information will be used. In general, a posted privacy policy (on a Web site) creates a binding contract between the user and the owner of the site. This means that users must review the privacy policy to ensure that they can comply with the details listed. One example of a privacy policy can be noted at Procter & Gamble's Web site, www.pg.com/privacy.htm.

Proper Use of Information

Another aspect of trust policies is the proper use of information. For example, can information be used against a person, such as in determining benefits for a life or healthcare insurance policy? One common business tactic is to screen and classify users of a particular service and sell that information or list of people with those criteria to another company (usually referred to as *affiliates* in legal documents). Such transactions open up problems such as unsolicited email, mail, or phone calls, preclassification for services such as credit cards, and more. This vague definition of "affiliates" presents perhaps the biggest loophole in trust policies, given that "affiliate" could mean, essentially, any

PRIVACY DEFENSE

Consumers can take several steps to minimize breaches of privacy including the following:

◆ **Avoid disclosing personal information.**

◆ **Use temporary or nonregular email accounts for email contacts to unknown parties.**

◆ **Lock down browser software by turning off cookies, ActiveX, Java, and other features. Turning them on only for trusted sites is the best way to prevent malicious software from stealing personal information or planting viruses on your systems.**

◆ **Read privacy policies on any site that may ask for personal information. If possible, never reveal information. (If forced to enter information, use fake information if it does not violate any laws or affect the outcome of the service.)**

Ironically, there are more standards and guidelines for online privacy policies than for physical merchant policies. For example, many stores ask for home telephone numbers to bring up a customer's purchase records. This allows the store to track purchase habits to a particular individual. Some grocery stores use "clipless coupon cards" or "club cards," which allow individual purchasing habits to be recorded and shared with affiliated partner companies (that is, they sell your personal habit history!). In addition, many organizations (like your local library) may ask for social security numbers that, legally, do not have the right to require that information. It is important that physical and online privacy defense measures are taken to prevent a loss of privacy or, worse, identity theft.

company that does business with that online merchant. Some companies entice consumers to reveal personal information in exchange for being eligible for sweepstakes or drawings. You stand a better chance of having your identity sold or stolen than of winning the sweepstakes!

Recourse in the Event of Breach of Trust

Given that it is not possible to maintain a 100 percent trusted environment all the time, what are some recourses for a user on a system claiming to be trusted? Generally, there will be some financial guarantees in the way of insurance (for the trusted merchant). Quite often, a policy will state that a dispute must be taken to arbitration (versus taken to a court of law). Arbitration generally tends to lead to far fewer consequences for the merchant than a court battle.

For large sites that take trust seriously, a Chief Privacy Officer or Chief Information Security Officer will be on staff to address misuse of information. Unfortunately, most often the only recourse for a breach of privacy is termination of use of the Web site's services.

Continuity of Trust

Internal mechanisms should be in place to ensure that trust is not an external promise, but also a vital part of the business's operations. Examples of internal trust mechanisms include strict employee background checks, secured physical facilities, and auditing of business changes. During the Enron/Arthur Andersen scandal of 2002, the major reason why Enron's irregularities were not found earlier was that a number of internal auditing processes were bypassed. Merchants must assure consumers that the company is taking steps to guarantee they have trusted employees and processes. Good trust policies will explicitly state if and how employees and affiliates of the site are trained to use the privacy policy.

User Consent

Finally, a mechanism for consent from the user is required. This is commonly referred to as *opting in*. Many organizations either do not allow for consent or do not have technology systems set up to monitor and comply with opt-in preferences. By certain laws, the concept of opt-in or the opposite, *opt-out*, can carry financial penalties if the merchant does not adhere to the posted policies. The difficult part for consumers is that most merchants will automatically assume an opt-in unless the user specifically asks to be opted out. This assumption puts the burden on the user and becomes quite complex if each affiliate requires a separate opt-out communication as well. Furthermore, changes to these policies are usually posted only at the privacy policy Web page, which, of course, may change without notice.

Trust Infrastructure

For most technical professionals, the most common area related to trust in digital transactions is that of creating trusted infrastructure. Trusted infrastructure is the implementation of systems, applications, and processes that allow for reliable, safe processing of transactions. Components of this infrastructure include firewalls, routers, virus scanners, vulnerability assessments, and hardened servers. Most IT expenditure occurs in this area as it is generally the most tangible area of trust protection.

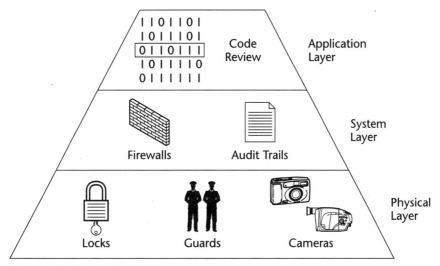

Figure 1.1   Trust infrastructure components.

We can look at trust infrastructure in layers, as illustrated in Figure 1.1. The simplest layer to lock down is the physical layer. Given that there are a finite number of risks associated with physical trust attacks, it is simpler to protect that layer over others. Methods such as security guards, locks, and alarms are all used to help ensure that physical access to a data center or similar resources will be difficult. One interesting problem that arises for the physical layer is that it might be difficult for someone to break into a well-protected site, but it may be easier simply to destroy it. Hence it is important to have a well-thought-out disaster recovery plan, including hot or warm standby data centers (which allow for backup facilities to take over in the event of a primary data center failure).

Physical Layer

Although we do not generally think of physical access as a realistic threat to modern day infrastructure, a breach of physical security can allow for a breach in logical security. In general, we need to ensure that the following have been implemented to guarantee a high level of confidence in our physical layer protection:

- Restricted access via multiple authentication mechanisms (for example, a biometric device and a card reader)
- Constant security monitoring including video, audio, and possible environmental sensor monitoring of outside and inside areas
- Trained security personnel
- Unalterable security logs of badge accesses, security guard patrol check-ins, and so on

System Layer

The next layer, the system layer, involves a number of systems interacting with each other. Generally, trust is more difficult at this level because each system individually must be secured as well as their interactions. At this level, we take steps like hardening an operating system and ensuring that only actively used ports are available. This means that only those applications and systems that require access get access.

The two key components that need to be protected at the system layer are the operating system and the network. Operating system flaws are the basis for many attacks against system infrastructure. Operating systems are vulnerable because they are constantly undergoing revisions. As a result, administrators are not always able to keep up with patches to fix vulnerabilities. In addition, security updates for operating systems like the Microsoft platform can sometimes break core functionality, causing many system administrators to delay security updates.

The network components are even more vulnerable than operating systems because there are so many points of compromise. A typical network will consist of multiple zones: intranet, Internet, and extranet. As a result, a complex set of technologies must be used to guard against attacks from both outside and inside the organization. Generally, most organizations are more vulnerable from the inside. A large number of studies have shown that organizations are more susceptible to insider attacks than direct attacks from the Internet. Keeping networks secure from insider attacks is a bit more difficult, but it is not impossible. Some key points in securing networks from insider attacks are as follows:

Ensure firewalls are used internally to protect systems from unauthorized users.   Such techniques help limit internal employee hacking and provide additional safeguards should the outside perimeters be breached.

Switched networks can minimize the efforts of network sniffers.   Switched networks make it more difficult for internal nodes to see all traffic across the network. Although it is possible to sniff the network at the wiring closet, the idea is to make this process more difficult in order to deter some attempts.

Strong access controls allow for increasing the level of trust the user requires to access the private network.   Whether the security policy calls for well-chosen passwords or biometric devices, access controls should be well defined and enforced. The greatest chance of breach is from the individual employee workstation because it bypasses most routers and firewalls set up to protect against breaches from the Internet. The most prevalent example of this is the use of personal digital assistants (PDAs). PDAs generally are attached directly to a node on a network, usually bypassing firewalls, routers, and virus checkers. Thus, a virus or other malicious code can be injected into the network directly.

Audit trails can be used to track down what happened after an incident or to detect suspicious activity.   It is vital that these log files be kept separate from the actual production systems. Furthermore, the logs should be stored in a manner that makes them unalterable (to prevent rogue system administrators from covering up their tracks).

Application Layer

The application layer focuses on those applications that utilize the system and infrastructure layers. This is perhaps the most difficult layer to secure and for which to provide trust. Given that the number of uses of an application, such as a software utility, is greater than in any other layer, the potential areas of security risk are greater. This is the layer where computer viruses attack systems, where exploits in browsers can be found, and where email can be intercepted and manipulated. To address security at this level, several technologies must be used.

Some of the key areas in which an application layer can be compromised include the following:

- Poor memory or user data management, which can result in buffer overflow or unintentional acceptance of malicious data (usually caused by inadequately screening user input or preventing more memory from being accessed than is actually available).

- Having too many features enabled. The greater the number of options in an application that are enabled, the greater the chance one of those options will be compromised (this rule of thumb can also be applied to the systems layer).

We can essentially break up defensive tools at this layer into the following categories:

- Defensive software (for example, virus blocking or scanning)
- Proactive software (for example, vulnerability scanning or testing)
- Human review (for example, manually reviewing application code for possible security issues)

Because this layer is the most accessible, the application layer is generally the most difficult layer to protect. After all, anyone who might access a merchant Web site, for example, will immediately have access to the application (that is, ActiveX) that allows the transaction to take place. Access to the system or physical layer is a bit more difficult.

Finally, it is important to understand that compromise in one layer can lead to compromise in another layer. It is common for the system layer to be attacked and then used to access application data. For example, a cracker may attack an operating system and use exploits in that attack to access customer data, such as credit card information, which resides at the application layer.

Trust Affiliations

In our daily lives we have always accepted transitive trust relationships. For example, if our friend gives a warm introduction to a person we have not met, we generally tend to accept this stranger with much more trust than if we had met this person on our own. In this case, because we trust our friend, we also trust that he or she will make a trustworthy choice for a friend as well.

Likewise, in the world of the Internet, a number of third-party trust associations or affiliations have appeared. Noted are affiliations for organizations, Web sites (specifically), and personnel. An ideal trust environment would have the ability to obtain affiliation certification for all three types, choosing the most stringent. Some examples of these associations are listed in Table 1.2.

Table 1.2 Trust Affiliation Examples

COMMON NAME	TYPE	FORMAL NAME	DESCRIPTION
BBB online	Web site	Better Business Bureau	Has programs for reliability as well as privacy
CCSA	Personnel	Certification in Control Self-Assessment	Systems audit focused
CISA	Personnel	Certified Information Systems Auditor	Systems audit focused
CISSP	Personnel	Certified Information Systems Security Professional	Broad experience and knowledge-based security certification
Common Criteria	Systems	Common Criteria (umbrella name)	Series of security practices and certifications focused for an international audience
CPP	Personnel	Certified Protection Professional	General security experience and certification
GIAC	Personnel	Global Information Assurance Certification	SANS Institute (series of technology-specific certifications)

Table 1.2 *(continued)*

COMMON NAME	TYPE	FORMAL NAME	DESCRIPTION
Good Housekeeping	Web site	Good Housekeeping Web Certification	Proper information and privacy disclosure and ease of commerce
SAS70	Systems	Statement on Auditing Standards No. 70	Audit of systems processes
TrustE	Web site	TrustE (founded by EFF)	Focus on privacy-related issues

Essentially the brand of these associations identifies the trust associated with their recommendations. Associations increase a level of confidence for the consumer when he or she encounters an unknown site; however, the value of this service lies in the success of the service and its history.

In general, most of these affiliations require a certain level of auditing and adherence to "good security" principles. Given that the definition of these principles varies greatly, the consumer must, essentially, guess at which affiliations carry the strongest meaning. The Better Business Bureau (BBB) has probably been the most successful. Given that the BBB is well understood in the physical world, it carries its brand name into the digital world. The actual adoption of the BBB and similar affiliates is still relatively low as compared to the number of Web sites — most merchants now rely on technology, such as SSL, which represents that data is protected in transit from the merchant's Web site to the user's browser. SSL, however, does not make any guarantees about how the information is treated and stored once it reaches the merchant. For example, if the merchant's computers are not well protected from hackers, the merchant may suffer an electronic break-in at its data center (which is far easier to do than breaking SSL).

The other thought to keep in mind is that most consumers purchase their goods with credit cards. Credit card companies have liability waivers for transactions and will allow a consumer to refute a charge with minimal or no financial repercussions. With this protection, many consumers may not even value the affiliations because they have financial protection. This, however, is definitely a false sense of protection. After all, if an identity is stolen, a waiver of responsibility will not solve a longer-term problem with destroyed credit. Identity theft is growing at an alarming rate in many countries; hence, the merchant is not only protecting a single transaction, but also ensuring the protection of an identity. Trust affiliations help ensure that there is less risk of identity theft at those affiliated sites.

Legal Issues with Trust in the Electronic World

One may argue that the biggest benefactors of the WWW revolution were lawyers. When the untamed domain of the Web was shown to be useful for business transactions, all sorts of laws (and lawsuits!) appeared. In many ways, lawmakers attempted to apply laws of the physical world to the online world. Given the distributed nature of the Internet our existing laws did not apply smoothly to the Web. An example is how some European laws affected what U.S. companies could sell or advertise on their Web sites. For example, in 2000, AOL ran into problems with decency standards when allowing content acceptable in the United States to be viewed in Europe. Although the services were hosted in the United States, the users were found all over the world. Privacy, consumer protection, and child protection laws varied around the world and thus had to be applied differently. This process of restricting the Internet continues with much debate.

Binding Trust with the Law

Generally, a compromise of privacy is a compromise of trust; therefore, trust relationships must also protect users' privacy. A number of the laws that have been developed around the concept of trust focus on this key area: privacy. The different areas in which legal issues affect trust and ecommerce can be broken down into three broad categories (there are many more, but we have chosen the most relevant for our discussion):

Consumer protection laws address the protection of consumer rights for online purchases.   Although these laws vary from country to country, some of the strongest consumer protection laws are in the United States. European and Asian countries do not have such strong recourse for consumers when a merchant violates certain policies or laws. In the United States, most consumers have multiple credit cards and use them more frequently for online transactions than their Asian counterparts because of strong consumer protection laws.

Privacy laws address the use and disclosure of personal information.   These laws also vary from country to country. In general, privacy laws are strong in Western countries, especially in the European Union. The United States is still catching up to European standards in key areas such as healthcare information privacy.

Contract formation laws address the legal enforceability of online contracts and transactions.   Luckily for online merchants, this has been resolved for most major countries in the world. In general, many countries now treat online transactions with the same power as paper transactions. This allows for all sorts of applications that can streamline lengthy legal document processes.

The following is a summary of some specific laws (that are more U.S.-centric) that fall under the three broad categories defined above:

- Electronic Communications Privacy Act regulates the monitoring of online information unless specific legal directives make exceptions.

- Computer Fraud and Abuse Act of 1986, 18 U.S.C. 1001, established felony penalties for breaking into federal interest computer systems and penalties for illegally obtained computer password trafficking. Essentially this law clarified that unauthorized computer entry was considered illegal. In the early 1980s, entry into U.S. federal computer systems was not considered illegal.

- Healthcare Insurance Portability and Accountability Act (HIPAA) provides guidance on how confidential patient information can be treated and accessed. We will discuss this in more detail in Chapter 5.

- E-sign Laws have become a necessity because several federal and state laws in the United States and in many other countries now grant digital forms of transactions the same power as verbal or written contracts (depending on the country). This provides for a powerful need to validate and trust online senders of documents and other materials.

- Children's Online Privacy Protection Act (COPPA) specifies practices for Web sites that cater to children age 13 and under. This is important for retail and toy sites that may try to attract children in the hopes of having them influence their parents to choose one product over another.

- Children's Online Protection Act (COPA) essentially provides restrictions for Web sites that require parental involvement and control to authorize either site access or some site transactions. This ensures that the child did not stumble across harmful or dangerous information or activities without the parents' consent. Note that COPA is under judicial review because the ACLU (American Civil Liberties Union) has brought the U.S. government to court on the legality of enforcing the law. A final decision has not yet been reached (it was sent to a lower court by the U.S. Supreme Court without judgment in May 2002).

- Financial Services Modernization Act (Gramm-Leach-Bliley Act) requires clear disclosure of financial institutions' privacy statements, including how private information is used with affiliates and third parties. The law requires opt-out ability, which allows consumers the right not to have their information shared or sold to unknown parties.

P3P

One key working initiative that focuses on applying privacy to the Internet is the Platform for Privacy Preferences Project (P3P). The P3P is a World Wide Web Consortium (W3C) specification in development. The P3P's goal is to create standard Web site policies that can be read by a machine. This would allow the development of tools to measure, compare, and even filter privacy among different Web sites. In this manner, the level of privacy would have some reasonable method of comparison. Currently, trust affiliations (as discussed in the previous section) are the only safeguard for privacy; however, trust affiliations are relatively expensive and require constant updates. Furthermore, the value of the results of the trust affiliation review is very subjective and varies greatly from company to company.

Digital Trust Solutions

One of the key aspects of representing trust in a digital format is the ability to show some type of digital credential for that trust. Whether the need is to authenticate a user of an Internet resource or to maintain the privacy of a communication, a digital credential is required on the Internet. An encrypted email or a merchant's Web site may look legitimate, but how can we increase our level of confidence and know that we have gone to the right place?

Generally, the most accepted form of this digital credential has been built on the foundation of a technology called Public Key Infrastructure (PKI).

IE 6: P3P IN ACTION

Microsoft's IE (Internet Explorer) v6 allows for the use of controlling information as per the user's preference on privacy. In addition to providing preferences for privacy components, users can get a report for P3P-compliant Web sites to determine the site's privacy policy in a quick and efficient manner.

The concept of privacy on the Web revolves around the exchange of and access to cookies. Cookies help maintain the stickiness for a site by storing some information on a user's computer for later access. IE 6 allows the user to control privacy options by increasing or decreasing the ability of a site to manipulate these cookies. Some options for controlling cookie behavior include the following:

- ◆ Blocking all cookies
- ◆ Allowing cookies for only those sites that have a privacy policy in computer-readable form (aka a compact policy)
- ◆ Blocking cookies that broker personal information to third-party Web sites (this is especially useful for those sites that collect information on the user's Web surfing habits and relay the information to a third party, such as an advertising agency)
- ◆ Allowing all cookies regardless of use or policy status

Summary: The Need for Solutions

This book focuses on using solutions that are built on PKI. Trust solutions describe practical applications of security built on PKI that increases levels of trust in transactions and services utilizing those solutions. Many solutions, though, do not use PKI; however, PKI has proven to be the most robust technically as well legally for serious applications. Chapter 2 describes the technical foundation of PKI to provide a technical base of understanding. In later chapters, we will explain how trust solutions are built on top of PKI to provide a complete umbrella solution to trust issues.

Complexities of PKI

Understanding the need for trust solutions requires comprehending why PKI can be complex and why it alone cannot solve security issues. As an underlying technology, it requires a complex range of features that must be customized from organization to organization. This chapter will review the various aspects of PKI and provide a solid base for understanding how solutions can be built on it.

PKI: A Basis for Digital Trust

PKI, simply defined, is an infrastructure that allows the creation of a trusted method for providing privacy, authentication, integrity, and nonrepudiation in online communications between two parties. By itself, PKI does not have much utility; however, combined with some trust applications, it can create a powerful foundation for increasing trust in electronic communications. For example, imagine being able to walk through an airport with an electronic card that can identify you with a high degree of confidence. That same card could be used to authorize a bank transaction. Although various applications are being utilized, including different technologies (biometrics, smart cards, and so on), all of them would be based on some form of PKI.

Why Is PKI So Complicated?

The challenge with PKI is that it is an underlying infrastructure, not an end-user application. Imagine if you walked into a car dealership and were asked what type of engine you wanted. Once you understood the type of engine you needed, you were sold the engine and given a list of manufacturers (chassis makers, tire makers, electrical motor makers, and so on) to work with to build the car. Until recently, this is how PKI has been positioned. Effectively, most PKI vendors expect users to take this engine and hire special mechanics literally to build the rest of the car on a custom, one-off basis.

Essentially, we can summarize the challenges with PKI as follows:

- Not all applications are already PKI-enabled or PKI-aware. Given that PKI is an underlying infrastructure, nonintegration with various applications makes it more difficult to deploy.

- PKI is based on the authentication, or trust, of the digital credential. The amount of effort for authentication can be significant for higher levels of trust.

- Generally, consulting or specific skill sets are required for most major PKI implementations (whether they are outsourced or done in-house). Not all applications or PKIs are seamless and user-friendly due to poor integration with other applications.

- The return on investment (ROI) for a PKI alone is zero given that it is an infrastructure and not a direct end-user application. The ROI must be based on the applications built on top of PKI. This is dependent on the points made previously.

In addition, PKI, whether insourced or outsourced, can have a relatively high cost if not effectively utilized. In the recent past, PKI systems were not delivered effectively with proper ROI models. Today, though, *PKI has become recognized as a piece of a puzzle that provides trust*. The trust concept has given rise to the idea of solutions selling. Solutions selling is a method in which a user works with a vendor to solve a specific business problem with one or more integrated technologies. The key word is *integrated*. Anyone can sell separate pieces of technologies and require the customer to do the integration. The real effectiveness comes when the customer does not have to do the integration and can use a solution immediately. Integration before the PKI solution reaches the customer can help solve the challenges mentioned previously.

Solution selling can do the following:

- Increase the ease of use because the interface and the functions of the core application are the focus of the user experience (versus the PKI engine). In this manner, the user can be trained on the end application, which reduces the skill set and time required for the organization to become productive with the business application.

- Decrease the expense required for authentication as more and more applications are used for the same digital credential (via economies of scale). A good example of this can be seen in the United States' custom of using the driver's license as a uniform identifier. The driver's license is used for authentication not only for driving, but also as proof of age to allow purchase of age-restricted items, proof of identity for credit card or check transactions, and even as partial proof for eligibility for employment. PKI, through its use of digital credentials, has this ability to be a universal credential among many different applications ranging from email to network sign-on.

- Decrease in consulting or specific skill sets because the PKI is already predeployed due to the integration. Consulting resources, if needed, can then focus on custom applications for specific companies, as opposed to deployment or implementation consulting.

- ROI can now be focused on the applications and the business problems it solves, just as other IT projects are viewed today. Examples could include saving expense report processing by moving from a physical, paper-based process to an online, all-digital process. The digital credential issued through the PKI can be used to bind the information on the expense report legally, as well as make post-signature changes evident. An ROI in this case could easily be measured, unlike the case if only the PKI was being examined.

Security Issues

PKI encapsulates four basic principles for secure ecommerce:

- Privacy
- Authentication
- Integrity
- Nonrepudiation

The basis of PKI technology lies in the use of public and private key pair technology. Simply described, it allows data to be exchanged securely over an insecure medium, like the Internet. This concept is analogous to that of a door with a mail slot. Mail (like an email message) can be addressed to that location (like the public key) and slipped into the slot. Only the person with the key to the door (like the private key) can open it and retrieve the mail. How do we know where the address for the mail slot is located? There is a chance that if we get the address from an untrusted source, we may put our mail into someone else's mail slot (because we may have been given a wrong address). In this case, the privacy and possibly the integrity of the mail have been compromised. If, however, we use an address book from a trusted source that verifies the proper address (like a digital certificate), then we can be confident that the mail has been sent to the right mail slot.

When a digital credential, also called a digital certificate, is created, a randomly generated public and private key pair is created. The private key is known only to the certificate requestor. The public key, along with details on the requestor — for example, name and email address — are sent securely to a third party for creation of the certificate. The certificate then remains a public document that acts as a verifiable credential. Why do we need a certificate when we already have the public and private key pair? Because the public key could be manipulated, a mechanism is needed to maintain its integrity. The certificate is that method.

Privacy

Privacy is the concept of keeping communication private from all parties except the intended recipients. A common application requiring privacy is email. The tricky aspect of privacy is that we must maintain it at all costs, no matter how high. Current PKI implementations and applications require a shift in how a user must think about privacy. It is not apparent when an email is sent, for example, that there is no privacy, so how can a user know to take additional steps to encrypt the message? Good security policies and key technologies must be in place, along with internal company education for users and the threat of stiff penalties to enforce the idea that communications should be kept private.

Good security practice demands that all communication be encrypted, or kept private, so as not to reveal specific information that can be targeted for attack. Many systems and vendors have a range of solutions to enforce such practices. Two forms of privacy are these:

- Privacy of the information
- Privacy of the sender and the recipient

Current major standards like S/MIME, which define how email can be encrypted (for privacy), do not encrypt email headers. This means that anyone can tell to or from whom an email was sent. Other information revealed can include the time, date, and even the subject.

ENCRYPTION OPTIONS

Many different protocols can be used for encryption to maintain privacy. The most common protocol is the Data Encryption Standard (DES). It is the basis for the most common variation 3DES, which was considered, until recently, the U.S. government standard for private encryption. The U.S. government agency NIST (National Institute of Standards and Technology) has selected the next generation of more secure encryption, called AES (Advanced Encryption Standard). AES is not widely used yet as software, and hardware makers will have to migrate their platforms over to using it slowly. Make sure that you ask your vendors if they support AES standards or when they plan to start using it as their basis for encryption.

Other commonly used algorithms include the following:

◆ **MD5 (a 128-bit hash algorithm)—used in creating digitally signed messages**

◆ **SHA-1 (a 160-bit hash algorithm)—used in creating digitally signed messages**

◆ **RSA (digital signing algorithm with usually no fewer than 1024 bits)— used in encrypting and transmitting data**

Authentication

Authentication refers to the ability to verify the identities of all parties involved in a message transmission. In the physical world we use items like passports for identification. The online world requires a combination of personal presence (physical authentication) and some level of digital authentication. Application enablers, such as biometrics (discussed further in Chapter 5) and smart cards (discussed further in Chapter 7), can help in this area.

The challenge with authentication in ecommerce is that it can be expensive relative to the cost of the ecommerce transaction itself. Furthermore, authentication requirements vary from industry to industry. Consider tobacco sales. In the United States, a person must be at least 18 years old to buy tobacco either in person or online. The in-person authentication requirement is resolved by requesting a physical identification (usually a driver's license). Aspects of the identification make it difficult to forge credentials. Online, however, we do not have the same ability for strong authentication without PKI. A number of services are available to provide online authentication for items such as age. Aristotle, a company that provides age verification, provides an "18 and over" or "21 and over" age verification when given certain information about an individual. Aristotle charges by transaction, thus making it useful only when transactions are few and the value of goods is high enough to justify the cost of the service.

We can employ three key methods of authentication to identify an individual:

Something you have.   Examples of this type of authentication include official credentials such as a passport, driver's license, and corporate ID badge. Each credential is vetted and issued by a trusted third party. The credentials, although available for anyone to see and verify, are designed to be difficult to forge. In the case of credentials, like passports, the ability for authorized personnel to do a real-time validation or revocation of those credentials is important.

Something you know.   The most common example is a password or a PIN. It is commonly accepted that using only a password or PIN is a weak form of authentication because someone can easily steal it or guess it.

Something you are.   One of the most difficult types of authentication to forge is authentication through a physical attribute of an individual, which may include the person's face, fingerprint, iris, and hand geometry. Each specific type of biometric authentication has its pros and cons; however, this method, combined with the previous two authentication types, creates a very good authentication strategy.

Integrity

Integrity refers to the ability for a message to travel from one party to another with a confirmation that the message has not been altered in transit. This concept is not the same as privacy, which cannot always guarantee that the message was not changed. Integrity is usually determined by a checksum or hash algorithm technology, which checks and verifies the message after it has been received. Applications such as browsers and email clients can perform these tasks automatically.

Common techniques for verifying integrity include the use of hash algorithms such as MD5 and SHA1. Both parties (sender and recipient) run the transmitted message through this hash algorithm. Then the hash numbers are compared between the parties, and, if identical, the claim of integrity can be made. One key advantage of hash algorithms is that they produce a small, fixed-size output. This output can be used for all sorts of applications, such as integrity checking for transmitted emails and verifying that document signatures have not changed. The properties of these hash algorithms ensure that there is a very low probability of being able to derive the original text from just the hash output. We will see more examples and details on how this can be applied to key applications like secure messaging (email, for example) in Chapter 8.

Authorization

In most companies, the levels of access or authorization of activities is a key element in good security practices. Depending on the access control policies, authorization may be as broad as "let all employees access this information" or as granular as "let only VPs from the Sales department access this information." Generally, PKI provides the raw data for authorization applications to make policy decisions. Products from companies such as IBM, Netegrity, and Oblix include robust and sophisticated authorization control software built around digital certificates. In these applications, presentation of the certificate is tied to a business rule stored in the authorization software.

An important technology in the space of authorization is the concept of SSO (single sign on). The nirvana of this area of security is the ability to present a single credential, such as a digital certificate, and have it authenticated to all aspects of a user's systems including applications, network resources, databases, and more. PKI can provide a major piece of this solution, but it cannot provide SSO on its own.

MICROSOFT TRUSTBRIDGE

Microsoft announced in mid-2002 that it was embarking on an ambitious project called TrustBridge to tie authorization from the desktop through the Internet. Microsoft already had the "passport" concept that allowed users to use multiple Microsoft Web services with a single sign-on capability. TrustBridge extends this concept through to the enterprise.

Using a combination of various technologies revolving around the protocol called Kerberos, certificates are used to authenticate users and obtain a Kerberos ticket. This ticket is a digital authorization to access various Microsoft-related services in a secure manner. This ticket-based authorization concept can then easily be implemented in the enterprise by the addition of related servers for Kerberos, allowing for a seamless single sign-on solution.

One key issue with the current version of TrustBridge is how do users get these certificates and under what authentication policies? Also, the whole system is based on the use of the Microsoft Active Directory, which may not be the preferred directory for an enterprise. Finally, the TrustBridge architecture relies on the mass adoption of "Web services" standards such as "ws-security," which has not yet shown widespread success.

Competing solutions from the Sun-led Liberty Alliance utilize technologies like smart cards that allow for a roaming credential (a certificate whose private key can be accessed from any location). It remains to be seen which technology will mature and if TrustBridge will evolve into a success story.

Nonrepudiation

Nonrepudiation is the concept that binds a party to a transaction. This is similar to a notary public witnessing the signing of a legal document. If there is a dispute, the notary can attest to the fact that the relevant parties were involved in that transaction. In online transactions, form signing and workflow applications manage this well.

A certificate authority (CA), a trusted third-party organization or company that issues digital credentials, is responsible for protecting its root private key. That is the most critical aspect of its business. Some techniques to increase security include the CA's use of hardware encryption devices, breaking up and storing the private key in pieces, and keeping the root key offline until needed.

Maintaining nonrepudiation in PKI is complex and centers on the protection of the private key. The biggest weakness in a PKI system is in its ability to protect and prove possession of the private key used in signing transactions. Because the private key is just a data file on a computer, it is vulnerable to theft or attacks. Generally, the protection of the private key is managed in several ways:

- Using password protection (as shown in Figure 2.1).
- Using biometrics or smart cards (this will be discussed further in Chapter 5).
- Separating the signing and encryption certificates. In this scenario, only the encryption key is escrowed and therefore vulnerable to compromise. The signing certificate's private key never leaves the possession of the owner of that key.
- Using shorter life spans for certificates in order to mitigate the impact of a compromised private key.

The challenge, despite the variety of methods, is to mitigate the risk of compromising the private key and the associated cost in protecting the key. Other technologies, such as those from ActivCard and RSA Data Security (two leading security companies), have been developed to create a one-time password concept for authentication. Those technologies, however, cannot easily replace PKI with stronger nonrepudiation claims.

An additional method used to bolster the nonrepudiation claim is to provide outsourced digital notary functions. Some PKI vendors offer a service in which once a digital document has been signed, certain information can be transmitted securely to the third party. This third party then uniquely identifies the document, digital certificates tied to the transactions, and the date and time of the transaction. In this manner, the service creates the equivalent of a "digital receipt."

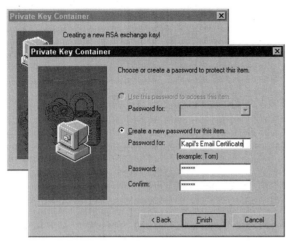

Figure 2.1   Microsoft password protection of the private key.

Applications of PKI

In Chapters 5 through 10, we will highlight many end-user applications for PKI. From a technology perspective, how can we leverage PKI? What can other technology vendors build on top of PKI that would allow them to deliver richer and more sophisticated applications? In this regard, PKI gives us several key benefits:

- Simple and easy management of digital credentials
- Effective auditing capability
- Multiple use of single infrastructure
- Ability to leverage stronger authentication mechanisms

From a technology perspective, applications can take advantage of PKI by not having to manage authentication or any of the requirements around that. For example, it would be very useful for a Web portal simply to accept a trusted digital credential, go to a trusted source, and check for the validity of that credential. Otherwise, the portal software would have to create its own authentication system, database, and auditing systems. A parallel analogy is exemplified by how the driver's license is treated in the United States as a trusted credential for authentication of a wide range of applications. For example, the driver's license is used for admittance into age-restricted venues, as proof of identity for checks or credit card transactions, and even as proof of identity to government authorities. The advantage today is that many applications are using PKI as a method for providing digital credentialing systems.

In any PKI system, the most vulnerable aspect of the system lies in how the private key is protected. The private key is required to decrypt messages, digitally sign messages, and generally maintain the validity of the digital credential. The private key is simply a small, specialized computer file. Most applications rely on the fact that the private key is kept, as the name implies, private and is known and accessed only by the key holder. In general, there are several methods to protect the private key:

- Requiring that the user enter the correct password or PIN before allowing any functions to use the private key
- Forcing the user to present a biometric credential to activate a private key
- Placing the private key on a removable device kept separate from the main system being accessed

This method of using a password or PIN to restrict access is built into all of Microsoft's operating systems as well as into many applications that utilize PKI. Passwords and PINs, though, are the least desirable method of protecting private keys. The fault in this method is that we rely on the user to choose a good password or PIN to protect access to the digital credential. In addition, if the private key is stored on a system (like a laptop) that is later stolen, the thief may use programmatic methods to guess the password.

Using biometrics as an additional authentication step provides stronger authentication. The primary advantage of this method is that it does not rely on user input such as a password or PIN. Furthermore, while a PIN or password may be stolen or guessed, it is more difficult to manipulate biometric devices. Although biometric devices are not foolproof and in many general applications do not have 100 percent accuracy, for single-use purposes in controlled environments (like an office or home), they do work suitably well. Depending on the complexity of the biometric device, cost can be a key factor in how widely this system is used.

Perhaps the best method for protecting the private key is to place it on a removable device. Because the removable device can be physically locked, it adds another level of protection. Technologies such as USB tokens and smart cards can store the private key or utilize various methods of keeping it safe. One challenge with this is that there has not been wide adoption or wide standardization. For example, only computers made after the mid-90s support USB. This is a challenge in many healthcare organizations where there are older technologies, some incompatible with USB devices and smart cards. In addition, the cost per user is driven up due to implementation, device, and device reader costs.

So how do we support nonrepudiation if there is a chance the private key may fall out of the possession of the intended owner? A combination of the methods previously described can increase the confidence of nonrepudiation. In addition, strong audit records of how private keys are generated, delivered, and stored can also track their use in the event of a dispute. Finally, legal infrastructure is essential to ensure that the burden of the private key's protection falls on the end user. The user is more likely to protect the private key if the liability for its loss is increased. This liability model is similar to that used for credit cards, where the user is required to protect credit cards (physically) as well as the credit card numbers. In the event of compromise, the end user is required to notify the credit card company of the compromise within a defined period of time.

XKMS

Given that the current methods and tool kits utilizing PKI for developing applications are not easy, the industry has developed a new method for leveraging PKI for applications called XML Key Management Specification (XKMS) that uses Web services technologies to register and manage keys. It has been designed to do the following:

- Make it easier for developers to use PKI essential functions by eliminating proprietary tool kits and special plug-ins.
- Speed up deployment by moving most PKI functions to the server side and away from relying on client integrations for PKI.
- Move application development into open standards, which allows developers to build reusable applications and modules.
- Allow for PKI development and deployment onto smaller processor devices, like PDAs and mobile phones. Given that most of the PKI functions occur on the server side, the mobile device does not need much processing power.

PKI Functions

Despite the variances in different PKI systems, they all consist of several key components that control how digital certificates are issued and managed. As with any security system, a series of checks and balances ensures the right mix of flexibility and control necessary in an operating environment. A PKI system can be broken down into three main elements:

- Certificate authority (CA)
- Registration authority (RA)
- End-entity

Certificate Authority

A certificate authority performs the following functions:

- Issues digital certificates (creates them and sends them to the intended recipient) in a secure manner

- Hosts a repository for valid and invalid (revoked or expired) certificates and makes this information available to third-party requests for validation

- Maintains the integrity, security, and real-time availability of the issuing systems

Essentially, the CA is a back-end function that must be available with the same reliability and speed of a public utility. Certificates can be issued to individuals, like employees of an organization, or to devices, such as a VPN device. In all cases, the individual or device must present the CA with sufficient information needed for unique identification, as per the policies set by the CA.

The actual method of issuing certificates involves the CA using its private key to digitally sign the incoming request for a certificate. By using the CA's public key, anyone can verify the contents of the certificate, ensure that the contents have not changed, and ensure that the certificate was issued from a trusted source. The value in the entire CA process is in its brand and its ability to protect its private key. Should the private key be compromised, it would cast a shadow of doubt over all the certificates issued by the CA, especially if the exact time of the compromise could not be established. Furthermore, many certificates issued after the CA private key compromise would have to be revoked, creating a massive end-user logistical problem. Realistically, a compromise of the CA private key would most likely lead to the end of the CA's business because the brand would be severely tarnished.

To accomplish the task of computing large numbers of requests for signing, the CA uses dedicated cryptographic hardware that allows its private key to sign requests quickly and more securely. Because these hardware devices are designed to be very secure, they can further enhance the protection of the private key. Well-designed CAs will create a *trust hierarchy*, which consists of a root with a number of subroots, to further enhance protection of the private key. In this manner, the root key can create the subroot, and then the root can be retired to a secured location and kept offline. In this model, only the subroots need to be online at all times for signing requests. In the event of compromise of the online subroots, the damage could be limited to a particular subroot. Furthermore, many CAs have various levels or types of certificates. This concept of subroots can create different types of certificates, each with its own policies and conditions for issuance. Some CAs also offer insurance in the event of a mistake by the CA. The insurance policies could also vary by subroot.

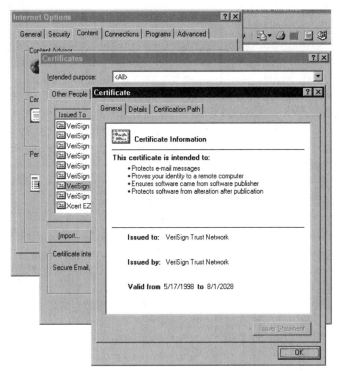

Figure 2.2 Example of CA certificates in Internet Explorer.

Why can't just anyone become a CA? It is true that to be a CA, all you need is Internet access and some cryptographic generating software or hardware. To be a successful CA, though, an organization requires the following:

Strong branding and trust by all parties involved (requestor and user of the certificates). Without the trust of the CA, no relying party will use or value the certificate when it is presented.

Presence of the CA's public key in popular applications. For example, Web browsers (see Figure 2.2). Because a certificate requires the public CA to be verified for security's sake, the CA certificate must be either delivered in a secure manner (this involves extra steps for the end user) or stored or bundled with trusted software (as in the browser software). Given that most users do not upgrade software like their Internet browser more than once every few years, a new CA would have a long lead time before being used by a majority of users.

A high level of security and availability. Because the certificates issued by the CA may be used in a range of applications, it is important to always be able to issue and check the validity of certificates consistently and reliably.

Cross-Certification

Ideally, we would like a single root certificate for all PKI applications; however, this is not practical because organizations have different implementations and variations of PKI and variances in their trust policies. As a result, for many applications it is important to cross-certify or create a bridge between various CAs. Cross-certification is the method in which the root of one CA trusts, or cross-certifies, with the root of another CA. In this manner, two independently constructed CA hierarchies can be linked together. One practical example is the merger of two companies, each having its own CAs. One solution would be to revoke and reissue all certificates so that all employees, vendors, and customers from the merged companies have certificates that belong to one of the merged companies' root CAs. The other method is to create a level of trust by cross-certifying the two root CAs. This would allow any certificate in either hierarchy to be trusted equally. The actual mechanism of the cross-certification would be to bring the root CA keys online and have them digitally sign each other's root CA. This would allow a path, or hierarchy of trust, to be established. The additional complexity introduced is that additional certificates would have to be issued for the purposes of trust within the new mesh of CAs (as shown in Figure 2.3).

The challenge of cross-certification is that the organization is claiming that the security policies and certification guidelines are the same for the entire cross-certified hierarchy — which may or may not be true. In addition to the cross-certification of the CAs, security policies will need to be synchronized to a common platform.

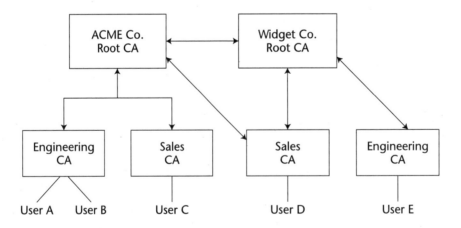

Mesh design allows two recently merged companies to leverage each other's PKI. Note that each user in either company can communicate via this design.

Figure 2.3 Example of mesh CAs.

Another approach of interoperability between different CA hierarchies is the concept of bridging CAs. In a bridge model, the different CAs are linked together by a central bridge CA. The bridge CA does not issue certificates as in the case of cross-certification, but rather acts as a trusted intermediary. This is useful for linking large numbers of different CA hierarchies, as is proposed in the U.S. government's Federal Bridge Certificate Authority project.

A trend that has come up in recent years is for a government to control the root CA for any CA that operates within the government's borders. Such restrictions can completely change the approach that an enterprise in that country is allowed to take. Given that control of the root CA controls the entire hierarchy of that CA, PKI can become a political influence. Take, for example, a CA based in country X that issues a CA subroot certificate to a company in country Y under the CA's hierarchy. Should the political situation change between countries X and Y, X may decide to exert pressure on the CA to revoke the root certificate issued to that enterprise. In this regard, the control of the CA's root can be both a business and political decision. Other factors of concern include the financial collapse of the CA. After all, if the CA goes bankrupt, all related CA operations will cease. Therefore, the value of the CA will quickly diminish as key functions such as revocation checking, searches for certificates, and other vital operations cease to exist.

In the described scenarios, the enterprise needs to establish a new root with another CA, revoke all existing certificates, and reissue new certificates. Enforcing the revocation status of the certificates is challenging given that the CA may not be available. Most likely, the enterprise will have to wait for the expiration of the certificates (as opposed to the revocation) until it can be reasonably sure certificates from the old CA have been taken out of circulation. Other options include having the dying CA cross-certify with another CA to help the transition for customers. This would not be an option for a political situation in which a CA terminates or revokes all certificates from that foreign country.

Registration Authority

Because the CA's main function is to issue the certificates, the registration authority (RA) component is required to provide for the authenticity of the individual or device requesting the certificate and ensure it has a right to it. In the example of a corporation issuing certificates, that corporation may require employees to receive only certificates that may be used to identify users to a portal. In this case, users must identify themselves to, say, an administrator at the company who will verify that the users are, in fact, current employees and then notify the CA to issue the certificate.

To prevent a rogue RA from falsifying and issuing certificates, the RA can approve or reject a certificate. Upon approval, the CA sends the certificate directly to the requestor. In this manner, an RA administrator cannot pretend to be that other user because the certificate will be sent directly to the end user. Furthermore, many CAs will have strong auditing capability, which will document all the activities of an RA, without the RA's being able to modify them. Some systems may require approval from multiple administrators.

What authentication does an RA perform? While specific authentication criteria will vary from application to application and organization to organization, the typical RA authentication usually uses the following criteria:

User name (first and last).   For certificates tied to individuals this is necessary to bind the identity to a particular user.

Email address.   This, combined with the user name, creates a unique credential throughout the organization.

Organization/department.   Although optional, this is usually determined for large-scale deployments because there may be multiple groups and/or administrators.

Generally the RA administrator will go through a strong level of authentication. After that, the RA will use a highly authenticated certificate, perhaps vetted and issued by the CA, to identify itself to the CA for approval and rejection commands.

For some systems where large numbers of certificate requests must be processed (for example, at very large global corporations), automated methods may be employed for the validation and approval or rejection of certificates. In these cases, the CA will issue an RA certificate (which is just a certificate that provides the identity of the RA administrator) to a device. That device will contain software that will do certain checks. For example, at a very large company, users may be asked to fill out a form that asks for information that would be known only to them (name, address, social security number, previous addresses, and so on). The submitted information would be automatically checked against a database that would have the correct information for that user. If the information entered matches the database, the RA certificate on that device would then sign the request and send it off to the CA for issuance.

Note that the CA can also serve as an RA. For example, for SSL certificates, which are used to create encrypted channels of communication between merchant Web servers and clients, the outsourced CA generally does a high level of vetting before issuing the certificates. Given that the RA function can be data intensive and require manual processing, this function can be costly if done completely by an outside agency. In addition, an organization has access to HR and other confidential records that could be used for authentication, unlike an outsourced agency.

End-Entity

The end-entity (as shown in Figure 2.4) is defined as the user or consumer of the certificates but is not issued to a certificate authority. The end-entity maintains the security of the private key associated with the issued certificate. This obligation is similar, for example, to the obligation of a credit card holder to maintain the privacy of the card and confirm possession of it at all times. The content of the certificates allows the user to uniquely identify the holder of the certificate and then make some security policy decisions based on that information.

Types of Certificates

A certificate may be issued as a digital credential to either a person or a device. In Chapter 3 we will discuss the best practices for which a particular certificate should be used, how it should be issued, and what contents it should have.

One interesting note to be made is that certificates can be generated for digital signing, encryption, or both. Such a distinction is useful when an organization wants to maintain two certificates, allowing the signing certificate's private key to be kept by the owner for nonrepudiation and allowing the encryption key to be escrowed with the organization for data recovery in the event the owner's key is not available.

Figure 2.4 Example of an end-entity certificate.

There are numerous types of certificates, each having a unique role in its use or its type of authentication:

Client certificates.   These certificates are used by individuals. Applications include access to intranets and extranets, internal corporate resources, and digital email signatures and encryption. Client certificates have, at a minimum, an email address and a person's name that, together, can uniquely identify that person. Other data could include organization or department affiliation and contact information.

VPN certificates (IPSec).   These certificates are generated using information about the device (like IP address) and submitted by a human (either manually or through some automated process) on behalf of the device.

Device manufacturing certificates.   These certificates are tied to a particular device (like cable modems), and generated and placed physically into some permanent memory on the device. These certificates generally have long expiration periods that usually are sufficient for the useful life of the product (that is, these certificate are generally not renewed because it is not easy to replace this certificate).

SSL certificates.   These certificates are generated by a Web server and used to associate a particular Web server address to a particular Web server software. This certificate not only provides for an encrypted SSL tunnel to a requesting client browser, but also helps identify if a particular URL belongs to the organization claiming to host the URL (it prevents spoofing). Recent developments in the industry have created the concept of "shared certificates," which allow a single SSL certificate to be shared among many Web server machines (as in the case of a Web farm set up for a high-traffic merchant site).

Code signing certificates.   These certificates are used to ensure the integrity and source of software code. These certificates can help end users prove that downloaded software has come from the claimed source and ensure that nothing was altered in the transit.

Wireless device certificates.   These certificates are designed to allow for SSL-type functionality, but with the computing and unique requirements that are associated with small devices and processors. Short-lived Wireless Transport Layer Security (WTLS) certificates are examples. These certificates essentially create a master SSL certificate, and then a middleware software system issues temporary, smaller certificates to the end device. In this manner, the computing power required to handle the smaller certificates is more manageable for the smaller device. When the master certificate is revoked or expires, the middleware software ceases to issue any further certificates.

Custom organization certificates. These certificates have been developed for specific organizations such as the U.S. government's ACES initiative (which allows U.S. citizens and businesses to conduct trusted and secure transactions with the government). Generally these certificates have specific, unique authentication and issuance criteria.

Qualified certificates. These types of certificates are compliant with European Directive 1999/93/EC, which dictates the format and content for legally binding certificates in the European Union. This directive gives the status of any transaction conducted with the certificate just as if a paper transaction had taken place. The qualified certificates consist of specific mandatory and optional fields to be placed in the certificates, the responsibilities of the owner and relying party of the certificate, and technical stipulations for other aspects of the certificate creation and digital signature process.

Implementation Issues

As with many enterprise-wide applications, implementation truly becomes the deciding factor between the success and failure of an implementation of a PKI management system. The three key areas of an implementation are these:

- Setup (rolling out the system)
- Administration (maintaining the system)
- Exception handling (dealing with business continuity issues)

Although there are can be many components and details in the rollout of a PKI, there are some key decision-making criteria:

- Audience
- Time allotted for rollout
- Ability to control the user's environment
- Expertise available during and after deployment
- Funds available for purchase and rollout

Setup

Setup of a PKI involves the setup of the CA/RA hardware and software as well as the user setup process. These steps must be accomplished before the PKI can be used.

Back-End Setup

Setup of a PKI deployment generally varies in intensity based on whether an outsourced or in-house model is chosen. Simply defined, an outsourced PKI is one in which the core CA functions are managed by a third party. In the simplest outsourced services, the enterprise can access all of the certificate life cycle management functions through a Web page and an Internet connection without any specific hardware or software at the enterprise's site. Generally, however, the outsourced model involves a few hardware components to manage some sort of auto-issuance of or customization for the life cycle certificate management.

An in-house model is defined as one in which an enterprise hosts the core CA functions within the control of the enterprise. In this model, the root CA, sub CAs, and certificates are all created within the domain of the enterprise. This allows greater flexibility but also requires the enterprise to ensure a high level of security to protect the root certificate as well as the issuance process. More on these topics will be discussed in Chapter 3.

User Setup and Registration

Part of the setup process for users is the registration process for certificates. In this process the enterprise must decide what information to collect about the user to determine sufficient confidence for authentication. There are two key methods for such an authentication:

- Identification of an individual based on personal information (known only to the RA and the registering individual)
- Identification of an individual through a passcode scheme in which a secret code is generated prior to the registration process and delivered to the registrant prior to registration through an out-of-band mechanism

The challenge is how to approve or set up all these registrations, especially for high numbers of registrants (such as very large corporations). A single user may request several certificates in a single year, requiring on average of at least two or three registrations per year.

The manual process of registration, a process in which each request is queued up for an RA administrator to either reject or approve, can provide the most control but also the most work. Other types may include automatic methods of administration that would compare the given information during the registration process to a trusted database and provide for an approval, a rejection, or a manual review. This method offers less control but can be useful for large installations.

Certificate Policy and Certificate Practice Statement (CPS)

Given that a certificate can be used to conduct legally binding transactions, the rules under which the certificate is issued and the rules under which a relying party of that certificate can use the certificate must be well documented. A certificate policy (CP) provides the level of trust a relying party can place in a given certificate based on the conditions in which the certificate was issued. For example, if an organization chooses an outsourced CA and requires a very trustworthy certificate, the organization may request the highest-level certificate from that CA. In this case, the CA will perform numerous, rigorous checks before issuing certificates. The other extreme is a minimally validated certificate that may prove only that the certificate holder has a valid email address. Based on the CP, the relying party can then decide how much trust to put into that certificate and make some type of business decision. For example, a poorly qualified certificate would be used only to access small sections of a portal, whereas a strongly authenticated certificate would be used to allow access to confidential areas. Every standard (X.509 v3) certificate carries information about the CP and details for the relying party. These are done through standard extensions available though the X.509 standard.

One key factor in deciding how to set up CA functions is to consider whether an organization needs to have a custom CP or use an existing CP from the outsourced CA. If the organization must have custom authentication procedures, then it must write its own CP. Writing a CP is not a trivial task because it can be challenged in a court of law. Generally, legal firms that can write good CPs will charge upward of $400 an hour! For smaller organizations, it is more cost-effective to go with an outsourced CA that can also provide a ready-made, tested CP.

A certification practice statement (CPS) defines the processes and procedures a CA requires for certificate operation and issuance. While a CP describes the level of reliability of a particular certificate, the CPS describes the reliability of the CA itself. Again, for an organization to host its own CA function, the organization will need to consider if it can develop its own CPS.

Administration

Most PKI systems do not require too much maintenance beyond normal system maintenance. The function of the RA administrator, which is more of an operational function than a maintenance function, will become the most significant aspect of maintaining a PKI. Regular audits, personnel background reviews, and good security practices of the facility housing the PKI systems must be scheduled and performed on a regular basis.

Renewal

Given that most certificates expire on an annual basis, a system must be set up for renewal of certificates. Renewal can take the form of two options: issuing a certificate with a new expiration period but with the same registration information and public key as the expired one, or issuing a whole new certificate with a new public key but with the same registration information. Renewal strategies should be implemented so that there is sufficient time to allow the user to operate with his or her existing certificate and obtain a new one without a lapse period in between. Generally, certificates are issued with an overlap period of four to six weeks to provide a smooth migration.

The other aspect of renewal is user education and training. The process of renewal effectively requires the user to identify himself or herself to the CA within a certain amount of time. Generally most PKI systems can be set up for auto-notification, but usually they do not push out a renewed certificate unless the user specifically asks for it.

One complex area is what is called "dual key pair renewal." In this variation, two certificates are issued to each user: an encryption certificate and a signing certificate. We discuss this in more detail later in this chapter in the discussion of escrow. At each renewal period, the user must renew two certificates simultaneously. Essentially, the user may have up to four certificates for one particular application, such as email, during a renewal transition period (one pair of expiring certificates and one pair of new certificates). In theory, the user may have additional certificates for things like extranet access and VPN access. As you can see, the number of certificates that needs to be renewed can add up quickly. Unfortunately, there is no easy method to deal with this issue other than good user training, support, and documentation.

Some PKI vendors provide software clients that can simplify the process of renewal. In these cases, the client software sends a signed message (corresponding to the certificate to be renewed) to the CA. The signed message is verified using the public key contained in the copy of the associated certificate. If the signature is confirmed, then it is assumed that the user generating that request is the rightful owner of the original certificate. Then the CA generates another certificate with the same user credentials and public key, but with new expiration dates.

Search

During the course of the use of a PKI system, users need to identify and use other users' certificates. Generally most organizations store certificates in a commonly accessible directory. Applications or even other users can query the directory and retrieve the certificate associated with that person or device. For applications like email, plug-ins can seamlessly tie the certificate to a user — for example, in the address book for Microsoft Outlook and Exchange users.

The challenge with search is that if the directory is accessible to everyone, then the credential information stored in the certificates is also accessible to everyone. It may be necessary to restrict access to the directory of certificates to, for example, hide which employees work at a particular organization.

Applications like Microsoft Outlook automatically attach a user's certificate to outbound email when a message is digitally signed. The recipient can then grab the certificate and verify the email without performing any extra steps. The certificate is also stored locally (as a copy) for future validation. Unfortunately, not too many applications currently provide this feature, so the necessity for an accessible directory is very real.

Exception Handling

With any security, despite the care taken in protecting and auditing the systems, there must be adequate safeguards and personnel to respond to a detected incident. PKI systems must be available all the time because they not only will issue certificates, but also may verify them, requiring constant uptime for real-time validation. In addition, given that the protection of the root key of the CA is perhaps one of the most important functions, exceptions or security incidents with that function are the most critical. Generally, for outsourced systems this is not an issue because the CA focuses on protection of the root key. For in-house systems, extra security and precautions must be managed to ensure that the root is not compromised or, if it is, that immediate steps are taken to mitigate the damage (like revocation and reissuance of certificates from a new root key).

Revocation

The concept of revocation of digital certificates is similar to that of revoking a government-issued passport. Although a government may wish to revoke a citizen's passport, it may not be possible to seize the passport physically. If the passport holder attempts to use the revoked passport at a border station and the border agent fails to check a computer listing the numbers of revoked passports, the citizen may be able to slip past the border agent and out of the country. Likewise, in some situations certificates will have to be revoked before their natural expiration period. In these cases, the RA must notify the CA about which certificates must be revoked.

In PKI there are several options for tracking and verifying revoked certificates including the following:

- Real-time validation, which provides for up-to-the-second validation of revoked certificates. This type of certificate authentication is essential for high-value transactions, such as financial transactions.

- Delayed checking, which is suitable for low-value transactions such as access to an employee portal or extranet. In this option the list of revoked certificates gets updated in 1 to 24 hours.

Real-time validation is usually done through a common protocol for this purpose called OCSP (online certificate status protocol). OCSP helps define a standard method for real-time revocation status checking.

Escrow

By separating the function of signing and encrypting, an organization can escrow or keep a copy of the private key associated with the encryption certificate's public key. Should the private key be lost or the user leave the organization, the data encrypted with the encryption certificate can be retrieved. The loss of the signing certificate does not matter because another signing certificate can be issued. In addition, the signing certificate does not need to be escrowed because the user is simply identifying himself or herself through a signing process and not encrypting data for which the private key would be required.

In general, any organization using PKI for critical business needs, especially email, should provide for dual certificates and escrow capability of the encryption certificate. Generally, most PKI systems (even outsourced ones) allow for private keys to be escrowed and stored within the organization's own network. One typical method for keeping the nonrepudiation claim strong is to use a symmetric key to encrypt the private key and then encrypt that symmetric key with the CA's public key. If the RA requests an escrow recovery, then it must ask the CA to decrypt and send back the encrypting key. At that point the RA can recover the desired key. In addition, the CA cannot recover the keys because it holds only the ability to decrypt the recovery symmetric key; it does not have direct access to the encrypted database of keys.

The concept of separating the ability for the RA to recover the key and allowing the CA to be involved creates an audit trail and provides for more accountability for how and why the keys were recovered. Some CAs will not, for example, allow mass key recovery, but rather force the RA to make individual requests for key recoveries. This mitigates the risk of a rogue administrator attempting to steal all the keys in an organization.

NOTE If an organization decides to use smart cards, it is even more critical to keep a backup copy of that key. In a smart card, typically, once the private key is generated (usually on the smart card directly), it cannot be copied or extracted from the card. Because loss or destruction of the smart card is a probable occurrence, it is essential to have a key escrow service generate the key and send it to the end user. The end user then imports the public/private key pair into the smart card.

Audience

The broader the audience for a PKI deployment, the fewer options and features we can implement. We can break down our audience into three broad categories:

- Mass market
- Enterprise
- Extranet

Mass markets refer to a wide deployment involving many users remotely located without a common desktop standard — for example, Internet banking customers. When rolling out to a mass market, there is generally little or no control over a user's desktop. Such restrictions require users to implement a public CA that can be applied for and installed in two or three steps. In addition, the whole process must be Web based and flexible for both Netscape and Microsoft browsers because of how certificates are created, requested, and delivered through a browser interface.

Enterprise users are often members of a common organization. This association allows the user desktop to have a more uniform environment and gives some control over what the user can and cannot do. Such deployments, depending on the size, may allow for private or public hierarchies. In addition, such deployments permit the use of proprietary client software that can assist the user in managing his or her certificates. For example, both Entrust and VeriSign, two leading PKI vendors, allow the use of a proprietary client so that the user can manage his or her certificate with functions such as renewal and automatic presentation when requested.

Finally, extranet users are affiliated with a common organization, but they do not have a controlled or similar desktop or environment. This occurs commonly in vendor/buyer relationships when an extranet is created to share information. In this case, we must treat this community as mass markets with respect to a lightweight client on the desktop approach; however, we can take advantage of the fact that the number of users will be much smaller than with a mass market approach. This allows us to use either public or private hierarchies with potentially additional single sign-on or other supporting entitlements systems.

Time Allotted for Rollout

Given the potential complexity of deploying PKI, it is always reasonable to obtain the maximum allowable time for a rollout; however, the challenge occurs when technology changes so quickly that the "final" implementation may never occur. For shorter deployments (three months or less), it is usually advisable to go with an outsourced or managed PKI. For longer deployments (more than three months), it may be feasible to use an in-house solution; however, the extent of customization and integration may be limited. We will cover some best practices for these areas in Chapter 3.

Expertise Available

As with any IT systems rollout, on-site expertise is essential for a successful rollout. Generally, most in-house PKI systems require the most effort because software, servers, and clients all need to be installed and configured. In addition, the ability to provide reliable and constant uptime can add to the expertise necessary. Larger companies can generally piggyback on existing IT staff to maintain the PKI systems. Smaller companies may need to hire consultants or outsource most of their PKI needs. Running a successful PKI system without information security professionals on staff is not feasible.

Funds Available

Depending on the factors mentioned previously, funds could be required in two places: upfront high costs or even payments over the life of the service. For in-house and large mass-market deployments, upfront costs will be relatively high, with economies of scale eventually bringing the costs per user down. For smaller rollouts and outsourced options, payments will be, generally, even over time. We will discuss more details of the financial aspects and decision-making skills required in Chapter 4.

Integration Issues

It can be argued that the single factor in slowing down PKI adoption is the issue of integrating and enabling applications for PKI. PKI can be integrated in the following ways:

- Through applications (for example, email clients)
- With third-party data (for example, authentication database)
- With stronger authentication options (for example, biometrics or smart cards)
- Through legacy systems

Integration with Applications

Not all applications are PKI aware. For example, Microsoft Word does not have out-of-the-box capability to use PKI. Why would Word need PKI? Well, imagine that you wanted to create a contract and ensure that the document did not change in transit and that the recipient did not make any unauthorized changes. The most secure and legally binding method would be to allow Word to accept a digital certificate and digitally sign the document before it was sent to the recipient. Although third-party applications exist as add-ons to applications like Word, they add cost and require user intervention.

There are several ways to PKI-enable an application for internal use. The most common method is to use the PKI vendor's tool kit for integration. The tool kit manages the core details of the PKI functions such as key generation. The developer can then adapt the user interface for the PKI-specific functions, such as certificate requests (as shown in Figure 2.5). Recent versions of most Web servers, for example, have greatly improved the ability for a Web administrator to request a certificate from within the administrator consoles. Earlier versions required multiple steps outside of the administrator's console.

Some vendors provide middleware for PKI integrations, effectively making calling and using PKI functions easier. (We will discuss these in more detail in Chapter 10.)

Integration with Third-Party Data

Good, strong authentication is the basis of a good PKI deployment model. The key component in good authentication is integration with reliable data sources. Generally, PKI systems will allow data integration and access with Open Database Connectivity (ODBC)–compatible databases, Lightweight Directory Access Protocol (LDAP)–compatible databases, and text file-based data. In many enterprises this integration is used to associate the authentication to a trusted source—for example, the personnel database. Given the complexity of most enterprise databases, tweaking is required at the PKI software to ensure that access is proper and schemas synchronize with the requirements of the PKI system.

To provide strong authentication, especially to a mass-market audience, it may be necessary to integrate with third-party data providers, such as credit bureaus, for example. Some data providers, such as ChoicePoint, provide third-party tool kits that can allow integration (for the authentication) as part of the Web site enrollment experience. In Chapter 10 we review additional solutions that can provide even stronger authentication with biometrics. The use of biometrics tied to good data authentication practices can greatly mitigate risks associated with the false issuance of certificates. For VPN and related products, each vendor has its own method of generating a certificate request and importing the certificate.

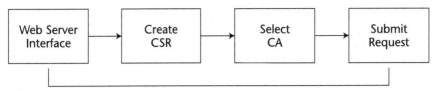

Figure 2.5   Example of an integrated Web server request.

PKI systems do not necessarily issue certificates automatically, even after data authentication. It is possible to require authentication and then request that a human administrator manually review the request. For high-value or specific areas, it is advisable to require administrator approval. For the bulk of requests, most enterprises would do best by relying on a semi-automated system that generates PINs out of band (in other words, a channel of communication separate from previous communications) or perhaps does the data authentication described in the previous paragraphs.

Integration with Stronger Authentication Options

As enterprises begin to realize the necessity for strong authentication, options like smart cards and biometrics become increasingly essential. Generally, integration with a biometric device requires the device vendor to do most of the integration, rather than the PKI vendor. Hence, it is important to choose a PKI vendor that has good partnership programs or ISVs, so that end users have more options for out-of-the-box solutions. Biometric vendors generally need to add a client on the desktop to control access to the certificate store, which is used to store all certificates on that machine. A registration process (to keep in memory the correct pattern for comparison) is required, which will be accounted for during deployment and support activities. Smart card vendors can use general Microsoft readily available standards such as Cryptographic Application Programmer's Interface (CAPI) and PKCS #11 (an industry level cryptographic token interface standard). Smart card initialization and life cycle management will require client software, and most smart card readers will require additional drivers. Again, setup and integration costs and time must be taken into account.

Integration with Legacy Systems

Given that any enterprise will evolve its IT infrastructure, integration with legacy systems will also be an issue. It has generally been accepted that PKI systems can affect only PC-based systems and PKI-aware applications. Although the PKI system may run on a UNIX or a mainframe system, most PKI vendors do not provide support for it. Integrating with mainframe systems usually requires some middleware software or a manual data transfer.

Integration with Single Interface

Perhaps the most overlooked aspect of a PKI system is the user experience. Given that certificates must be managed for things like requests, revocations, and renewal, there must be a simple method of managing certificates. Most PKI vendors have some interface; however, these interfaces tend to be client-based applications, which may not be available on all platforms (PC, UNIX, Mac) or for all versions.

Cost

PKI systems cannot be characterized as the massive ERP deployments we have seen in the past that cost millions of dollars and took several years. Nevertheless, it is easy to spend a fair amount of money and time on a system and not effectively deploy or use it. Tables 2.1 through 2.4 show an approximate idea of how costs will be amortized based on whether a system is outsourced or implemented in-house. In Chapter 4 we will discuss how to justify these costs with some ROI analysis. Essentially, we can break down our discussion into setup and ongoing costs.

Setup costs consist of personnel, hardware, and software. Tables 2.1 and 2.2 show the typical setup cost components. Costs are generally higher for the initial setup for in-house systems versus outsourced systems.

Table 2.1 Setup Cost Components for a Typical In-House PKI System

COMPONENT	SETUP COSTS	COMMENTS
Hardware	High	Computer hardware, including redundant systems and security infrastructure. Hardware consists of at least two or three servers, related networking gear, and security infrastructure, including firewalls.
Software	High	PKI software, including initial license and maintenance fees. Software consists of CA software, RA administrator console, and related OS and Web server software.
Consulting	High	Required expertise for setup and installation of PKI systems. Initial consulting is used for physical setup of hardware and software. Also general business analysis may be included to determine how the CA hierarchies are set up. Initial integration with databases or client desktop applications may also be done at this stage.

Table 2.2   Setup Cost Components for a Typical Outsourced PKI System

COMPONENT	SETUP COSTS	COMMENTS
Hardware	Low	Computer hardware, including redundant systems and security infrastructure. Initial setup includes basic hardware (usually for the Web servers) for redirection to the outsourced CA. Also includes redundancy for Web server hardware where certificate lifecycle management functions are controlled. Administrator console may also be included (a PC).
Software	High	PKI software, including initial license and maintenance fees. Includes some software used for local customization or management. Additional components to customize authentication may be included.
Consulting	Medium	Required expertise for setup and installation of PKI systems. Business analysis to guide CA setup and authentication processes. Customization of life cycle Web pages and/or security policies.

Given that a PKI system is an essential part of a company's infrastructure, the system must be available on a 24×7 schedule. In addition, costs of maintaining an RA administrator must be accounted for as a purely automated authentication system would be too difficult to set up. Tables 2.3 and 2.4 show the ongoing costs for components and relative costs for in-house and outsourced systems.

Table 2.3   Ongoing Cost Components for a Typical In-House PKI System

COMPONENT	SETUP COSTS	COMMENTS
Hardware	Medium	Computer hardware, including redundant systems and security infrastructure. Hardware may need to be replaced or upgraded over time.
Software	Low	PKI software, including initial license and maintenance fees. Software becomes cheaper over time as most of the investment is made up front. There are still ongoing maintenance fees on the software.
Consulting	Low	Required expertise for setup and installation of PKI systems. Generally, unless further integration is needed or business process changes significantly, consulting is not generally required after the setup stage of a PKI system.

Table 2.4 Ongoing Cost Components for a Typical Outsourced PKI System

COMPONENT	SETUP COSTS	COMMENTS
Hardware	Low	Computer hardware, including redundant systems and security infrastructure. Hardware may need to be replaced or upgraded over time, but an outsourced PKI requires less hardware.
Software	Medium	PKI software, including initial license and maintenance fees. Ongoing fees for the managed PKI system.
Consulting	Low	Required expertise for setup and installation of PKI systems. Generally, unless further integration is needed or business process changes significantly, consulting is not generally required after the setup stage of a PKI system.

Summary: Best Practices to Reduce Complexity

As we have seen, a PKI system has a wide range of options and, likewise, a number of complexities. Given the utility of PKI, it is necessary to find a way to ease the complexity and enhance the use of the benefits PKI can provide. As a result, best practices of PKI can help reduce the difficulty in the various stages of a PKI deployment. Best practices can provide a good foundation for building trust solutions that, in the end, provide for easy deployment and use of PKI solutions.

CHAPTER 3

Best Practices of PKI

Given that PKI is a time-tested technology, a number of best practices have been developed in the industry over the years. Because various solutions will be built on top of this PKI base, it is critical that we have a well-designed and well-implemented PKI. This chapter describes the various aspects that should be considered in developing an effective, reliable, and secure PKI.

Insource versus Outsource Factors

One of the key decision-making criteria in building a trust infrastructure based on PKI is whether to host the CA function (insource) or have a third-party run the CA functions (outsource). The decision to choose insourcing or outsourcing must be established before embarking on the design and implementation of a PKI solution. This decision may affect the scope, costs, and even the choice of possible vendors. A summary of pros and cons is listed in Table 3.1, with a more detailed discussion to follow throughout the section.

Table 3.1   Comparison of Insource versus Outsource Benefits

AREA	INSOURCE BENEFITS	OUTSOURCE BENEFITS
Authentication policy	Custom; allows easily changeable policies	Leverage already established and functional policies
Customization	Maximum flexibility, but longer deployment time	Minimal ability, but quicker deployment time
Deployment	Requires more effort up front, but less work ongoing	Minimal effort, but may require more integration
Cost	Moderate upfront costs, lower ongoing	Lower upfront costs, moderate ongoing
Personnel required	Significant numbers required to run, secure, and maintain CA and RA systems	Lower numbers required to run and maintain RA systems only

Public and Private Hierarchies

A key concept to understand in determining if an organization should out-source or insource is the idea of public and private hierarchies. Public hierarchies, simply defined, are those hierarchies that chain up to a root that lies in a common, public application (like an Internet browser). Figures 3.1 and 3.2 show some examples. The advantage of this chaining is best seen when a certificate, issued under this public hierarchy, allows the application (such as the browser) to automatically verify the validity and issuer of the certificate. This allows for a smoother user experience because the root of the CA is embedded in the application. In the case of Microsoft-based operating systems, the certificate is stored in the registry, which can then be accessed by other applications, such as Microsoft Outlook. Public hierarchies are usually required in cases where information or authentication must be solicited from nonaffiliated parties (such as via Internet email). Levels of trust for nonaffiliated parties must be relatively high, and therefore a common party to establish that trust must come from an outsourced CA.

Private hierarchies chain up to a root that is not found in common, publicly available software. In these cases the verification of the hierarchy is not important (when used for authentication to a portal, for example). It is possible to install the root of the private hierarchy manually either at the time of the certificate delivery or at any other time. The consequence of this, of course, is that the end user bears more of the burden in terms of user administration (although it is only a one-time event per machine). Private hierarchies are most useful for closed, affiliated communities, such as an employee portal.

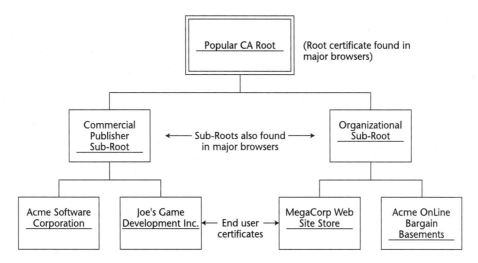

Figure 3.1 Examples of public hierarchy.

It is important to note that access control to protected resources is not usually based solely on verification of a certificate chain up to a trusted root CA certificate. Authentication applications, such as extranets, usually have authorization modules to allow software to read the contents of the presented certificate and make access control decisions based on an access control list.

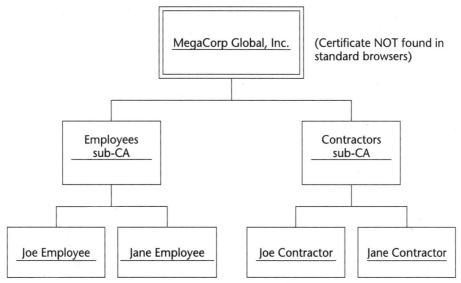

Figure 3.2 Example of private hierarchy.

Control and Flexibility

A key decision-making factor in a PKI design is the level of control and flexibility an organization needs in its CA operations and authentication requirements. Generally, insourced options give maximum flexibility because the CA operations are managed and controlled by the enterprise. In addition, the authentication processes and mechanisms can be fully defined by the organization. This flexibility is critical when defining legal documents such as the certificate practice statement (CPS) and certificate policy (CP), as introduced in Chapter 2. By definition, an insourced PKI will have to be created under a private hierarchy. The consequence of this approach is that end users will have to install the CA's root into their applications to ensure that the applications recognize those certificates.

TIP There can be several types of root certificates including one for a CA and one for an organization (like your company). For public hierarchies, the organization's root is created and signed by the CA's root. For private hierarchies, the organization's root is the highest level in the chain. See Figure 3.3.

An outsourced model provides less flexibility because certificate hierarchies are created at the time the CA is set up. Additional changes require more time and money. If an organization does not have specific requirements for authentication, the CP and the CPS are willing to accept the CA's CP and CPS, then the burden of creating the CP and CPS is lifted from the organization. In addition, the outsourced model moves the burden of the protection of the root key for the organization to the outsourced CA. In this regard, most outsourced CAs provide some level of insurance for breaches of security.

Cost and Deployment Time

The outsourced model permits shorter deployment times due to fewer hardware and software requirements for setup and management. In addition, with outsourced models, personnel and secure infrastructure requirements decrease as the CA bears more of this responsibility. The costs of such a system are amortized over a longer period of time, versus a larger capital expense with software and hardware for an insourced model. Generally, this model works well for small to medium, and some large, enterprises.

For very large installations, insourced models may be favorable as secure infrastructure, data centers, and personnel may already be available. In this manner, larger upfront costs can be leveraged to provide decreasing costs over time due to economies of scale. In addition, large installations will more likely have to create their own authentication requirements and more hierarchies, which would be relatively expensive for a given equivalent outsourced model. The major downside to insourced models is the longer deployment time required (large implementations usually last more than six months).

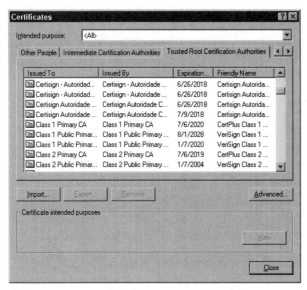

Figure 3.3 Example of some common public root certificates.

Vendor and Technology Selection

The purchase and implementation of a PKI solution involves significant time and expense. As a result, choosing the right vendor and technology for an organization's needs is critical. To choose appropriately, it is important first to map out the selection criteria. These criteria can then be applied to each vendor to determine the right fit.

Determining the Selection Criteria

To ask a vendor the right questions, you must first start by developing good selection criteria. These criteria include the following:

- Financial strength
- Scalability
- Security
- Operations
- Support
- Consulting Strength

Financial Strength

In all cases, especially in the turmoil of rough economic times, it is critical that the chosen CA remains financially soluble and is able to provide enhanced technologies as standards and customer needs change. Currently a number of PKI vendors are suffering major financial issues that make them less attractive as vendors.

Whether or not you have a financial background, nothing is more important than being able to ascertain the financial viability of a PKI vendor. Because only public companies are generally accountable and required to publicly disclose financial statements, a conservative approach is to select a PKI vendor that is a public company. Unlike many other technologies, PKI can become the basis for all aspects of an enterprise's mission-critical applications. Some of the key elements to look for in a potential PKI vendor include the following:

- A strong balance sheet, including sufficient cash flow and assets to sustain the business.

- A good acquisition strategy because it is difficult for any company to adapt to quick technology changes without looking at acquisition.

- A seasoned management team. The computer security business can be a complicated business with constantly changing market and customer needs. The management team should be up to the challenge of such a dynamic business environment.

Scalability

Given that an enterprise may grow over time and its suppliers, vendors, and customers will increase, it is essential to pick a scalable solution that can manage thousands or maybe even millions of certificates over time.

Many PKI implementations need to manage larger and larger numbers of certificates. Consider that in the typical life cycle of a certificate, multiple certificates may need to be issued to the same person because certificates may be lost, certificates may expire, and a variety of other events may occur.

TIP An estimate of two or three certificates per user per application is a good yardstick for measuring the number of certificates that will have to be managed.

In addition, deployment methods will affect whether thousands of certificates need to be issued in a short period of time or if only hundreds of certificates will be issued at a time. As a result, it is considered best practice to plan for the largest bandwidth required and implement for a smaller bandwidth.

Scalability issues occur for the RA functions as well as the certificate issuance functions. As the number of certificates to be managed grows, so does the burden on the RA. In addition, as the number of certificates grows, so does the need for dedicated certificate issuance cryptographic devices (such as hardware signing modules). The PKI vendor must be able to provide solutions for small-scale deployments as well as manage certificates for millions of issuances. Finally, scalability is an issue for directory and database storage. When dealing with large numbers of certificates, such as for a national root certificate, the directory (or database) system employed will be critical for large numbers of certificate issuances and verifications. The directory or database is used for tasks such as storing certificates, retrieving certificates, and checking for revoked certificates.

Security

If we consider that a chain is only as strong as its weakest link, then it is important to look at a PKI solution as a sum of various components. For example, compromise of the enterprise's root certificate can potentially invalidate all certificates issued under that root (because a relying party may not know which certificates were fraudulently issued). Although this may appear obvious, it is critical to determine and examine the various components and subcomponents of a vendor's product line for security strength. To help mitigate risks from insecure designs, look for security affiliations such as the FIPS or European Union (EU)–related security standards. For example, a key certification (especially for outsourced CA vendors) is the BS7799 certification (security-focused certification for people and processes). The BS7799 investigates the operations of a company and determines if they are reasonably trustworthy. Although trusted operations do not necessarily imply secure software, the BS7799 does show that the vendor has thought about security from the ground up.

Operations

For an outsourced CA model, it is critical to choose a vendor with a very reliable and solid understanding of CA operations. CAs should perform regular audits by outside auditors, create well-documented procedures, keep separation of duties for all back-end CA operations, and develop business continuity planning. In addition, CAs that perform root key generation for enterprises must keep a well-documented trail of how the keys are generated, the chain of custody of the keys, and key signing procedures. Some of the industry-leading CAs will go so far as to videotape and notarize all aspects of the key generation process.

For an insourced CA model, the operations of the vendor are not as essential because all of the CA functions happen within the enterprise. In this regard, it is important for the enterprise to ensure that it can do as effective a job at the operations aspect as an external CA.

One important certification for reliable operations is the Statement on Auditing Standards No. 70 (SAS70) audit. The SAS70 audit gives an independent auditor the ability to formulate an opinion on the controls of an organization. While the SAS70 is not a pass/fail checklist, it does give a third party the ability to understand how well run an operations center or company is. Generally, SAS70 audits should be done once a year through a trusted outside agency.

Support

As with every vendor, support is a critical component of vendor selection. With a PKI, good support is even more critical given its complexity. There are several aspects of support including the following:

- Coverage period
- Service Level Agreement (SLA) for escalation
- Technical competency
- Support restrictions

The following are best practices generally required for medium to large enterprises for PKI systems in production (smaller enterprises will require reduced amounts of these parameters):

24 × 7 coverage.   Because a PKI system is involved in the issuance and revocation checking of certificates, the reliability of the system must be maintained at all times.

Service level agreement (SLA) for escalation.   In general for high-severity issues, escalation should be immediate or, at the most, an hour after the initial call. Less severe issues should be escalated anywhere from 4 to 24 hours after the initial call.

Technical competency.   Because many customer support centers have high turnover or are outsourced, it is important to understand the level of technical understanding the customer support representatives maintain. Without good technical knowledge in the front-line response teams, problem resolution can take days. Well-planned technical support centers will have well-designed knowledge management systems (KMSs) to ensure that they will always have initial and immediate guidance, even if the first person taking an issue does not have an answer.

Determine how many callers can use the support line.   Many vendors have a "named caller" policy, which means only a predetermined set of people may access the support line. This could be difficult to accept, especially if you have a wide geographical dispersion of your PKI infrastructure and have regional administrators.

TIP Carefully review your support contracts. SLAs and the service costs are detailed in the vendor's contracts. Consider negotiating maintenance or support costs to get either a lower price or an increased level of service for the same price.

Consulting Strength

Many vendors will not have the ability to do PKI implementation and application integration. Vendors with good consulting relationships will be able to help enterprises deploy and customize PKI and related solution systems through consulting partners. A good consulting partner will be able to minimize rollout and maintenance costs through knowledgeable architecture and implementation.

Given that PKI solutions involve many different components and integration issues, it is essential for a PKI vendor to have consulting strength on which it can rely for implementation and customization and integration projects. PKI integrations, and knowledge of integration, usually requires expertise beyond the vendor's capability.

In general, several key actions can be taken to understand the consulting strength of a vendor:

- Look for relationships with some of the top consulting firms.
- Verify the training programs used to train the consulting teams. Generally, the vendor will have a channel program that will cover various aspects of training, including certification of consulting personnel.
- Look for tool kits for integration with the vendor's software or back-end. Well-designed tool kits provide an easier interface for consultants to use to implement customization and execute implementations.
- If possible, attempt to talk to other companies that have worked with the consulting companies of the prospective vendors. Look for length, cost, and quality of the engagement. PKI consulting projects can easily run into cost overruns due to their complexity, so ensure that the consulting company has been successful in the past and has a proven methodology.

■ Ask to see the credentials and history of all consultants who might be used for a PKI engagement. Many times, large consulting firms send in junior consultants to train at large corporations, counting on long and large engagements. If an engagement is big enough, you may use the experience and background of consultants to your advantage and negotiate a lower consulting engagement fee for junior consultants (provided you are confident they can still do the job right!).

Vendor Vetting: How to Ask the Right Questions

In general, the best method of surveying various vendors is through a request for proposal (RFP) process. This section will lay out the basis of an RFP designed for PKI implementations. Specific examples are given that highlight the type of questions that need to be asked. Although this is by no means a complete trust solutions RFP, it does provide some basic fundamentals.

Executive Summary

The executive summary describes the overall direction and purpose of the RFP by indicating deadline dates and general submission contact information. Generally, this section lets the vendor quickly understand the resources it will need to work on this project. Remember that in planning for delivery dates and costs, decreasing the time does not necessarily decrease the costs. Certain activities will incur fixed costs (like purchasing software and maintenance and support costs). An example:

Acme Co. is soliciting proposals for a PKI to be deployed for internal use for its offices in Europe and Asia. With this PKI system, Acme is looking to develop substantial cost savings by automating and moving routine, but costly, online tasks, such as expense reporting and purchase requisitions. Acme is seeking proposals until July 1, 2003, 5:00 p.m. Proposals may be sent to Acme's headquarters...

Introduction

The introduction provides a description of the enterprise, including the size of the organization and its geographical sites. This information is especially important because the organization may require several physically separate sites to be involved. In addition, with respect to security, laws vary from country to country, and, thus, the vendor may need to understand what compliance requirements will be necessary at each site. The industry the organization is involved in is just as critical. Certain industries, like finance, have specific laws that must be taken into account during the rollout of the PKI. The more detail the enterprise can provide, the easier it will be for the vendor to get an accurate assessment of the project. An example:

> *Acme Co. is one of the largest manufacturers of cyber widgets and has offices and plants in Europe and Asia. Acme is aiming to reduce its expenses through easier and more secure authentication mechanisms and by moving processes to online forms. Currently Acme has 3,000 employees distributed across Europe and Asia with more than $10 billion in annual revenue. Acme's manufacturing process relies on the ability of plant employees to access the intranet and email 24 hours a day, 7 days a week, to match its production schedule.*

Scope of the Project

This section describes the overall parameters, including allowed time of rollout, number of users, and key applications that will be used for the PKI. Based on this information, the vendor can create a more accurate response to the RFP. As much as possible, precise numbers and timelines should be listed. Keep in mind that internal project and budget planning should allow for time and cost overruns. Typically overruns of 20 to 30 percent for cost and time are a good margin for planning. Note that some vendors will use a per-seat charge model, and some may charge on a per-certificate basis. The per-certificate model implies that every certificate (VPN, email encryption, extranet) that a user may require will incur a level of cost. Usually, however, this model is reserved for outsourced CAs. Insourced models usually charge a fixed fee and ongoing maintenance costs so that the costs are set up per seat, especially because most insourced models require a client component per desktop. It may be advisable to present information for and solicit responses to both scenarios for comparison. An example:

> *Acme Co. plans to deploy a PKI for its worldwide employee base, consisting of 3,000 users in several countries in Europe and Asia. The goal is to deploy all phases of this project by the first quarter of 2004 for Europe and by the second quarter of 2004 for Asia. Training and user documentation should be completed prior to the rollout of any systems for production. The main applications will consist of secure email, form signing, and intranet portal access. The bulk of users will fall into a generic access level as they will need basic authentication; however, we expect about 600 management-level personnel to require strong authentication to receive their certificates that provide them with increasing levels of access to the corporate portal.*

Project Organization and Management

This section of the RFP explains the requirements for project management. Large-scale or complex projects may require that the vendor provide a project manager. Some sample requirements are as follows:

Describe how changed management procedures are dealt with after signed authorization. Because most proposals are based on certain assumptions, it is important for both the vendor and the organization to ensure that if changes are to occur, the impact on cost and time is understood.

Include project methodology and projected timelines for milestones of the deployment of the solution. This information will also reveal how much experience the vendor has with this technology.

Security Architecture

This section of the RFP contains a description of the security requirements for various components of the PKI architecture, including the need for industry or government certification standards. Some sample requirements are as follows:

Describe how the proposed solution will manage the storage of Root CA signing keys on hardware devices that comply with FIPS 140-1 Level 3. FIPS 140-1 Level 3 is a high level of security for a commercial hardware device.

Describe the support for secure communications among the various components of the solution. Many PKI solutions and trust applications are built with modular components. As a result, these components may need to communicate sensitive information to one other.

Describe how the proposed solution stores data in an encrypted format to protect against unauthorized changes. A key vulnerable point in a system could be the data stored regarding the system, including escrowed keys and temporary tables used during transactions. Encrypted data makes it more difficult for the security of the system to be compromised.

Security Policy

The security policy section describes the need for security policy development or conformance to existing corporate security policies. This section is especially important if an organization already has well-developed security policies, as any new system should not force an alteration of business practices.

How does the solution provide for restricted delegated privileges to users? In large installations it is not possible for a single administrator to perform all CA/RA functions; as a result, there must be a mechanism for delegated administration with, perhaps, restricted functionality.

Describe the methods for password management controls such as length of password, password history maintenance, and account lockout for excessive failed attempts. Although most systems should use digital certificates in all aspects of their security, some vendors will still use passwords as a protection scheme for the private key of a certificate or as an interim access control method until a user gets a certificate.

Describe how the solution would allow for the use of authentication and access control methods to prevent unauthorized access to administration resources. This is critical because if the administrator access is weak, then the entire system may be compromised.

How will the proposed solution display notices and legal banners warning users of misuse and possible monitoring of activities on the related systems? Certain laws require a notice stating that the user is accessing a private system. Without such banners it is possible for a user to claim that he or she was not aware of attempting to access a private system. These laws strengthen anti-hacker laws.

Standards and Security Design Guidelines

In complex RFPs, it may be necessary to spell out the actual design and security specifications of the vendor hardware or software. This section can be eliminated if the Security Architecture portion is sufficient. Otherwise, detailed software development processes, information classification schemes, and code audits may be specified as a prequalification for vendor selection. Some requirement examples include the following:

Describe vendor's participation in support of open standards such as PKIX, X.509v3, X.509v2, OCSP, X.500, RSA algorithms, ECC, DES, 3DES, RC4, AES, MD5, SHA-1, and PKCS standards. Your particular organization may require interoperability with more or fewer standards. The more standards-based technology a vendor uses, the easier it is to perform integration and customization tasks.

What are the specific vendor variances to the previously listed standards? The beauty of standards is that there are so many to choose from. Make sure that you understand how vendors may have "tweaked" standards.

Operational Guidelines

This section is a requirement for an outsourced CA function (rather than an insourced CA function). Detailed questions should be designed to investigate the reliability and security of the vendor's back-end processes. Some examples include the following:

Describe how the solution provides for backup of all data, including data files, programs, application system software, and operating system software.   Some vendors provide complex and integrated components for their PKI that make it difficult for backup strategies to be developed. Understanding these business continuity features is critical for a reliable system.

Explain provisions to log access of all events, including administrator logins/logouts, user logins/logouts, system process events, and error reporting.   This statement helps explain how insider attacks can be mitigated or at least detected. You do not want the administrator to be able to perform an action and change the logs of that action.

Describe how maintenance and downtime activities are scheduled and how customers are informed of data center activities.   For outsourced CAs, understanding availability and downtime procedures is critical for creating your business continuity plans.

Describe facilities and processes for maintaining a 24 × 7 reliability and 99.9999 percent uptime.   Realize that the more reliability you require, the more expensive the solution. This statement essentially asks an outsourced vendor for the highest level of availability. Likewise for insourced solutions, you are asking the vendor to prove that it is possible to run your data center with this level of reliability and availability.

Audit

This section specifies the types of audits required or asks about the various audits a CA undergoes. This can also apply to insourced CAs as they may undergo auditing of their software development processes.

The vendor should describe any audits done by outside parties on a regular basis, including BS7799.   Outside audits help ensure that an objective party is monitoring the vendor and its operations. These audits are very important for an outsourced vendor, but they are also important for an insourced vendor's operations and secure software development process.

Describe any compliance with relevant ISO standards.   Depending on your industry and/or geographic location, it may be important to note ISO standards that the vendor may meet.

Security Awareness and Training

This section includes inquiries about the breadth of services the vendor may provide to help train and educate the enterprise. Given the complexity of trust technology, it is critical to be able to assess the vendor's ability to train your staff.

The vendor should provide recommended training programs for both system administrators and end users.   This helps you get an idea of the complexity of the vendor's solution. In addition, it can help in properly budgeting for training, a key aspect of any enterprise deployment.

Describe the amount and content of training provided as part of the professional services deployment.   It is important to understand whether the professional services team will take the time to train in order to pass on knowledge during the implementation phase. Without such knowledge transfer, supporting the initiative may be difficult.

The vendor shall provide system administration guides, user training manuals, application software documentation, and system software documentation.   This statement ensures that there is sufficient information for the organization's own IT staff to be able to maintain the PKI successfully after the vendor's PKI deployment team has left.

Consultant Profiles

This section asks the vendor for samples of the professional biographies of the consultants who will be doing the implementation of the PKI solutions and/or the custom integration work. Some examples:

Provide a list of the professional service consultants who will be involved in implementing this solution. Include name, title, and relevant professional experience.   Do not assume that any consultant that the vendor may send directly or through a third party can do the job. Carefully screen consultants based on their resumes. Remember that you are buying a consultant's experience, so each consultant can be very different.

Describe the lead times and other requirements in initiating implementation once the solution has been accepted.   Some companies will have scheduling or travel issues that may result in lag time before a project can be implemented. Also realize that you will pay for travel and expense costs, so planning can help bring down unnecessary travel and lodging costs.

Project References

Ensure that you are able to find the vendor's past or current clients who are willing to talk with you and describe their experiences with the PKI vendor. Of course, this may not be very effective given that, most likely, only customers with positive experiences will be referenced. Their answers to your questions, though, will help you understand the PKI vendor's vertical expertise and experience with organizations of your size. An example:

> **Provide at least three references of companies in different industries that would be willing to talk about their experience with your company.** Ensure that the responses include the names of senior managers because it will be the business decisions makers who will ultimately decide whether the project was a good decision.

Design

A key aspect of a PKI is its design and architecture. PKI technology allows for flexibility in design regardless of the specific technology chosen. Choosing the best set of options will vary from organization to organization, but a number of best practices can provide guidance.

Elements of a PKI Infrastructure

Although we briefly discussed the various elements of a PKI in Chapter 2, it is important to understand how all the aspects of the overall infrastructure must work with one another to ensure a solid, well-implemented PKI. This section presents various best practices for how each element should be planned.

CA Hardware and Software Architecture

One of the first elements you will need to select will be the CA hardware and software. Based on the particular vendor and whether you have decided to outsource the CA function, the design will vary. Let's examine some common points, regardless of the vendor or model for hosting the CA:

- Ensure that your hardware has validation for FIPS-140 Level 1 (Federal Information Processing Standards Publications 140-1) or above for any key generation signing capability for RA functions. FIPS-140 Level 1 refers to security requirements that are to be met by a cryptographic module used within a security system protecting unclassified information. FIPS-140 Level 1 is the minimum standard any organization should accept.

■ Ensure that your CA hardware has validation for FIPS-140 Level 2 or above for any key generation signing capability for CA functions. FIPS-140 Level 2 goes beyond Level 1 by indicating for software-based cryptographic functions how role-based authentication (that is, authenticating the specific user) is performed.

TIP Watch out for FIPS-140 "compliance," "conformance," and "compatible" designations as they are not the same as actual validation. These terms refer to FIPS-140 "like" standards, but not necessarily validation through testing.

■ The RA components should be separated from the CA components on different machines and possibly in different data centers. Given that we do not wish to have an insider breach, RA and CA functionality should be physically separated with multiperson access required for CA components.

User Setup/Registration Definitions

Because registrations usually occur through a Web server–based system (the top PKI vendors have this functionality), it is important to have a Web server machine that is hardened. To ensure a smooth user experience, it may be necessary to incorporate the look and feel of the general site into the registration server. In this case, it is advisable to have a jump point from the main portal system to a separate Web server that manages the registration. Then the registration, once completed, can jump back to the portal. All this can be done seamlessly, using the same look and feel consistently. This allows a more secure Web server to manage the registration process, but it provides user convenience through the use of a common look and feel.

Legal Policy Development

PKI has many applications that require legal backing, including digitally signing documents and recovering private keys through an escrow process. As a result, the legal policy development is a key aspect of the design of a PKI. Perhaps the simplest method to use for legal policy development is to use an outsourced CA and rely on the CA's policies. While this does not provide very much flexibility in the development of custom legal documents, it does decrease design and deployment costs for a PKI project.

If an organization decides that custom legal policies must be developed, then some key areas to develop include the following:

■ Certificate policy (CP) and certificate practice statement (CPS)

■ Authentication policies

- Privacy statements (for mass market applications in which authentication data must be collected)

- Private key liability (to ensure that the user bears responsibility for the protection of the private key and notification in the event that the key is lost)

Business continuity policies (above and beyond a normal IT strategy) to protect against downtime of the PKI infrastructure are critical. The organization hosting the PKI must provide some sort of SLA to its end users, whether they are internal or external.

Insurance, one aspect of the legal framework, is a critical piece of the legal infrastructure. Because problems will occur from time to time, it is important that the organization can afford to minimize damage to a trusted brand or solution. In addition, the legal documents are critical for shifting the burden of protection of the private key to the end user. The type of insurance that usually covers such claims is called Errors and Omission (E&O) insurance.

Three types of agreements (as shown in Figure 3.4) need to be established:

- An RA agreement

- An RA/end-entity relationship, which covers the relationship between the end user and the administrator of the PKI

- The subscriber/end-entity agreement, which covers the relationship between the CA (and its conditions for issuance) and the end-entity (that is, the user, whether a device or a human)

In outsourced models, these agreements are pretty well defined already. In insourced models, all of these agreements will need to be crafted. Such agreements would also include the RA agreement because different departments or administrators may manage the RA and CA function even though they are both contained within the enterprise.

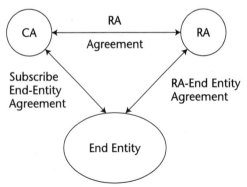

Figure 3.4 Legal relationships among main PKI entities.

RA Agreement

The RA agreement covers the aspects of the RA and CA relationship. If the RA and CA are part of an insourced model, then this agreement can be simplified. In any case, this agreement should be established, even in the case of an insourced model, as generally this will serve as an internal SLA between the CA (usually run by a production IT team) and the RA (usually run by an operations or administrative team). Main points in this agreement would include the following:

- Indemnification of the CA by the RA to ensure that (especially in the case of an outsourced model) the CA does not bear an infinite risk of liability should something go wrong.

- Description of a surety policy that would allow for certain financial guarantees for the CA to function even in spite of financial problems on the CA's part.

- Limits on third-party (that is, relying party) claims against the CA. This will ensure that financial retribution against a CA issuing a false certificate contains a ceiling to prevent the financial shutdown of the CA (again, this is more important for an outsourced model).

RA-End-Entity Agreement

The RA-end-entity agreement describes the relationship between the user of the certificate and the RA, the organization that issued the certificate. The key aspect of this agreement is that it should include statements that will do the following:

- Ensure that the user provides truthful statements about the information used in the approval of the certificate

- Ensure that the user uses the certificates as per the guidelines provided

- Ensure that the user requests revocation of his or her certificate if the private key is lost or otherwise compromised

- Ensure that the user discontinues use of all expired public-private key pairs (and not try to pass them off as legitimate)

Subscriber-End-Entity Agreement

This agreement can also be referred to as the "relying party" agreement. Essentially, a certificate must be accepted and acted on once presented. Certain clauses must be contained in this agreement, such as the following:

- The relying party must check the certificate's status (that is, ensure that it has not expired or been revoked).
- Rely on the certificate for only the purposes stated in the CP or CPS (for example, the certificate, if issued with very weak authentication, can not be used for high-value transactions).
- Put limits on the liability of the RA or CA in the event of a falsely issued certificate. There also must be some insurance guarantees that cover such scenarios and can compensate the victims of bad certificates.

Best Practices for PKI Selection

Although PKI deployment can vary depending on the industry, local laws, and, of course, the organization's specific business requirements, a number of best practices can be applied for the majority of PKI installations.

Personnel

One of the most difficult challenges in rolling out and successfully using PKI is the ability to hire and retain trained, qualified professionals in this area. Several key characteristics should be noted when looking to hire (either permanently or on a consulting basis):

- Well-recognized security certifications (some examples were given in Chapter 1), such as the CISSP
- A background in security (almost a necessity)
- Software development experience (this is helpful due to the integration efforts usually required)
- The ability to be available or, at least, work with IT personnel to ensure 24×7 reliability

Secure Infrastructure

Many organizations believe that a PKI in and of itself will create a secure infrastructure. This, of course, is not true as PKI provides only the basis for a trust solution. Secure infrastructure components, like firewalls and routers, are still required. In general, it is best to separate the CA and RA functions physically by logical firewalls. In addition, the RA system should be well protected physically and logically from outside attacks and insider abuse. If a compromise must be made in terms of speed versus security, always err on the side of security. Given that certificate life cycle functions, such as issuance and renewals, occur only a few times a year per user, an extra wait due to multiple checks proves to be a worthy trade-off.

Generally, some aspect of the registration process must be accessible to a large group of people, whether internal or external to an organization. As a result, the registration server (usually a back-end or front-end add-on to a Web server) should be set up in a DMZ with possible IDS and auditing capability. Any RA functions should be safeguarded with external devices, such as smart cards, requiring some level of dual factor authentication.

One easy way to minimize security loopholes in the supporting security infrastructure equipment is to purchase security appliances. Security appliances are simple, one- or two-function hardware boxes that are designed to operate in a data center. Firewalls and virus checkers have security appliances, which allow for quick deployment and ready-to-go hardened systems.

Legal Aspects

Looking at a PKI system should also include examining the legal aspects. Although more relevant for outsourced deployments, legal CPS and CP, liability, insurance, and relevant issues must be considered. If your organization has knowledgeable legal resources, then it may be possible to develop your own legal documents. Investigate whether the legal documents will have to be created or if can you leverage what the vendor can provide.

Deployment Time Frame

Regardless of whether an insourced or outsourced model is chosen, plan on a timeframe deployment of no less than one month. If contract and other sales-related issues are included, add another two to four weeks. In addition, depending on the complexity of the project, ensure that the project consultants provided by the vendor or through a partner consulting firm are scheduled and available as soon as the sales contracts are signed.

Here are some key areas that affect the deployment time and costs of a PKI implementation:

> Larger and more customized deployments can take six months or more. Insourced models can usually take at least three months, if not longer, considering the hardware and software setup. Generally, certain activities can be planned in parallel, including the following:
>
> - Consulting statement of work reviews (these define what the consultants will do, in what timeframe, and in what budget).
> - Creation of CA hierarchies (if you do not have any idea of how to structure these, then see if you can get some pre-engagement consulting time to help plan this).

- Personnel training. Ensure that your administrators are well prepared to interact with the consultants so that your organization's personnel can do future upgrades/changes as necessary.

- Scheduled downtime in product data centers for installation or modification of hardware and/or existing software (such as Web servers used for registration servers for the PKI). Many organizations have planned, fixed maintenance windows into which the deployment will need to fit.

Costs

We will cover more details on cost in Chapter 4; however, good estimates to use for costs depend on some key factors:

- Number of users

- Number of applications (because more applications may mean more certificates)

- Whether the CA service is being outsourced or managed fully in-house

TIP Ensure that the amortized cost for your PKI does not exceed more than 10 percent (ideally) or no more than 25 percent (maximum) of the cost of the overall application you are trying to trust-enable with PKI.

In general, the best estimate to use for security-related applications is that the cost of the security should not be more than a fraction of the overall cost of the application to be secured. For example, if your automobile insurance costs exceeded the costs of the automobile itself, it may not make sense to own or operate that vehicle because the utility and expense of the car are overwhelmed by the insurance costs. Likewise, if the costs of certificates or related infrastructure services exceed 10 percent of the overall cost of the application, then the ROI becomes increasingly difficult to show. Costs can range from $50 per user to $200+ per user when software, hardware, consulting, and other hidden costs are amortized.

Implementation

We have seen a number of best practices throughout this chapter. Choosing a PKI architecture and vendor is only half of the work. Most IT-related projects fail during the implementation phase as a result of cost overruns or inaccurate estimates of deployment time. Generally, a pure PKI implementation is only part of a larger project. Most PKI implementations are associated with other trust-solution rollouts (for example, form signing or VPN deployment).

The two key areas that are most impacted and will affect the cost and deployment success are the resources available and the project management of the rollout. This section covers some of the best practices for implementing PKI trust solutions.

Project Management

It is amazing to see so many companies jump into major rollouts like PKI without aligning the proper resources. Here are some common mistakes many companies have made when deploying PKI:

Not planning for router/firewall rule changes.   Depending on the particular system and implementation, pieces of the PKI system may have to reside in publicly accessible places on the network. The registration server, for example, typically resides in a DMZ. Communication between modules, including the registration server and the RA components, may require specific ports to be available through the router or firewall.

Not planning for downtime or maintenance windows.   In almost all cases, modifications to a Web server will be required as part of the PKI deployment. As a result, there may need to be a reboot of the Web server software or the machine that hosts the core software, or both.

Not involving IT personnel early to allow for adequate training.   Although specific consultants may assist in the implementation, it will be IT personnel who maintain the systems, so IT should be involved early in the project, during the implementation phase.

Inadequate allocation of resources to end-user documentation.   Because, eventually, all this infrastructure will enable certain applications for the end user, it is very important the end user understands the changes that will be coming and how to manage through them.

Not identifying designated administrators ahead of the PKI deployment.   Establishing RA and system administrators for the system should be done well ahead of deployment. RAs must have specific certificates, and for outsourced models getting the certificates could take several days during the vetting process.

Resources Needed

Another key area where many organizations fall short is in identifying and employing the right personnel to design, implement, and maintain the PKI system. The unique aspect of PKI is that while it does solve security issues and requires knowledge of the security space, it also relies heavily on software integration. As a result, several types of people are needed to implement a PKI project successfully. A sample team for a PKI deployment would include a lead architect, a directory specialist, a software developer, and a security professional. The lead architect is responsible for determining the technical requirements based on the various business issues, including authentication requirements, insurance requirements, and end-user requirements. The directory specialist would be responsible for creating and maintaining a directory to hold vital information, such as authentication data and certificates in a common repository. Tasks for this role include creation of the directory schema and possibly integration into existing databases (for example, the personnel database for authentication data). For smaller projects, the lead architect could also serve as the directory specialist. The software developer is required to ensure that integration with various trust applications (such as form signing), can be accomplished as and when needed. Again, for smaller deployments, this is not much of an issue; however, for larger deployments, customizations can be the bulk of the effort. Finally, given that PKI requires security infrastructure and good security processes to ensure the credibility of the certificates and issuance process, the security professional needs to ensure that good security has been implemented. The security professional performs duties, such as interfacing with IT staff to ensure that firewalls, access control systems, and database security are all in line with the risk model the organization is willing to take.

Timelines

Perhaps the most difficult aspect of any deployment that has a wide impact across an enterprise is enabling a smooth rollout. Planning for timelines required to implement PKI will greatly enhance the success of the project. An efficient deployment would take advantage of the ability to execute several tasks in parallel to minimize deployment time.

A typical PKI implementation falls under a few basic phases (as shown in Table 3.2):

1. **Preparation.** This stage requires the organization and the vendor to agree on the scope and details of the implementation before any deployment work begins. Detailed tasks include purchase and shipment of product, a kick-off meeting to ensure that the organization and PKI deployment team understand the project requirements, and the review and acceptance of the agreement between the deployment team and the organization (that is, a statement of work).

2. **CA generation.** Before any certificates can be created, a root CA must be generated. In outsourced models, this process can take one or more weeks. For insourced models, higher security standards will be needed and may require scheduled time for root creation. Detailed tasks include creating a naming hierarchy (for root and intermediate CAs) and preparing and generating the root.

3. **Setup for production.** Basic software installation and preparation are done at this stage to prepare for a production rollout, although at this point the software is not put into production mode. Detailed tasks include enrolling and installing the administrator certificate (that is, the RA certificate) and ensuring that the root CAs are ready to be placed online.

4. **Setup and deployment for the test environment.** When possible, the environment meant for production is duplicated and placed into a fully functional test environment. For most PKI vendors a "test" environment means simply signing certificates with a test root CA versus the product root CA. Detailed tasks include duplicating the steps in phase 3, but actually bringing the test root CA online and implementing testing.

5. **Setup and configuration of registration modules.** Generally, this phase is used to customize the user experience and describe what the enrollment pages for the end user will look like. Web server plug-ins or customizations may also be done at this stage.

6. **Installation of optional modules.** Additional modules that need to be installed are handled at this stage. Examples of optional modules include escrow services and roaming services. Specific tasks will vary based on the customization and optional modules required.

7. **Moving system to production environment.** With a successful completion and install in a test environment, the system is then moved into production. For most PKI systems, this is simply replacing the test root CA certificates with production root CA certificates.

8. **Training/knowledge transfer.** Last but not least is the transfer of knowledge from the deployment consulting team to the organization. Without this transfer, it will be difficult for the organization to maintain the infrastructure.

Table 3.2 A Sample Project Plan

ID	TASK NAME	DURATION	START	FINISH	PREDECESSORS
1	**PKI Trust Solutions Project–Project start**	**19.5 days**	**Mon 3/24/03**	**Fri 4/18/03**	
2	**Preparation**	**15 days**	**Mon 3/24/03**	**Fri 4/11/03**	
3	Order and ship software and hardware	5 days	Mon 3/24/03	Fri 3/28/03	
4	Kick-off meeting	1 day	Mon 3/31/03	Mon 3/31/03	3
5	Review/agreement of statement of work	5 days	Mon 4/7/03	Fri 4/11/03	4FS+4 days
6	Request and install secure server ID to enable SSL	1 day	Mon 3/24/03	Mon 3/24/03	
7	Config server for certificates	1 day	Tue 3/25/03	Tue 3/25/03	6
8	Complete pre-engagement checklist	1 day	Wed 3/26/03	Wed 3/26/03	7
9	**CA generation**	**5 days**	**Tue 4/1/03**	**Mon 4/7/03**	
10	Identify hierarchy and naming	4 days	Tue 4/1/03	Fri 4/4/03	4
11	CA generation	1 day	Mon 4/7/03	Mon 4/7/03	10
12	**Setup for production system**	**4.5 days**	**Tue 4/8/03**	**Mon 4/14/03**	
13	Enroll for administrator certificate	1 day	Tue 4/8/03	Tue 4/8/03	11
14	Authenticate order	3 days	Wed 4/9/03	Fri 4/11/03	13
15	CA loaded on production machines	3 days	Wed 4/9/03	Fri 4/11/03	13
16	Approve/pick up administrator certificate	0.5 days	Mon 4/14/03	Mon 4/14/03	15
17	**Setup and deployment for test/staging system**	**3.5 days**	**Tue 4/8/03**	**Fri 4/11/03**	

Table 3.2 *(continued)*

ID	TASK NAME	DURATION	START	FINISH	PREDECESSORS
18	Enroll for administrator certificate (test system)	1 day	Tue 4/8/03	Tue 4/8/03	11
19	CA set up on test machine	2 days	Wed 4/9/03	Thu 4/10/03	18
20	Approve/pick up administrator certificate	0.5 days	Fri 4/11/03	Fri 4/11/03	19
21	**Setup and configuration of registration modules**	**8.5 days**	**Mon 3/24/03**	**Thu 4/3/03**	
22	Install and customize software	0.5 days	Mon 3/24/03	Mon 3/24/03	
23	Develop registration verification function (including automated verification)	5 days	Mon 3/24/03	Mon 3/31/03	22
24	Test registration	1 day	Mon 3/31/03	Tue 4/1/03	23
25	Run script against policy to configure Web pages for modules used	1 day	Tue 4/1/03	Wed 4/2/03	24
26	Download and install policy file	1 day	Wed 4/2/03	Thu 4/3/03	25
27	**Installation of optional modules**	**2.5 days**	**Fri 4/11/03**	**Tue 4/15/03**	**20**
28	**Email server Integration**	**2.5 days**	**Fri 4/11/03**	**Tue 4/15/03**	
29	Verify configuration of needed servers	0.5 days	Fri 4/11/03	Fri 4/11/03	
30	Make necessary changes to the mail server configuration	0.5 days	Mon 4/14/03	Mon 4/14/03	29
31	**Testing – PKI integration with Microsoft Email Platform**	**1.5 days**	**Mon 4/14/03**	**Tue 4/15/03**	

(continued)

Table 3.2 *(continued)*

ID	TASK NAME	DURATION	START	FINISH	PREDECESSORS
32	Create Outlook profile on two end-user machines	0.5 days	Mon 4/14/03	Mon 4/14/03	30
33	Enroll and issue certificates to each end user	0.25 days	Tue 4/15/03	Tue 4/15/03	32
34	Set up Outlook (email client) security profile to use the new certificate for signing/encryption	0.25 days	Tue 4/15/03	Tue 4/15/03	33
35	Exchange encrypted email between the two end users	0.25 days	Tue 4/15/03	Tue 4/15/03	34
36	Verify that decryption is successful for both end users	0.25 days	Tue 4/15/03	Tue 4/15/03	35
37	**Key escrow service (depending on PKI vendor)**	**2.5 days**	**Fri 4/11/03**	**Tue 4/15/03**	
38	Verify the database schemas	1 day	Fri 4/11/03	Mon 4/14/03	
39	Set up configuration files	1 day	Mon 4/14/03	Tue 4/15/03	38
40	Install optional hardware for crypto functions (key generation)	0.5 days	Tue 4/15/03	Tue 4/15/03	39
41	Configure the certificate renewal process	0.5 days	Fri 4/11/03	Fri 4/11/03	
42	Create and configure the key escrow data source (on database system)	0.5 days	Fri 4/11/03	Fri 4/11/03	
43	**Testing — key manager**	**1.5 days**	**Fri 4/11/03**	**Mon 4/14/03**	
44	Enroll, delete, and recover a certificate and key pair	1.5 days	Fri 4/11/03	Mon 4/14/03	

Table 3.2 (continued)

ID	TASK NAME	DURATION	START	FINISH	PREDECESSORS
45	**(Move) Activate system for production**	**4 days**	**Fri 4/11/03**	**Thu 4/17/03**	
46	Configure Web pages to point to production system	1 day	Fri 4/11/03	Mon 4/14/03	20
47	Enrollment/approval for production RA certificate	1 day	Mon 4/14/03	Tue 4/15/03	46
48	Install RA (administrator) certificate	1 day	Tue 4/15/03	Wed 4/16/03	47
49	Test certificate enrollment/revocation/renewal	1 day	Wed 4/16/03	Thu 4/17/03	48
50	**Training and knowledge transfer**	**1 day**	**Thu 4/17/03**	**Fri 4/18/03**	
51	Documentation	1 day	Thu 4/17/03	Fri 4/18/03	49
52	Administrator and end-user training	1 day	Thu 4/17/03	Fri 4/18/03	49
53					
54	General Availability	0 days	Wed 4/16/03	Wed 4/16/03	48

Summary: Choosing the Right Partner

Choosing a PKI vendor is similar to choosing any other vendor for your organization. The specific focus on security and operations does make it more essential that a vendor is closely scrutinized. This chapter has covered how PKI should be implemented correctly and what questions to ask vendors to ensure that they are using best practices. The discussion here provided a base to build upon and to get started in analyzing various approaches to PKI. The next chapter looks at the financial aspects of PKI; as any PKI system, and the trust solutions built on that system, requires substantial financial commitments.

Selling PKI

Designing and implementing PKI provides only a partial picture of what is involved in deploying a successful trust solution based on PKI. Selling PKI to customers, vendors, and internal groups is a significant aspect of the PKI deployment process. As we have seen in previous chapters, PKI provides a base technology that can touch many aspects of a company's infrastructure. As a result, it is necessary to have the right tools to prove that solutions built on PKI can provide a strategic advantage through cost savings, increased productivity, and new applications and services.

ROI on PKI, ASAP

Security used to be a technology that was easy to sell with stories of scary hackers creeping into a company's network in the middle of the night. Although the scary stories still have an impact, the number of security technologies considered a "must have" has been reduced significantly. PKI has now evolved from a technology to keep hackers away to a business tool needed, for example, to comply with government or company standards. The legal support for PKI gives any solution built on it the power to leverage years of legal work to move archaic processes online for efficiency and cost savings.

Reactive versus Proactive Selling Models

Reactive selling can be defined as a method of selling a product or service after an incident has occurred. Personal injury lawyers are perhaps the most infamous of reactive sellers. The probability is high, for example, that an event such as a car accident was caused by a driver's mistake, and thus a case may be made against one party to seek compensation. In this mode, a strong case can be made by the salesperson because the loss can be measured almost immediately.

In security, reactive selling occurs with the examination of how and why an incident occurred; the sales pitch may include managed services to restore and implement lost or damaged resources. Reactive selling models tend to be high-margin products because the service or product is required in a short period of time and to remedy a loss has already occurred. In addition, because the business may be inoperable, services or products may be needed to mitigate further effects.

Proactive selling can be tied to those security services or products that provide preventive measures against security breaches; show an increase in revenue, customer satisfaction, or other business metrics; or provide a competitive edge by enabling new services. Examples of proactive-selling products and services include firewalls and similar perimeter protection devices, as well as enabling technologies such as digital signatures. The best examples of proactive selling in PKI are compliance models. Given that numerous regulatory compliance factors exist in various industries for security and privacy, such as HIPAA in healthcare and the Gramm-Leach-Bliley Act of 1999 (GLBA) in finance, compliance is clearly a proactive-selling approach (companies institute these measures before a determined deadline out of necessity).

PKI essentially can be viewed as either a proactive sell, if sold as a business process enabler, or a reactive sell because the defense of digital signatures in court and audit trails created with digital certificates can aid in forensics.

Why is understanding the reactive versus the proactive sell important for PKI? Depending on the need and audience for the PKI solution justification, whether this will be an internal sell to management or a sell to a customer, the approach of the analysis and selling points will vary. For example, if an organization had been hacked and information was stolen, forensic analysis would be far easier if digital certificates had been used to create audit trails to dispute any nonrepudiation claims. On the other hand, a bank, for example, looking to provide new services online, would view PKI as an enabler to offer new, secure services online.

Success Criteria

How do we measure success or convince a third party of the advantages of PKI? There are, of course, qualitative metrics, including ease of use for single-sign-on technologies built on certificates. In this manner, a single user can access multiple sources with a single credential. In addition, we have the reassurance that our identity and communications are secured from snoopers. (We will discuss the qualitative selling points of PKI in more detail later in this chapter in the *Nonfinancial Benefits* section.)

We can also measure the success of the PKI deployment itself. After all, "shelf ware" (that is, software that is purchased but never fully utilized) has become quite a problem for IT organizations. Deployment success in PKI can be measured by the number of PKI-based trust solutions. For example, while digital form signing will add value to an organization, using that same infrastructure to do portal access and secure messaging provides even more value and, thus, success.

Finally, success in the world of PKI can also be measured in terms of raw dollars—that is, the return on investment (ROI). ROI is a metric used by business professionals to gauge the impact of investing money in a particular project. In this case, it allows us to show quantitative benefits, such as cost savings per person and increased revenue. It is evident that additional monies put into a PKI can increase the value of the trust solutions that are built on top of the infrastructure.

Although it has been traditionally used for financially oriented investments, ROI has become popular over the last several years as a tool to justify IT and corporatewide projects. This type of internal ROI is called an internal rate of return (IRR). After all, if the IT strategy is not aligned with business goals, a fair amount of the expenditure will be wasted.

ROI IN ACTION: STATE OF IOWA ROI PROGRAM

The state of Iowa, to ensure that expenditures on IT-related projects were fruitful, created a process for measuring ROI. The state did ROI analysis on projects such as PKI and form signing. Because of the state laws that required it (as per House File 2205) to conduct all transactions with the state electronically by July 2003, the state explored new technology based on PKI. The state's Uniform Electronics Transactions Act (UETA) recognizes that a physical signature can be replaced by a digital signature. Although the laws do not explicitly state that PKI must be used, the analysis done by the state showed that PKI is the most widely accepted technology to implement digital signatures.

Before being able to use the ROI models presented here, you should establish a baseline for your current process, application, or organization. It is against this baseline that any improvements can be measured. If there are no baselines to be established (because you may be launching new services), then looking at non-implementation and opportunity cost can settle as a baseline. In large or inefficient corporations, establishing a baseline can, itself, be a major undertaking. This effort could also be added into the cost of the solution, and then a more accurate ROI can be calculated with this taken into account.

Implementation ROI

Interestingly enough, even if we justify a PKI trust solutions deployment with the ROI models that we will discuss later in this chapter, the actual deployment of the system must be successful. Therefore, creating success factors for a deployment and an "implementation ROI" is critical. Several essential success factors can be used to measure a deployment:

Deployment schedule.   The on-time deployment of all components helps keep the expenditure within budget and, therefore, is a critical factor in determining success. In addition, any ROI calculation that may focus on cost savings as a result of the PKI will be skewed if the deployment is not on schedule.

Number of trust applications enabled.   Given that PKI is a basic infrastructure, its deployment is not exclusively useful. Combined with specific applications, such as form signing and secure email (as we will discuss in more detail in later chapters), PKI becomes increasingly useful and important. Thus, by leveraging more applications on the same infrastructure, our efforts become more significant.

Number of certificates issued.   Scope of deployment can be measured by the number of certificates issued. The greater the number of certificates, the more extensive the use of the PKI. A number of companies will purchase and set up a PKI but never issue the planned number of certificates. Such a scenario reveals a lack of planning or low utility of the infrastructure.

Number of users and devices covered in the deployment.   A variation of the number of certificates is the number of users and devices affected by the PKI. The greater an organization's participation in the deployment, the more likely the success and importance of the project will be felt.

Number of customers and partners adopting the system.   Most systems utilizing PKI will usually have a migration plan in which users are encouraged to use PKI systems to provide trust in an application. The number of users choosing the PKI method (for example, presenting a certificate for portal access as opposed to using a user name and password) serves as a good measurement of not only the utility of the technology, but also of the training, education, and awareness users have about a more effective method of conducting online transactions with increased confidence.

TIP Remember that a single user may require multiple certificates, such as for secure email, Web portal access, or VPN access. Plan on four certificates per user, including replacement certificates due to lost certificate private keys.

The implementation ROI concept can be applied not only to initial deployments, but also in subsequent years to measuring the growth and utility of the PKI. For example, in most PKI systems, certificates are to be renewed once a year (typically). As a result, measuring any of the previously mentioned factors on the certificate renewal dates can reveal the success of the deployment. Outsourced vendors completely rely on these factors for future business. After all, if they sell customers the ability to issue certificates and customers do not deploy and expand the use of certificates, then naturally future (also known as renewal) business declines.

One important variation on an ROI model is a total cost of ownership (TCO) model. A TCO can be viewed as an ROI analysis over many years, whereas an ROI is perhaps tied to a shorter timeframe or perhaps a single use or purchase event. Given that TCO requires a sustained view of three to five years, we do not cover the TCO approach in this chapter. In recent economic times, most companies are looking at a timeframe of six months to two years; therefore, an immediate ROI is needed to push through PKI. In addition, TCO includes many "soft" or hidden costs, such as administrative overhead and additional processes, associated with a security deployment. The ROI model gives us a good estimate in a quick, easy snapshot.

Creating ROI Models

There are several ROI models on which we can focus to build a case for deploying PKI:

Cost savings per transaction.   Whether the transactions involve establishing a new customer account or completing an internal expense report process, moving processes online with the confidence of PKI-enabled security can save money on a per-transaction basis.

Reduced processing time per transaction.   It goes without saying that the more efficient a process, the cheaper it becomes. In addition, you can leverage shorter transaction times as a key differentiator for products and services to customers, whether the customers are internal or external.

New services.   With the ability to provide secure, legally binding transactions online, companies can offer a range of new services. For example, the ability to provide digital receipts for online transactions can easily be done using PKI as an underlying technology.

Reduced exposure.   Given that we can fix a cost associated with hacking or insider misuse of information resources, we can, thus, create a model in which we can show that investment in security can prevent a certain amount of lost revenue. We can view this model as an insurance or defensive model.

Regulation compliance.   In regulated markets, certain security tools and processes must be in place to avoid financial penalties. As a result, choosing PKI to meet those regulatory markets lets you save on non-compliance fees.

Cost Savings per Transaction

Incrementally reducing costs on a per-transaction basis can lead to significant savings over a long period of time. For example, consider a typical purchase order process for a company. The purchase order (PO) request is made, via paper, and routed to one or more managers for approval. Once approvals are given, the finance department reviews the order for accuracy and appropriate authorization signatures. Finally after approvals and authorizations, the PO is issued. This process may take days or weeks for larger companies. The process could be done online through an online application, for example. This new process would allow digitally creating and signing a PO request, so that the process could be done electronically in minutes. In addition, if the vendor accepts a digitally signed and created PO, then the product can be ordered faster. The cost of a typical PO-generation process can range from $50 to $150 per PO. Any digital solution would effectively be cheaper for anything requiring more than a few POs. In addition, reduced paper archiving costs, order form printing costs, and errors can result in significant savings.

It is important to note that cost savings on a transactional level can be an effective ROI only if the volume of transactions is large. In this regard, target this type of ROI model for mass-market or other wide-audience applications.

EXAMPLE: COST SAVINGS PER TRANSACTION ROI

A classic example of cost savings is the use of VPNs to replace dial-up modems as a method of accessing a corporate network from a remote location. Traditionally, corporations had large modem banks in which affiliated personnel would connect and supply some type of authentication, usually a user name and password. The cost of long distance calls, overhead to administer the large modem banks, and user issues involved in maintaining the whole system usually led most companies to set up a VPN.

We can make some basic assumptions on costs for a hypothetical company with the following parameters:

5,000 users (representing a small- to medium-sized global corporation)

Dial-up (phone) costs of about $100 a month per user (some users, such as sales people, spend much more than other users). Note that international dial-up costs could easily double this cost.

$200,000 in modem bank, server, and related hardware. This includes the modems, servers, and authentication devices. Personnel costs are not factored in because personnel costs will remain with a PKI system (to a degree depending on the model chosen).

Based on these parameters, and using the following formula:

$$\text{ROI (Cost Savings)} = \frac{\text{(ISP Cost)} + \text{PKI Cost} + \text{(VPN Software Cost)}}{\text{Traditional dialup costs without VPN}} \times 100 = \% \text{ return}$$

ISP Cost = \$30/user/mo for ISP Service × 12mo/year

PKI Cost = user/year PKI outsourced seat cost

VPN Software Cost = user/year for VPN software

we can calculate a per-user cost (per year) of about $1,240. The calculation used to arrive at this figure is (5,000 users * $100/month dial-up costs * 12 months) + ($200,000 setup and hardware costs) = $6.2 million / year. Divide this by 5,000 users to get $1,240/user/year.

Now if we apply a PKI solution by creating a VPN that allows a user to use a local ISP (wherever in the world the user might be) and then use that local connection to access the Internet to communicate with the home office, we can show significant cost savings. Let's assume the following parameters for a PKI solution:

◆ 5,000 seats purchased (to correspond with 5,000 users)

◆ Dial-up ISP service at $30/user/month

◆ $100/user/year for outsourced PKI service

◆ $10/user/year for VPN software (backend and client)

This results in a cost of $520/user/year per employee, based on the following calculation:

($30/user/month for ISP service * 12months/year) + $100/user/year PKI outsourced seat cost + ($100/user/year for VPN software)

(continued)

EXAMPLE: COST SAVINGS PER TRANSACTION ROI *(continued)*

Compared to our non-VPN solution, this yields a cost savings per user/year of ($1,240/user – $560/user) or $680/user/year! The ROI can then be calculated with specific input numbers based on the original investment, but it will no doubt be in the double digits.

Please note that broad assumptions were made in this analysis by averaging typical hardware, software, and other costs across a range of vendors. Your specific solutions will depend on volume discounts, number of users, and existing resources such as personnel and hardware. The idea of this example was to show the logic that could be used on a very common scenario to justify the expenditure for a PKI system.

Reduced Processing Time per Transaction

Take an internal example such as a consulting firm with thousands of consultants roaming the globe who have to submit expense reports by fax or postal mail. In this case, processing time would have to include postal mailing time, approval time, and authorization time. A more efficient process would be to allow the consultant to digitally sign an expense report, route it to the authorizing agent, and then forward that information electronically to the financial department. Receipts or supporting documents could be sent via postal mail to be double-checked at a later date. In this manner, we can reduce the transaction time from weeks to days. An external example may include the online enrollment of customer accounts. Take, for example, a bank that would like to sign up customers. If we take the old model of initiating a request online and then sending, via postal mail, a large packet of information to be sent back, customer activation would hover in the low double digits. If we can take that same process online, the customer could enable his or her account in 30 to 60 minutes, and customer activation rates could soar to 50 percent or more.

EXAMPLE: REDUCED TIME SAVINGS ROI

As we reduce the amount of time a particular process takes, we can, of course, reduce the expense involved in the workflow. Consider that the average Fortune 500 company creates and receives more than 60,000 documents a year. An average document life cycle cost is nearly $10 a document in addition to the $75 a document for searching archived documents. (Silanis Corp, 2001, http://www.cio.gov/fpkisc/business/silanis-pki/sld007.htm). Based on these numbers, it is obvious that an enormous amount of time is spent on processing paper during the course of business.

In this example of how PKI can produce a time savings, we look at an expense-reporting process in which a filer needs management approval before sending the document on to a finance department for processing the check reimbursement. Let's examine some basic assumptions for our example:

◆ Global corporation with 5,000 users worldwide.

◆ Average document takes two to three days to be approved by manager.

◆ Mailing time for remote users and road warriors to send in their reports for approval is about four to five days, depending on location.

◆ Average document then takes three to four days to be approved and reviewed by finance department.

In this scenario the average expense report would take about 9 to 12 days to get processed. This translates into almost half a billing cycle for a credit card. In other words, the traveler expensing certain items may actually have to float, out of his or her own personal funds, the expenses for at least one credit card payment until reimbursement is issued. Check advances can help mitigate such issues, but they too require several days of processing and approvals! Figure 4.1 shows how this sample flows in the pre-PKI mode and how it flows after the use of PKI.

Pre-PKI Flow

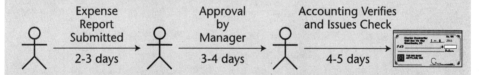

Expense Report Submitted	Approval by Manager	Accounting Verifies and Issues Check
2-3 days	3-4 days	4-5 days

"With PKI" Flow

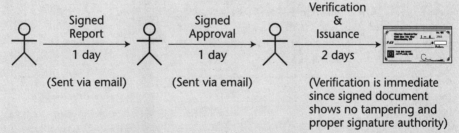

Signed Report	Signed Approval	Verification & Issuance
1 day	1 day	2 days
(Sent via email)	(Sent via email)	(Verification is immediate since signed document shows no tampering and proper signature authority)

Figure 4.1 Form signing flow.

(continued)

EXAMPLE: REDUCED TIME SAVINGS ROI *(continued)*

With PKI, let's make the following assumptions:

◆ **5,000 seats for the PKI**

◆ **Average time to sign a document is less than one minute (using a digital certificate for signing)**

◆ **Average time to send a document for approval is less than one minute (document is digitally signed and emailed to approver)**

Average time to approve and send the document to finance is less than one day (document is digitally signed and emailed to finance department). Because the document has been digitally signed, it is easy to review given that email can be checked from any location in the world.

Average time for finance review and approval is less than one day. Because the document has been digitally signed, verification happens instantly given that an altered document (after the approval signature from the manager) would result in a software-issued warning to the finance department in the document. In addition, everything is done via email so audit capability is increased.

Based on the following formula:

$$\text{ROI (Time Savings)} = \frac{\text{time per transaction without PKI}}{\text{time per transaction with PKI}} = \text{time savings per transaction}$$

we can claim our ROI is as follows:

ROI (Time Savings) = [9 days * 8hrs/day] / [2 days * 8hrs/day] * 100 = 450%

To demonstrate a financial gain, we could take this ROI further with the following analysis:

ROI (Financial Gain) = [time for transaction without PKI per transaction * cost/time unit] / [time for transaction with PKI * cost/time unit] * 100.

For our example, we can assume that an average employee overhead is $100/hour. This would result in our financial gain ROI being:

ROI (Financial Gain) = [[72 hours * $100/hour] / [16 hours * $100/hour] * 100] = 450 percent (which is the same as expected, but with more details about the cost per transaction we may get different results from the time-savings and financial gain analysis because we may differ in our per-unit cost if a transaction goes online).

New Services

If we position security as an enabler, then we can offer new and improved services with the confidence that PKI can provide for security. These services may include online digital receipts, digital notaries, and micro payments. Part of the selling value proposition is for a company to be able to offer strategically valuable services that, without PKI, could not be done effectively. New services give the organization competitive advantages, increase customer satisfaction, and provide new opportunities for revenue, among other benefits.

It is difficult to quantify the benefit resulting from being able to provide new services as a result of PKI. We can make some basic business assumptions, though, about a new service:

- 20 percent gross margin (at the very least) is what the organization seeks; obviously, the greater the margin, the greater the requirement for a return

- Six months time to market

- Volume from new service will be at least 10 times the paper volume (as a result of utilizing the Internet and other electronic channels)

- Customer acquisition costs on the Web are at least three to four times less than those of physical methods (such as direct mailings)

EXAMPLE OF A NEW SERVICE ROI MODEL

A technology company that sells PCs that has moved its operations online can most likely sell more bundled services online, at a lower cost, than it could in brick-and-mortar retail stores. For example, selling PCs online allows for the customer to upgrade software and/or hardware at the time of purchase, before any inventory is acquired or work is done. This allows new services to be activated without taking the risk of inventory, as is the case with a retail scenario.

- ◆ 50 percent is the certainty that new service development will take six months.

- ◆ Traditional customer costs refer to traditional media advertising, postal mailings, and so on.

If we take the New Service ROI model provided in the following equation:

$$\text{ROI (New Services)} = \frac{[(\text{Trust revenue}) \times (\text{Avail. \%}) \times (\text{Volume increases})] - (\text{Trust costs})}{(\text{traditional service revenue}) - (\text{traditional customer costs})} \times 100 = \% \text{ return}$$

Trust revenue = revenue enabled through trust services

Avail. % = 50% availability per year

Volume increase = 10 factor of increased volume

Trust costs = trust enabled services costs

then we can get the following formula:

ROI = ($800 for online customer revenue) * (20% margin) * (50% availability during ecommerce Web site development during the first year) * (10 factor increase in business)] / [($600) – ($150/customer costs for customer acquisition using direct salespeople and mailings)] = 10.7 × return for the first year

---

EXAMPLE: REDUCED EXPOSURE ROI MODEL

If we consider a Web site that devises all its income from its online presence, then we can safely say that any downtime would directly hurt the business. By being online, the company increases its chances of being hacked. We can estimate that there are an average of five breaches a year that, based on our information, would cost the business about $1 million/incident times the five breaches a year. This results in a cost of $5 million per year. We consider a sophisticated security system to cost an average of about $300,000 in hardware and $250,000 in software; we have a total cost of $550,000.

Let's apply our example to the Reduced Exposure ROI model, as shown in the following equation:

$$\text{ROI (Exposure)} = \frac{(\text{cost/breach}) \times (\text{\# of breaches per year}) \times (\text{\% probability of breach})}{\text{resources to defend against breach}} = \times\ 100 = \%\ \text{return}$$

For our example:
ROI = [[($1 million/breach) * (5 breaches/year) * (85% probability of breach)] / ($550,000)] * 100 = 727%

Reduced Exposure Model

The classic model for justifying security expenditure focuses on reducing liability or risk. As a result, we can relate financial costs to each security breach. The equation in the sidebar, "Example of a New Service ROI Model," shows the formula we can use to determine the quantitative costs for the breach. The specific parameters will vary greatly, but we can suggest the following parameters for the formula:

- Cost/breach = ranges from $150,000/incident (Department of Trade and Industry (DTI) of the United Kingdom) to $2 million/incident (Computer Security Institute 2001 survey)

- Suggested cost is about $200,000/breach including personnel and lost business for non-Web-based business

- Suggested cost is about $1 million/breach for Web-based business (based on an average of $125,000/hour cost for Web downtime as estimated by Cahners In-State group; see http://www.darwinmag.com/read/120100/worst.html)

- Number of breaches/year = suggested range of two to five, based on various surveys

- Probability of breach = 85 percent based on CSI survey (June 2002)

EXAMPLE OF REGULATION COMPLIANCE ROI

Let's take the example of an HMO that bills its customers for work not covered under its plans. An HMO may have more than 100,000 people as part of its plan. If the HMO violates a regulation, like HIPAA, for example, by selling its customer list that shows a patient's name and medical history (for example, to certain pharmaceutical companies), the fines would be enormous. According to HIPAA, a single incident per individual is $100. If we apply this fine to 100,000 people, this result is a fine of $10 million. Had PKI been used to encrypt data and ensure that access to the customer list was restricted (with certificate controls), such use would have been prevented. Most organizations violate regulations, not by a concerted effort by upper management, but rather by a smaller department unaware of its impact through certain activities, such as list rentals of customer information.

With the Regulation Compliance ROI model shown in the following equation:

$$\text{ROI (Compliance)} = \frac{\text{fines due to noncompliance}}{\text{investment in PKI and related security services}} \times 100 = \% \text{ return}$$

where:

♦ Fines due to noncompliance will vary from industry to industry.; generally, fines will run into the $100,000s over the course of a year.

♦ Investment in PKI and related security services can be estimated at $500,000 for medium to large enterprises.

we would get this formula:

ROI = [($10 million fines due to compliance violations) / ($500,000 cost of security and PKI)] ∗ 100 = 2,000%

As you can see, the investment in PKI and related security services becomes nearly trivial compared to the potential for massive fines that the organization faces.

Regulation Compliance Model

Given the increase in the push toward electronic transactions by government agencies, PKI is a natural fit to help organizations meet various regulatory guidelines. In this manner, noncompliance can cost organizations substantial amounts. For example, HIPAA violations are $100 per person per violation, and up to $25,000 per person per violation of a single standard for a calendar year.

In this model we look at the cost of being compliant versus the penalty for noncompliance.

Generally, if we look at regulation compliance, we do not usually bring up the concept of ROI. When companies break safety or related compliance laws, they are prevented from operating. Privacy and security compliance laws, though, do not fall under strict guidelines because they usually are accompanied only by financial penalties. For example, if an organization does not comply with, say, the HIPAA privacy regulations and allows customer transmission of personally identifiable data, then the organization would face a $100 fine per person per violation. If, for example, the violation occurred because of a mass mailing, the fine could literally add up to millions of dollars.

Nonfinancial Benefits

We have seen the analysis of quantitative benefits to building trust solutions on PKI. Let's examine in more detail some of the qualitative or soft metrics around PKI. We can breakdown the soft metrics into two main areas: FUD (fear, uncertainty, and doubt) and convenience.

FUD

FUD has been used as the most basic method to sell security. The concept of FUD is to create such corporate insecurity that technology is used to protect an organization "just in case." PKI clearly helps alleviate the FUD factor. Given that PKI has been tried and tested both technologically and legally, most business managers can sleep at night a bit better knowing that liability and security issues have a means of being resolved.

How can we present and measure the FUD factor?

- Use industry peer comparisons to review the security issues of an industry in general and compare our particular organization to those factors.
- Perform security or vulnerability assessments to get the scope of the security issues the organization faces.
- Take internal surveys or surveys of our customers to understand what areas are of most concern.

Industry Peer Comparison

Each industry faces specific and unique challenges. The type of customer, price point of the products, and government regulations all factor into the specific security challenges an industry will face. For example, in the financial sector, the issues of fraudulent information in the process of applying for loans and bank accounts make it a critical need to fill. In our organization we can examine the areas in which we collect personal information in the process of authenticating an individual. By combining better, stronger forms of communication and then representing that effort in the form of a digital credential, we can alleviate, qualitatively, an area of concern. In our discussion of trust solutions for verticals later in this book, we will examine some of those specific requirements for security for each vertical.

THE BACK-TO-SCHOOL-SALE METHOD

Note that consulting companies may view vulnerability assessments as loss leaders (used extensively in retail stores to attract customers into shops—for example, luring customers into a store for basic school supplies, such as paper at low prices, but upselling them to more lucrative, higher-margin items) and may offer very low prices. Why? Because invariably most organizations will have a number of security issues that the consulting company will offer to fix— at prices that can make up for the loss-leader assessments. If you hire a consulting company for your vulnerability assessments, make sure that you build in the costs for fixing them. In addition, after an assessment has been performed and the results presented to management, the organization that received the results now is obligated to fix certain security issues. If a breach occurs after this awareness, the company could be found to be negligent and may lose insurance coverage, face compliance penalties, and even face lawsuits by affected users.

With these issues in mind it is prudent to build into your PKI deployment process an initial assessment and regular ongoing assessments. These costs should be factored into the deployment costs to help obtain a more accurate ROI.

If you don't know what your peers are doing or the challenges they are facing, ask! Many trade groups and associations share information about the common problems they face. The FBI has working groups to help companies share information, confidentially, with each other regarding security issues and resolutions.

Vulnerability Assessment

Hiring a security firm, performing analysis internally, or contracting with a managed security services firm are all ways in which an organization can understand its security risks. Taking these vulnerability reports as a basis for implementation is a good way of selling security technology such as PKI. For example, if a controlled hacking exercise shows that email is easily spoofed or snooped, then we have a clear case for establishing policies and technologies to encrypt email (which is based on PKI). Other examples include showing weakness in access control (in other words, points in the network that can be accessed by guessing passwords), which could be strengthened through the use of PKI.

Vulnerability assessments are ongoing snapshots of an organization. These should be done on a regular basis to maintain a ready state of alert and keep current with information. Regular assessments can also help justify the need for technologies like PKI on a regular basis. After all, if a PKI gets installed and never used, the organization will not see the consequence of that action until an assessment shows areas of security weakness.

What can a vulnerability assessment firm check to ensure that your PKI is secure? Actually, the tests will focus on the infrastructure that supports your PKI. This will include assessing the ability of your firewalls, routers, and other devices to prevent unauthorized access to core network services. To specifically address the security of the PKI components, some key elements to check include the following:

- Make sure that the operating systems of the systems that host the CA and/or RA functions are hardened. (In other words, make sure that unnecessary services are removed from the system to prevent hackers from having more opportunities to break the security.)

- Ensure that communications between the various PKI models, such as the CA and RA, are encrypted.

- Determine how PKI database information is being stored (in other words, is the data being encrypted?).

- Ensure that administrators are required to have strong authentication (biometric devices, for example) to access the RA and/or CA modules.

- Verify that all systems related in the PKI are housed in secure facilities.

Internal Surveys

The most direct method for positioning security technology like PKI is to ask your employees and customers about what keeps them up at night. Regular internal or customer surveys can provide a reality check for how best to deploy, manage, and sell PKI technologies. For example, through internal surveys you may discover the key applications that should be enabled for PKI. In addition, you can determine areas where training may be required based on users' current habits. Here is a list of questions that can be used on security surveys:

- Do you lock or log off your terminal when you leave for lunch? For the day? (These questions determine the security-consciousness level of your audience.)

- How often (number of times per day) do you exchange emails with confidential data? (This question assesses the need for security in communications. Generally, this will vary based on the individual's role and level in the organization. Certain levels of the organization, like executive management, will almost constantly communicate confidential data.)

- Do you download software from the Internet from Web sites you have never been to? (This question determines risk factors for the introduction of viruses into your network from within the network.)

- Do you secure your laptop when you step away from your desk? (This question describes the possibility of theft of the entire system. Using a stolen system may make it easier to break into a network because passwords, cached files, and other material may reveal access codes and methods into the corporate network.)

- Do you frequently work remotely? (This question identifies any unique requirements for remote access security.)

Convenience

The convenience factor is a big sell for areas like biometrics. The idea here is that we cannot lose our physical aspects as we can an access card or password. By implementing biometrics, we are creating a simple (and strong) method for authentication. By locking down a digital credential with a biometric device, we can easily solve the challenge of protecting the private key in the PKI technology. This method creates a simple and convenient way to maintain nonrepudiation.

The challenge is in managing the idea of convenience to sell PKI. One approach is to position the technology as a method for reducing the complexity of tasks. Take, for example, a road warrior who constantly moves from city to city, dialing up to the corporate network for email, portal access, and other resources. A typical remote user will have to remember and manage more than five passwords (the computer password, the network password, the remote access password, the portal password, and the email application password). Replacing all these passwords with a single certificate reduces the time needed to log in and access data. Furthermore, PKI can be used to authenticate and/or protect data on devices such as wireless PDAs or phones. For a road warrior, being able to use a phone or PDA to access email is an enormous time saver. After all, checking email via a traditional laptop modem can take more than 15 minutes. Road warriors also benefit from being able to fill out and digitally sign and submit an expense report, thereby eliminating mailing time and minimizing long authorization times for reimbursements.

A good example of the use of convenience is Checkpoint's remote access (VPN) solution. This solution uses digital certificates to authenticate the user to the network. In this manner, the user, on dialing into the corporate network, can establish a secure connection and identify himself or herself, all without entering a single password.

Case Study: Anatomy of a PKI Sale

To better understand how PKI can be sold to customers or to internal decision makers, we will take a look at a typical sales cycle for a PKI system. The idea is to lay out the components of a sale to convey appropriate expectations for vendors and customers.

The Prospect

Generally, PKI sales are well over $100,000 and average about $200,000 per sale. This makes the sale a direct sale managed by an outside or direct salesperson. The first step is in developing prospects for such deals to generate leads. Most vendors have found success in providing business strategy white papers, free industry consulting, or road-show seminars that explain how specific business problems can be resolved using the vendor's solution.

The Pitch

Given that most PKI sales are large enough to warrant upper management signatures, the sale usually involves multiple presentations to various levels of staff at the customer's organization. Internal pitches are usually done to the management decision maker with a buyoff from the technical staff or an outside consultant, or both. Almost every single sale will involve a technical discussion, including a review of the completed RFP (request for proposal). An RFP requests, usually, far more features than are actually required. Initial technical meetings in the presales process determine the specific focus and scope. Prepare to have technical staff with knowledge about PKI either as the vendor or as the customer.

The Closing

Approval levels in most companies for typical PKI sales usually require senior management approval. As a result, a typical closing time ranges from two to eight weeks, depending on the organization's review and approval process. Ensure that, even as a customer, you allocate appropriate time for the internal approval processes.

The Payment

Regardless of whether an insourced or outsourced solution is chosen, add-ons, such as maintenance or support contracts, are invariable. Determine the realistic need for things like 24 × 7 support because it is costly to obtain. For outsourced models, ensure that the SLAs (service level agreements) reflect the value of what you are paying for. For insourced models, ensure that internal SLAs match what the vendor can provide in support. After all, if the internal process is slower than the vendor support, a quick vendor response time to an incident is a waste of money.

The Delivery

Given that most PKI-based trusted solutions will require consulting, scheduling, and planning, a consulting engagement is the final step in the sales process. If your vendor allows you to download software as the method of delivery, you will save money by not having to pay sales tax on the product aspect of the sale. If the product is physically shipped to you, you will incur sales tax. Make sure that you can download software to avoid paying excessive taxes (in many U.S. states, but this may not apply to all regions of the world). The most difficult aspect of the PKI delivery process is scheduling the right resources at your site and matching that schedule with the consulting/deployment team (usually from the PKI vendor). Ensure that the deployment of your chosen PKI, if it involves outside consulting help, starts very soon after the signing of the contracts. Some vendors require the use of the professional services and/or customer support within the first six months of the purchase.

Summary: It's All about the ROI

In the end, choosing a measure of success depends on the audience and how PKI is deployed and used. For internal selling, ROI models are recommended because, assuming an organization is already considering PKI, the soft, qualitative metrics are probably not necessary. For external selling (that is, consultants and vendors), a blend of qualitative and quantitative metrics would work best. Companies may feel that an ROI can be better obtained through other means such as financial investments; therefore, it is necessary to show both the need to provide security and a financial benefit. This combination makes it easier to obtain management approval. Thus far we have covered a basic understanding of the technology in previous chapters and the business aspects of PKI from this chapter. We will examine specific solutions and drivers for PKI solutions in the next several chapters, starting with healthcare solutions in Chapter 5.

Solutions for Trust

Healthcare Solutions

No industry is more challenging for technologists than healthcare. Solutions in the healthcare sector need to navigate a sea of government regulations, legacy systems, and unique user requirements to work successfully. This chapter will cover some of the applications built on PKI in the healthcare sector. We will examine the key drivers and influencers of technology, including one of the biggest legislative drivers, HIPAA (Health Insurance Portability and Accountability Act).

HIPAA

The biggest driver of security technologies in the healthcare space is the Health Insurance Portability and Accountability Act of 1996 (HIPAA). HIPAA was originally intended to protect the right to healthcare for workers when they changed or lost their jobs. A by-product for the technology industry was the recognition that HIPAA would place a large administrative burden on the healthcare system. As a result of this view, the Administrative Simplification set of provisions allowed for the creation of requirements to move a number of administrative healthcare functions online. In summary, these provisions included the following:

- Standards to enable electronic exchange transactions
- Creation of unique identifiers for individuals, employers, health plans, and health providers
- Sets of codes identifying specific medical services that can be used to simplify billing
- Security standards for the management of health information that describe how healthcare information and IT systems involved with that information are to be protected
- Use of digital signatures
- Ability to transfer information between health plans (to ensure continuity of coverage)

In order to accommodate the various players in the healthcare sector, standards and compliance vary depending on the participant and type of description. Healthcare plans and clearinghouses must comply with all of the security standards defined in the Administration Simplification provision. Because healthcare plans and clearinghouses deal with a large amount of confidential information, it is critical that they protect the data being handled. Healthcare providers are required to adhere to security standards if they manage or transmit personally identifiable healthcare information. "Personally identified healthcare information" refers to data that can be linked to a particular individual, such as a patient's X-ray results. Nonpersonally identifiable information may be statistics that can characterize trends in the aggregate, for example.

Many people have referred to HIPAA as the next Y2K for the healthcare industry. In some sense, yes, the compliance date of 2002, with an extension to 2003 (with smaller organizations having until 2004 to reach compliance), does present a hard deadline for the healthcare industry. The main difference in this comparison is that Y2K is an event that has passed. HIPAA is an enduring standard that organizations must plan for not only in preparation for the compliance date, but on an ongoing basis. Consulting-based solutions, however, will not allow an organization to sustain compliance. An investment in a system based on PKI is necessary.

One important distinction HIPAA makes is in terms of security versus privacy. Providers were required to comply with all security standards for all healthcare information. On the other hand, providers were required to comply with privacy standards for only protected healthcare information. Providers that do not use electronic methods for exchanging HIPAA information may still be required to comply with security standards, but not necessarily with privacy standards.

HIPAA REGULATIONS TIMELINE

HIPAA could be considered a work in progress. Here is a brief history of how the regulations were developed by the Department of Health and Human Services (DHHS):

- ◆ **November 3, 1999: HIPAA Standards for Privacy published in the Federal Register.**
- ◆ **December 20, 2000: Final HIPAA privacy regulations are issued in a 1500+–page document.**
- ◆ **February 28, 2001: HIPAA rules reopen for public comment. Compliance date is pushed back.**
- ◆ **July 8, 2001: DHHS releases the first HIPAA privacy guidance statements.**
- ◆ **February 20, 2002: DHHS releases further information about delay in implementation of HIPAA guidelines to April 2003 and to 2004 for smaller organizations.**
- ◆ **August 14, 2002: DHHS releases final HIPAA regulations published in the Federal Register.**

Throughout the history of the development of the HIPAA guidelines, confusion and politics molded the regulations. Compliance dates were pushed back, and numerous public comments and FAQs were issued to help clarify various pieces of the regulations.

The security standards were modeled after the National Research Council's report (National Research Council, *For the Record: Protecting Electronic Health Information*, National Academy Press, 1997). The standards specified security with references to the administrative procedures, physical safeguards, technical security services for computer security, and technical security mechanisms to keep data protected in transit over a network. Specifically, the security standards address the data integrity, confidentiality, and availability of the healthcare data that falls under the HIPAA regulation. Tables 5.1 through 5.3 show the very high-level summaries of the requirements and descriptions. The *italicized* rows are the requirements that may utilize PKI-related technologies.

Table 5.1 Summary of HIPAA Administrative Procedures

HIGH-LEVEL REQUIREMENT	COMMENTS
Security certification	Independent mechanisms for security compliance
Chain of trust	*Agreements establishing equal security and integrity protection between trading partners*

(continued)

Table 5.1   *(continued)*

HIGH-LEVEL REQUIREMENT	COMMENTS
Contingency plan	Covers standard business continuity plans
Processing records mechanism	Describes how information is manipulated
Information access control	Describes access authorization, establishment, and modification
Internal audit	Establishes how an organization will internally monitor compliance on a regular basis
Personnel security	Creates processes for ensuring that personnel are screened and trained
Security configuration management	Covers configuration procedures of hardware and software as well as security testing and virus checking
Security incident and management procedures	Refers to risk analysis, management, and relevant security policies
Termination procedures	Procedures regarding termination of resources
Training	User education and awareness on a range of security issues

Table 5.2   Summary of HIPAA Physical Safeguards

HIGH-LEVEL REQUIREMENT	COMMENTS
Security Role	*Assignment of the security role to particular organization or individual*
Media controls	*Protection of storage media used, for example, in backups*
Physical access controls	Physical controls for access to information systems
Guidelines on workstation use	Guidelines on the end user's role in security management
Training	Security awareness training for end users

Table 5.3 Summary of HIPAA Technical Security Services

HIGH-LEVEL REQUIREMENT	COMMENTS
Access control	Covers various types of role-, user-, and context-based access; treats encryption as optional
Audit controls	Mechanisms to log and record electronic activity to create audit trails
Authorization controls	Provide for user- and role-based access
Data authentication	Refers to message integrity; mentions digital signatures as a solution to maintain message integrity
Entity authentication	Includes PIN, tokens, and biometric devices for end-entity authentication

The most interesting and relevant aspect of the HIPAA as it relates to PKI and trust solutions is that the original draft included standards for the use of electronic signatures as having to use digital signature standards (in other words, PKI as we have discussed it thus far). The important point is that digital signatures are not required; however, without the use of PKI, it would be very difficult to achieve message integrity, access controls, and end-entity authentication. Some of the key aspects of the HIPAA rules are that a digital signature must allow for message integrity, nonrepudiation, and user authentication.

Table 5.4 Summary of HIPAA Technical Security Mechanisms

HIGH-LEVEL REQUIREMENT	COMMENTS
Communication/network controls	Refer to the use of message authentication and either access controls or encryption

When the HIPAA standards were originally written in August 1998, it was not clear how PKI technology would evolve. As a result, a number of stipulations were added to standards to allow for future changes. Some of the required key features included the following:

Ability to add attributes. Certificates can provide attributes that can describe information about the certificate holder. The ability to add attributes is part of the X509 v3 standard protocol, and, thus, most major PKI vendors can adhere to this requirement.

Continuity of signature capability. This feature allows documents or messages to be verified between signings. For example, managers may verify an employee's digital signature before signing the document with their own digital signatures.

Countersignatures capability. This feature allows for verification to determine the order in which signatures were placed on the document or message. In this manner, a chain of signature authorities can be established to ensure that a proper process had been followed.

Independent verifiability. Given that certificates can be used and validated by resolving the chain of trust for the certificate, it is possible to easily verify the digital certificate that was used in a transaction. Furthermore, with public key technology, anyone has access to a signer's public key, making this requirement trivial for certificates issued by public CAs.

Interoperability. Some PKI vendors do make deviations from standard X509 v3 certificates, which then can cause problems when the systems have to interact with each other. Interoperability is required to prevent the need for a single vendor. A number of standards bodies in other industries have attempted to create this "universal model" for certificates. For the most part, certificates can be used for standard applications, such as digital signatures, with good interoperability; however, some complex, custom applications may not work with all types of certificates.

Multiple signatures. Generally, in an approval or workflow process, multiple signatures may be required for approval; thus, a PKI would need the ability, either directly or through third-party applications, to show a chain of signing authorities. Most form-signing or workflow packages that use digital certificates have this ability.

Transportability. This is the ability to send a signed document over an insecure network (for example, the Internet) without the loss of message integrity. It is part of the basic functionality of a digital certificate, as it provides privacy and integrity by encrypting and signing a message.

HEALTHKEY

HealthKey is a multistate organization, funded by the Robert Wood Johnson Foundation, that creates secure infrastructure models for healthcare organizations. A key aspect of the organization is the definition of a PKI system that can be leveraged across the healthcare industry. Some key projects HealthKey has focused on include the following:

♦ Secure email between healthcare organizations. This initiative advocates using organizational-level certificates rather than individual certificates. This, of course, does not provide individual nonrepudiation, but it does protect sensitive information transmitted over the Internet.

♦ Bridge service for CAs (to allow different CAs to interoperate). The first example of this bridge service was executed in July 2001 with the HealthKkey Bridge Technology in Minnesota. The application sends secure email between different organizations using the bridge model.

♦ Immunization registry secure access. This project, launched with the name Provider Access to Immunization Registry Securely (PaiRS), allowed the North Carolina Department of Health and Human Services Immunization Branch to offer secure access to a common registry of immunizations. In this manner, citizens and healthcare workers could access immunization records. Challenges in using PKI were found when high mobility was required (as in the case of citizens). User name/password and PKI were implemented in parallel because of these challenges.

♦ Communicable disease information (sensitive information sent by the Center for Communicable Diseases to local agencies, for example, in the event of a epidemic). The key reasons for using a PKI-based solution include: secrecy (to prevent panic and false news reports) and speed (by using the Internet for information flow).

It is important to note that HIPAA does provide for the resolution of a number of privacy concerns; however, the resolution of the security requirements establishes a good base for privacy resolutions. In addition, various directives from other organizations, such as the European Union, affect how certain companies, like pharmaceutical companies, can deal with European customers. In general, an organization that is HIPAA compliant will have a much easier time meeting EU privacy directives.

PKI as a Solution to HIPAA

Given the requirements of integrity, nonrepudiation, and confidentiality that are imposed on a digital signature in HIPAA, it is clear that PKI is the only industry-recognized solution. HIPAA acknowledged that PKI would be the ideal option.

"Only digital signatures, using current technology, provide the combination of authenticity, message integrity, and nonrepudiation which is viewed as a desirable complement to the security standards required by the law...The use of digital signatures requires a certain infrastructure (Public Key Infrastructure) ..." (from 45 CFR Part 142 on 43260).

We have seen in previous chapters that PKI provides a robust method to manage digital credentials (also known as certificates). Let's review the features PKI provides and see how they relate to achieving HIPAA compliance:

Confidentiality (in other words, privacy).   Given that PKI provides for encryption of a message or transaction, parties in between the sender and recipient cannot easily decrypt the message encrypt using PKI tools.

Authentication.   Because the private key is considered a valid proof of a person's identity (because the private key is known only to the authenticated owner), messages signed by the key holder validate, digitally, the signer's unique identity.

Integrity.   To maintain message integrity—that is, ensuring that a message was not altered after it was created—hash algorithms are used within a PKI system to verify the integrity of each message.

Nonrepudiation.   As we noted in the comments for authentication, the holder of a private key is deemed to be the only owner of that key (unless it is reported lost or stolen, in which case the certificate associated with that private key would be revoked and invalidated), any signatures with that key are deemed to belong to the signer.

Access control.   Although PKI does not directly provide for access control mechanisms, it does provide for a good foundation. Certificates, treated as digital credentials, can be tied to biometrics to control access, or certificates may be used as proof of identity. The certificate can provide the basic information to help an access control system make an informed decision about access to some resources.

Some additional HIPAA-specific aspects make PKI a good technology to be used in HIPAA compliance objectives. They include the following:

- Provision of unique individual identification (in other words, each transaction is tied to a unique individual). Passwords and the like can be shared easily, and, thus, they alone do not qualify as unique identifiers.

- Persistent personal roles that tie a role to a person (for example, a doctor) regardless of the organization affiliation of that doctor.

- Support for proxy roles. Proxy roles are delegated, but authorized, roles (for example, a doctor gives an administrator proxy rights to submit a claim application for a patient).

Biometrics and HIPAA

Biometrics is the field in which devices are created that can identify individuals based on physiological or behavioral characteristics, or both. In theory it is easy to forge digital authentication such as user names and passwords, but it is very difficult to forge biometrically identifiable components, such as fingerprints. The advantage of modern biometric technology is that it is very convenient and provides for higher security than most other forms of authentication. Traditionally, these security techniques were used only in highly secure facilities; however, due to reduced costs in manufacturing and other advances, it is now affordable to bring biometrics to the corporation (and even to the mass market for some methods).

Biometrics have become interesting for the healthcare industry because they solve the key problems for security and privacy: cheap, mobile, and (relatively) very secure. To meet the requirements of HIPAA, organizations have begun to look at biometrics as a possible component. Biometrics by themselves won't solve HIPAA compliance issues. Additionally, healthcare organizations still have to create a method for nonrepudiation for digitally signed transactions. This, of course, can happen only through the use of digital certificates. By combining the access to the terminal or digital certificate with a biometric device, we have achieved good security practices and HIPAA compliance for many healthcare organizations' tasks.

NOTE Back in 2001 Frost & Sullivan, a leading market research firm, indicated that the total biometric market generated $66 million in 2000 and was expected to reach $900 million by 2006. Today, with HIPAA and other privacy and security regulations, the biometric market will most likely be much bigger than original forecasts. Another research study from Morgan Keegan and Company estimated that the biometric industry could see revenues as high as $2 billion, as soon as 2004.

Biometrics Overview

Biometric systems generally have some common processes that describe how the systems are enabled and used (as shown in Figure 5.1). In all systems, the device requires some type of enrollment from the user. (Note that, in some methods, the enrollment is done by a third party, as in the case of facial recognition systems scanning public areas by law enforcement agencies.) This enrollment generally consists of several samples from that device. For example, for a fingerprint scanner, this would require several reads of the same finger. This information is formulated into what is called a template. A biometric template consists of data points that can help the device uniquely identify a particular physical characteristic from a particular individual with a high degree of confidence. The size of the templates varies, from small templates for basic fingerprint scanners, to larger templates for 3D hand geometry scanners, for example. The size of the template matters only when storage or transmission bandwidth is an issue. Next, the template is stored in a master database for later retrieval and comparison against a future authentication candidate. Many biometric systems suffer their biggest weakness at this point because capture of the template database allows a hacker to imitate the user or reverse engineer the physical characteristics. Although some algorithms use a hash, it is a one-way function for preventing this security risk and is not implemented for all systems. Finally, when an application or resource needs to be accessed, the candidate authenticates to the biometric device, which takes a snapshot of the characteristics to be compared against its template database. For very large-scale systems (such as government citizen identification projects), speed and database management are major factors.

Many types of biometric devices can be used to authenticate an individual, but the most popular are these (see Table 5.5):

Fingerprint readers.   This technique uses an individual's fingerprint to authenticate that person. One or more fingers may be required for the authentication. This method is perhaps the cheapest among all the biometric options. In fact, fingerprint devices are being incorporated into other generic devices such as keyboards. For example, HP (its Compaq division) sells a Biometric Option Kit that includes a biometric keyboard.

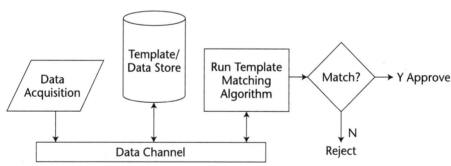

Figure 5.1   Process overview of biometric system.

Hand geometry. This method relies on the user to place his or her hand in a device that can measure unique aspects of the hand, including finger length and hand dimensions, among other characteristics. These devices are easier to use among a diverse population because they force the hand to be placed on the device for proper measurement readings. This is in contrast to, say, fingerprint devices, in which the rolling of the finger, the cleanliness of the device or finger, and other factors may slow down the time for authentication. Hand geometry devices can be several hundred dollars per device and usually require custom installation in a secured area.

Voice verification. Although we've seen this method many times in the movies (remember that line "My voice is my passport" from the movie *Sneakers*?), voice verification is not, perhaps, the best method for authentication (it was, in fact, the point of compromise in *Sneakers*). Due to changes in voice (for example, from colds), background noise, and other aspects, voice verification is usually limited to verification for specific workstations or a closed environment. Voice verification is perhaps the most convenient because as long as the user can speak, other disabilities do not affect verification.

Iris/retinal scanning. In both of these methods, an aspect of the eye is scanned and verified. Retinal scanning is more intrusive because the eye must be placed directly on top of the measuring device. This slows down the authentication process and brings up hygienic issues if multiple parties are to use the same authentication device. Iris scanning is more practical because authentication can occur from a distance. These systems, though, are not cheap or as easy to use as other devices. Trials have already been done with iris scanning for automated teller machine (ATM) usage (as was done by the Bank United of Texas). The concept of using an ATM card may be a thing of the past!

Facial recognition. Perhaps the most popular in the media, facial recognition has been used for a number of years by various law enforcement agencies to pick out suspects in public places. In London, for example, cameras are mounted throughout the city, and suspects' faces are compared to a known database of felons. If the software detects a possible match, a police officer is sent to investigate. Another example is its use in U.S. casinos for detecting known cheats and ensuring that suspects are not able to enter the casino without the knowledge of security staff. In general, this type of authentication is used for large numbers of people that require nonintrusive authentication. There are a number of questions about the accuracy of this method because these systems are more accurate for verification (for example, in entering a secured facility) than for identification (for example, picking a known criminal out of a crowd).

Table 5.5 Summary of Biometric Devices and Applications

TYPE	ACCURACY	ERROR FACTORS	EASE OF USE	COMMENTS
Fingerprint readers	High	Dirt, oil	Easy	Excellent for low-cost applications
Hand geometry	High	Age, injury	Easy	Ideal for small community, secured installation access
Voice verification	High	Cold, throat sickness	Moderate	Good as adjunct security mechanism
Iris/retinal scanning	Very high	Lighting	Moderate	Iris scanning is good for mass audience; retinal scanning is good for small group verification pool
Facial recognition	High	Lighting, angle of cameras	Easy	Good for small group verification; mass verification not as accurate

Other devices and techniques exist, but they are mostly niche authentication devices that most organizations will probably not use often. In general, most of the devices require a registration period for each user to be authenticated. This requires each user to register at the device, usually several times, and from this process a template of a "good pattern" is created and stored in a database or on the device. Naturally, the template database itself is a vulnerability because stealing this template could allow an attacker to replicate or fool other devices looking for the same template. High-end devices keep the template on the device itself and do not network with any other computers. In addition, a number of privacy issues arise when templates need to be created and stored for a mass population (like all Medicaid users). Currently, debates are raging in the government and corporate sectors on how biometric devices may be applied and yet maintain privacy for end users.

Some key aspects of biometric devices that implementers and users must be aware of include the following:

- Level of security
- Accuracy
- Costs
- User acceptance and ease of use

Level of security refers to how much effort would be required to fake the authentication and, thus, how reliable is the security of the biometric device.

Accuracy is measured in how often the device authenticates and rejects access attempts the way it is supposed to, as shown in the theoretical graph of Figure 5.2. For example, biometric devices are commonly measured based on their false acceptance and false rejection rates. False acceptance occurs when a biometric device authenticates a user who is not the appropriate user. False rejection occurs when the biometric device rejects a legitimate user. False acceptance provides decreased security and reliability. False rejection triggers poor user satisfaction.

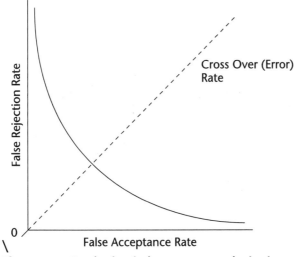

Figure 5.2 Graph of typical acceptance and rejection rates.

User acceptance and ease of use describe how intuitive and easy the device is to use. Obviously, the greater the effort required in authentication, the less likely users are going to choose that method voluntarily. In addition, for high-traffic, high-speed applications (such as authenticating employees during the morning rush into the office), speed is necessary. Thus, certain devices such as fingerprint authenticators are fast, but retinal scans are slow due to the necessity of each person to line up his or her eye against a machine and the need to sanitize the machine between users.

Hospitals, Doctors, and Managed Care

For any security solution to succeed in the healthcare space, it is important to understand the scenario in which these solutions must function. In general, though, we can describe the following characteristics of the healthcare sector:

- The industry is composed of many different stakeholders, including patients, managed care organizations, hospitals, doctors, nurses, and administrative staff.

- In general, the industry, as a whole, is risk averse and, thus, does not rely on cutting-edge technology. In fact, most organizations have to rely on legacy systems, which force many vendors to maintain backward compatibility for many products.

- In general, the industry is fairly well regulated with compliance issues ranging from security to privacy of patient information, both in transit and in storage. Both HIPAA (issued by the Department of Health and Human Services) and regulations issued by the Centers for Medicare and Medicaid Services stipulate specific guidelines for healthcare participants to follow.

Unique Security Requirements

Each party in the healthcare life cycle has specific needs and unique requirements that must be taken into account for security. Any successful solution must take into account these variances.

Doctors' Requirements

One important behavior of doctors is that they tend to be highly mobile. Doctors perform patient rounds in a hospital or travel from their offices to clinics or other hospitals. As a result, any solution must incorporate the mobility they require. Along with this mobility comes the challenge of being able to interface with various devices and systems. Given that hospitals, clinics, offices, and other places where doctors will need access to information will all have different systems, a solution for security must incorporate the factor of a homogenous system base.

Another aspect of doctor interactions is that many administrative tasks, such as claims processing and billing, are not directly managed by the doctor, but rather delegated to a trusted administrative assistant. As a result, issues of confidentiality and nonrepudiation must take into account that a patient's information will be handled by numerous individuals whom the doctor trusts to keep it confidential.

The last feature of doctors' requirements is that they often do not use dedicated terminals when going about their business. Most workstations are shared, sometimes among dozens of people (nurses, doctors, administrators, and others). As a result, doctors must be able to identify themselves at a shared terminal, with reasonably quick access time, and then terminate that access almost as quickly.

HIPAA guidelines stipulate the following additional criteria:

- Need for unique individual identification that identifies the specific person responsible for a transaction.

- Need for persistent personal roles. This means that a role (for example, of a doctor) exists regardless of the managed care plans the doctor is a member of. This is critical in the case that a doctor's license status has changed. For example, if a doctor's medical license has been revoked, all relevant parties need to know this information—this is a change in a persistent role, regardless of the doctor's patients or managed care plan. In addition, healthcare organizations may apply general policies to a role. For example, all doctors in a particular managed care plan may be required to have a certain level of authentication, which may include a check on the doctor's medical license and a verification of personal information.

- Need to support delegate, or proxy, roles. For example, many individuals in a healthcare organization, whether a hospital or a clinic, will delegate specific administrative duties to another, trusted individual. Doctors frequently delegate billing tasks to administrative staff; however, the billing tasks include references to diagnostic codes and other sensitive information.

THE FAX DILEMMA

It is no secret in the healthcare world that a bulk of communication occurs via the traditional fax machine. How is this affected by HIPAA? Quite a bit! Given that faxes will contain medical and billing information, confidentiality of these transmissions must be maintained, especially in the sending and receiving ends of the transmissions. Security in transit is not guaranteed with fax machines. One possible option for more secure fax methods is the technology called fax servers. Fax servers allow organizations to send and receive faxes more efficiently by sending faxes directly from a PC via a server to a physical fax machine (or possibly another fax server) on the other end. The opposite, receiving faxes from a physical machine and placing them as scanned images on a computer server repository, is also possible. In all cases, these documents now have become electronic media and therefore must be protected. Fax servers are clearly more secure than physical faxes as data can be locked down using some type of access control, including biometrics.

Hospital Characteristics

Hospitals are well known for being technology laggards. As a result, it is quite common to find older systems and software in operation in many hospitals. The challenge with this environment is that the "latest" solutions may not be feasible for most hospital environments. In addition, hospitals are not known for having large IT budgets because IT does not directly result in increased revenue (as is the case in other industries, like the finance sector). In fact, a September 2001 study showed that hospitals had planned their budgets for HIPAA compliance to be only about $450,000 when, in fact, the actual budget expenditure for HIPAA compliance was closer to $3.1 million on average (Duncan, Mathew, "HIPAA Survey 2Q01 Results: Spending and Consulting Use," Gartner, Inc., September 6, 2001.) Hence, any solution to help meet compliance regulations will invariably have to be low in capital expenditures.

Managed Care

Managed care organizations (like HMOs) spend quite a bit of money on claims processing and related administrative costs. These organizations are the greatest beneficiaries of any move to electronic transactions because electronic transactions can reduce costs and potentially reduce fraud. Given, generally, the large numbers of doctors and subscribers in the large managed care organizations, solutions must be highly scalable. Hence, deployment issues along with costs are the most critical issues to focus on in developing solutions for the managed care space.

SCARY STATISTICS

HIPAA, while overall a step forward in the U.S. healthcare system, comes at a steep price. As far back as 2000, an American Hospital Associations study estimated that hospitals (in total) would spend on the order of $22.5 billion between 2000 (when the HIPAA was first introduced) and 2005. The study highlighted that this cost was incurred to meet only a few of the privacy compliance provisions of HIPAA! More recent healthcare industry sources estimate healthcare compliance cost at more than $40 billion!

Cost and Other Factors

In addition to the usage factors we have described, several other factors must be taken into account before security solutions can be deployed in healthcare-related organizations:

Costs, which must be kept low on a per-user basis.   IT is considered a support function and not necessarily a method of generating more revenue in the healthcare space.

Deployment method and costs.   Given that there are many parties involved in a typical healthcare transaction (patient, doctor, nurse, administrator, HMO, hospital) having an easy-to-deploy system is essential. Frequent upgrades or replacements would become significantly expensive because most healthcare workers are so frequently mobile.

Compatibility with legacy systems.   For example, many hospitals still use Novell as their primary network operating system and management tool. Yet in the corporate world, Novell is considered a very small segment of the market. As a result, solutions must take into account that backward compatibility must be maintained.

Physical security of the security solution.   Any solution that may require hardware devices or tokens will have to incorporate the ability to physically secure that device as well. Because many healthcare workers are mobile, it is not trivial for them to be able to physically secure any authentication device, unless they can carry it on their identification badges or in their pockets. This requirement relates to the fact that a solution must be designed for high mobility.

Audit and compliance tools.   Given that audit and compliance are major factors in the healthcare vertical, security solutions must be able to provide strong tools to audit use and access to information, as well as tools to enforce compliance. For example, if token devices are issued for authentication to doctors, a chain-of-custody report must be maintained. In that manner, the device can be shown to be used by only one person (and thus that person bears the liability and burden of reporting inappropriate use of that device, including loss or theft).

Who Pays?

Perhaps the most complex aspect of the healthcare vertical is the payment systems. Generally, a subscriber to a managed care plan pays some deductible, with an employer of that patient paying the rest to the managed care plan. The doctors who are part of those plans bill the plan directly for services rendered. There may be intermediary services to which doctors subscribe to determine the eligibility of the patient. Hospitals also may bill patients and/or managed plans and have doctors, who may also be part of those plans, whom they need to pay. As you can see, the payment aspect can be quite complicated.

In the end, the question of who pays is perhaps best answered by asking who benefits from these security solutions. Beneficiaries can be examined in two categories: those parties who would benefit from more cost-efficient solutions enabled by security technology, and those parties who are required to adhere to specific compliance regulations.

Those gaining the most from cost efficiencies are the managed care providers. Due to the large volume of claims they must handle, fraudulent claims, and mistakes of processing claims for doctors not in their plans, any solution that can reduce costs and improve claims accuracy would be worth paying for. If claims submitted by doctors or hospitals could be done electronically, but with a legally binding digital signature, then the costs of claims processing would drop substantially. Based on a March 11, 2002, *Dallas Business Journal* article, on average, a paper-based claim process costs about $10 per claim. Electronic filings would reduce that number by nearly half, resulting in a 50 percent saving!

Multiple parties will need to be concerned about compliance. Mainly the managed care providers and hospitals need to do this because they manage thousands of patients and their related information. Hence compliance violations could add up to serious consequences. Doctors generally also must adhere to HIPAA and related compliance guidelines, but they tend to see far fewer patients; thus, noncompliance would have a lesser impact on them than on hospitals and managed care providers. (Of course, the patient impact is severe if privacy or security is breached regardless of who manages that information!)

PHYSICIAN AUTHENTICATION SERVICES

An interesting approach to ensuring the authentication of medical profession-als can be found in the VeriSign Healthcare Authentication Services. This service, a joint venture of VeriSign, a security company, and the AMA (American Medical Association), allows interested parties to authenticate a medical professional by accepting a pre-authenticated digital certificate (called the AMA Internet ID). The process of issuing certificates requires applicants to be listed in the AMA's Masterfile database, which holds information about the professional's identity and state licensing information.

In addition, the approved applicant using the AMA Internet ID can sponsor a delegated ID (called an "affiliate ID"), which allows a doctor's staff personnel to perform specific tasks with a trusted credential. For example, billing and patient communication may require support staff (as opposed to the doctor) to be involved.

The selling point of the service is that healthcare organizations that accept and use this ID can reduce their authentication costs because the authentica-tion has already been done against the trusted AMA database. The AMA makes the Internet ID available free to U.S. physicians and requires physicians to provide the following information when they enroll:

- ◆ Last year of residency
- ◆ DEA number
- ◆ License number for state in which currently licensed
- ◆ Social security number

Has adoption of this concept taken off? Clearly the adoption has been slow since its inception. The AMA Internet ID has been available since December 2000. Initially this service was offered by Intel (through its Healthcare Authentication Service) and then was purchased by VeriSign several years ago. So far the biggest customer of the service has been MedUnite, which announced back in June 2002 that it would offer the AMA Internet ID to its customers. MedUnite would leverage the ID to allow its customers stronger authenticated transactions for secure online access and secure transactions. Given the scope and promise of the service, more and more healthcare organizations will likely begin to sign on to the service.

Other similar services are available, including a notable one by MEDePass. MEDePass issues a digital certificate based on the authentication of a physician's license information and verification. This information, similar to the AMA Internet ID, can help healthcare organizations meet HIPAA compliance in the area of secure and confidential exchange of patient information. As of the writing of this book, MEDePass did not have a delegated credential (for example, one for use by a doctor's office staff), although it has been working on such an add-on to the service for availability in the near future. The MEDePass service was developed primarily through the California Medical Association and, in fact, provides this service (in other words, the issuance of a certificate) free of charge to its members.

CASE STUDY: HIPAA, PKI, AND BIOMETRICS

THE PROBLEM

A large pharmacy benefits management company with a dozen processing centers countrywide receives over 1.3 million drug prescriptions per year. A pharmacist must sign off on each prescription as he or she verifies each patient's existing drug profile and checks for drug interactions. Once the pharmacist signoff occurs, the actual fulfillment process kicks in, and eventually the drug in question shows up at the patient's doorstep.

To manage this huge volume of prescriptions, the company uses a custom prescription processing workflow solution that starts out by digitally scanning each incoming prescription. Scanned images of each prescription then make their way through this automated workflow system and are verified by a pharmacist and a supervisor, and they are finally fulfilled by an automated fulfillment system. At each step a user authentication must occur to prove that only authorized personnel are performing the transactions. In addition, given stringent laws and upcoming regulatory requirements like HIPAA, each such user authentication and associated transaction must maintain nonrepudiation in a court of law.

The current system uses user names and passwords to authenticate the pharmacists and their supervisors to the workflow system. The first problem with the current system is that the pharmacists and the supervisors must authenticate themselves using passwords for each individual transaction to associate a transaction with the corresponding authentication event. As a result, it creates inefficiencies in the system. The next problem is that, given the number of steps involved in the prescription fulfillment process, the pharmacists and their supervisors are assigned several different passwords to be used at different stages in this fulfillment process. It is common for these passwords to be forgotten, especially if IT policies require good passwords. Each forgotten password requires technical support intervention, which translates to lost productivity and fewer prescriptions being processed.

THE GOAL

The goal is to give the users of the workflow system a simple solution that is secure and can streamline the fulfillment process. All this has to be accomplished while conforming to the strict regulatory requirements of HIPAA.

THE SOLUTION

The final solution employs strong user authentication using (biometric) fingerprint devices and PKI capabilities for digitally signing transactions to satisfy the key productivity and HIPAA requirements.

Biometrics are employed to validate the pharmacist's and supervisor's identity at any workstation, desktop PC, or notebook PC they use to get to the workflow application.

Each workstation is equipped with a fingerprint scanner device. An authentication management infrastructure (AMI) product has been employed from BioNetrix Systems (a Vienna, Virginia-based, privately held company) to enable user credential information to be stored and managed from a centralized data store. BioNetrix also provides a secure single sign on (SSO) product and workflow capabilities built into its AMI and SSO products that allow easier system access and more convenient integration with the automated prescription management system.

THE NEW USAGE SCENARIO

It is common for pharmacists to travel between different processing centers across the country. In addition, each processing center may have fingerprint scanners from different manufacturers that are not compatible with each other (that is, enrollment on one scanner does not verify on another). To accommodate both these requirements, each user of the system is enrolled into the BioNetrix AMI product with all the fingerprint scanner devices being used. This enrollment happens only once but allows the users to roam freely as long as his or her workstations have TCP/IP connectivity to the BioNetrix server.

The new solution obviates the need for pharmacists to remember any passwords. In addition, several prescription validation transactions can be combined into just one. A single user authentication event can be tied to each such combined transaction using the digital signing capabilities that PKI offers. This creates nonrepudiation in the transaction record that conclusively ties the identity of the individual performing a transaction to the transaction itself.

A pharmacist or a supervisor can now walk over to any workstation with a fingerprint scanner and authenticate by simply placing his or her finger(s) on the scanner. Prescriptions are now batched together to decrease the number of overall transactions. Each batched transaction is now securely approved by the touch of a finger.

The pharmacy benefits manager sees the result of reduced password administration costs and improved productivity. As a result of this solution, more than $3.5 million per year in savings will be realized.

Summary: The Healthcare Prognosis

Given the complexity of the healthcare industry, coupled with the emergence of managed care and other healthcare organizations, adding privacy and security elements has indeed made the healthcare industry quite complex. For U.S.-based organizations, HIPAA will help bring the country within range of other EU Privacy Directives and standards for privacy, and this development will become an enormous benefit for the end consumer. Clearly, there are efficiencies to be gained through automation and moving processes online; with HIPAA as a guide, we can ensure that those processes remain secure.

Financial Solutions

The financial sector has long been known for its progressive stance on infor-mation technology. The combination of high-value transactions and the need for advanced technology to stay ahead of the competition makes the financial sector a natural fit for trust solutions. This chapter presents an overview of the sector, the various solutions, and case studies highlighting how the industry has embraced trust in its digital transactions. A key focus is the legal drivers and compliance issues that can be resolved using PKI trust solutions.

Financial Sector

Talking about the financial sector requires us to examine the space from two different angles. The consumer side deals with a mass audience and its unique set of issues. The commercial side generally has fewer customers to deal with but has higher requirements for performance and security. Let's examine the unique aspects of both types of financial communities.

Consumer

The consumer side has seen a recent acceptance of digital transactions. Most financial institutions now offer services, such as online bill payment and account balance statements. The majority of these services have taken off only in the last two to three years. There is a long way to go, though, before there is substantial acceptance of these services. Most analysts estimate that about 10 to 15 percent of the user base (relative to the potential market) has adopted digital financial services. This estimate is in line with past advances in the financial sector, such as with automated teller machines (ATMs). ATMs took nearly 10 years to become an essential method of transactions for the average consumer. Given that the Internet has been around for only a few years as a commercially viable entity, we still have far to go before mass adoption.

Some key areas in which financial firms look to increase digital services include the following:

- Automation of applications
- Contract signing
- Mortgage and loan approvals
- Self-service maintenance of accounts

Generally, consumers provide the most revenue for banks through loans. As a result, reducing the cycle time for obtaining these loans becomes critical. Furthermore, by creating more self-service features, firms ensure that very little money needs to be spent on customer service, the most expensive aspect of the business. In addition, with electronic transactions, fraud and credit checks can be performed much more quickly and yield more accurate loan positioning.

Commercial

Commercial-side applications have greater options for revenue, given that fewer customers with more revenue per customer are involved. This equation permits increased spending in customer service and information technology. The flip side of this opportunity is the increased need for more stringent security. In addition to the legal requirements, the value per transaction is generally higher with commercial activity. As a result, more secure solutions are necessary.

Increasing efficiency for commercial transactions translates into faster funding of loans, increased liquidity, and lower error tolerances. Some applications for trust solutions in this space include the following:

- Forex (foreign exchange) trading
- Escrow services
- Leasing
- Share trading

Generally, customer adoption in the commercial sector is less of an issue; however, integration and support for legacy systems remain as key problems. Because most large retail customers already have systems, the real issue lies in how to integrate them for maximum benefit.

Legal Drivers

Given the regulations that surround the financial vertical, technology solutions that provide non-epudiation and privacy have the most applications. There are a number of legal drivers in this sector, including these:

- The Gramm-Leach-Bliley Act (GLBA)
- The Fair Credit Reporting Act (FCRA)

The Gramm-Leach-Bliley Act

The U.S. Congress signed the Gramm-Leach-Bliley Act (GLBA) into law on November 12, 1999. The intent of the law was to encourage adequate competition among members of the financial services industry. The GLBA was similar to HIPAA (a healthcare legislation) in that both laws sought to encourage efficiencies in their respective industries. Similarly, both recognized the need for security and the privacy of the individual. The GLBA specifies, in seven titles, the specific requirements for all major financial players, including banks, securities firms, and insurance companies and the responsibilities of the financial community to protect the individual's right to privacy.

These are major parts (or titles) of the GLBA:

- TITLE I: FACILITATING AFFILIATIONS AMONG BANKS, SECURITIES FIRMS, AND INSURANCE COMPANIES
  - This title covers the inner details of the banking industry and the change that allows banks and brokerage firms to merge their operations (previously disallowed under the Glass-Steagall Act).
- TITLE II: FUNCTIONAL REGULATION
  - This title defines rules for functional regulation of bank securities activities (among other easing of restrictions).
- TITLE III: INSURANCE
  - This title deals with various aspects of the insurance industry, including brokers, insurers, and even rental car agency insurances.
- TITLE IV: UNITARY THRIFT HOLDING COMPANY PROVISIONS
  - This title disallows new unitary thrift holding companies and requires existing ones to be sold into only financial companies.
- TITLE V: PRIVACY
  - This title most concerns us in this chapter, as it directly deals with privacy issues.
  - Subtitle A — Disclosure of Nonpublic Personal Information.
  - Subtitle B — Fraudulent Access to Financial Information.

- TITLE VI: FEDERAL HOME LOAN BANK SYSTEM MODERNIZATION
  - This deals with certain operational details, including thresholds for certain asset and loan requirements.
- TITLE VII: OTHER PROVISIONS
  - These provisions deal with other aspects of banking services.

Title V impacts the consumer most from a security/privacy perspective (and is most relevant to this chapter). Title V has two key areas, privacy and security, in which it defines the scope of protection of consumers' (specifically individuals') information. This is perhaps the most complex aspect of the act because the consumer has the ability to control, to an extent, how information about him or her is used and in what circumstances. This puts the burden on the financial institution.

TIP When applying for sweepstakes, magazines, or other nonessential services, consider using an alternate address and phone number, such as your office, and abbreviating your name (for example, instead of Kapil Raina use K. Raina). Your information will still be valid, communications will still reach you, but you limit the scope of damage due to a disclosure of your key information. In addition, when you do get solicitations, you can immediately track the source based on the address and name variances you have given. This also helps mitigate identity theft damage should your information be stolen from the mail.

Privacy

A further clarification in the form of Regulation P (passed in 2000) was created to indicate that providers must alert their consumers of the policies available to safeguard customer information before making any purchases. This includes what information is being collected under what guidelines and to whom the information will be disclosed. Nonpublic information sharing is restricted, especially among nonaffiliates (that is, companies that do not have a direct relationship to account holders). Examples of this might be a bank selling names, addresses, and credit worthiness ratings to a luxury car dealership. Privacy policies must be developed, implemented, and clearly disclosed. Privacy policies must be made available on an annual basis to customers. Clearly guidelines must be followed in how information is classified (public or nonpublic) because many of these protections are for nonpublic information only.

Finally, consumers must have the ability to "opt out" of any disclosure of their nonpublic information (with third parties, for any purpose). This last piece is most noticeable because many credit card offers appear through this passing of information. In this manner, a third party can purchase the credit level and other information about potential customers. Opting out will actually make it harder for third parties to solicit this information.

WHAT IS PUBLIC AND NONPUBLIC INFORMATION?

As per the GLBA, the classification of information as public and nonpublic is important because most of the protection is for nonpublic information.

Here is an example of what would be considered public information:

- ◆ Information from an unrestricted Web site (including news postings)
- ◆ Information from the telephone directory
- ◆ Any public records (real estate transactions, liens, and so on)

Here is an example of what would be considered nonpublic information:

- ◆ Social security number
- ◆ Bank/brokerage account numbers and balances
- ◆ Personally identifiable information collected via cookies on a Web site
- ◆ Any information not available from public access means

As for information that may not be explicitly listed in the current GLBA, the guidelines for "Reasonable Belief" are defined by the SEC. These guidelines state that the financial institution has followed proper procedures in order to determine either from the consumer or on its own that public information is, in fact, available through normal public information sources. Essentially the responsibility falls on the institution to make the judgment, but if the consumer claims the information is not public, then additional proof must be provided to consider that information public.

An interesting side note is that these regulations will affect the type of information that can be contained in a digital certificate. A digital certificate can and should be considered a public record. As a result, names, addresses, or anything that might go into a certificate will have to be certified as public information or the person identified by that information will have to agree to waive his or her rights in regard to that information.

Security

The security aspects of Title V differ from privacy because privacy can be managed, for the most part, by policies and processes. Security, however, requires tools and solutions in addition to policies and processes. These guidelines are stated in the Title V Section 501(b). The basic aspects of these security guidelines include the following:

- Security and confidentiality of consumer information must be maintained.
- Protection is provided against any anticipated threats or hazards that may affect the security or integrity of these records.
- Protection is provided against unauthorized access that could result in harm or inconvenience to the consumer.

A number of financial agencies (SEC, FTC, and others) developed specific guidelines for regulating financial institutions to develop comprehensive security programs to address the administrative, physical, and technical safe-guards to protect sensitive consumer information. There are several main com-ponents to the information security program guideline: assessment of risk, control of risk, supervision of service provider arrangements, revisions of the guidelines, and finally reporting of this information to the board of the finan-cial institution.

Assessment of Risk

This guideline is meant to ensure that threats, internal and external, have been identified and rated based on the likelihood of their actually occurring. This information can be contained by a thorough security audit. In addition, the adequacy of mitigating controls needs to be determined (for example, Intru-sion Detection Systems [IDS] or alert systems to warn against active or impending threats).

Assessment of risk becomes easier when using audit trails that are digitally signed. In this manner, file checksums, directory contents, and access dates and times can all be recorded and then digitally signed. This will allow imme-diate comparison between audits of what has changed and narrow down the scope and effort of the audit. The use of time-stamping servers (which, in turn, use PKI or related technologies), as mentioned in Chapter 8, can supply legally binding transaction times and dates for notices to consumers.

Control of Risk

Control of risk includes scaling risk mitigation and program guidelines appro-priately for the size of the institution. In other words, an annual audit that can be done in a day for a small bank will probably not be appropriate for a large multinational bank. Logical access controls (passwords, smart cards, and so on) must be tested periodically for effectiveness. In addition, this regulation requires encryption of data while in transit or in storage. Although PKI is not explicitly called out in the regulations, there are very few options to effectively encrypt data and manage that encryption without PKI. Finally, control of risk covers physical access controls, ranging from locks to biometrics.

This section requires that data be encrypted in transit and in storage. PKI and related solutions are a natural fit for this type of effort. Many tools exist that allow a desktop or data store to be encrypted. Many databases now also provide for encrypted functionality. Finally, protecting data in transit can be done through SSL, VPNs, or some type of content protection scheme (like set-tings policies on documents and information on who can see the content and under what conditions).

Supervision of Service Provider Arrangements

Organizations can no longer shift liability completely on an outsourced provider. If a bank's Web site gets hacked — for example, if the data is taken from the bank's hosting company — the bank itself could also be liable. Under GLBA, the bank has to seek out providers that offer adequate security mechanisms (physical and logical). Contractual obligations between the provider and the financial institutions should stipulate this commitment and execution of security at the provider.

If the financial institution is using a hosting provider or otherwise needs to communicate to sensitive servers (like Web server administration consoles), then a secure mechanism will be needed. SSH, SSL, or some similar protection will be needed to protect administrator access information to or from the service provider–based systems.

NOTE Guidelines for service provider contracts initiated on or before March 5, 2001 are grandfathered until July 1, 2003. After that date, GLBA applies to new and renewed contracts.

Revisions of Guidelines

GBLA recognizes that, with technology constantly changing, threats change as well. As a result, organizations are required to update security policies and processes as per the evolution of security technologies. In some sense, this is perhaps the most difficult aspect of GLBA to manage properly. After all, how aware must an organization be to changing threats before it is considered negligible? Generally, if basic prudent security principles are followed, such as encryption, logical security access, and so on, the scope of what needs to be tracked (such as changing viruses) is reduced. This allows organizations to focus on changes in a smaller area.

Reporting to the Board

In order to increase the effectiveness and awareness of GLBA, the act requires that the board of the financial institution be aware of the status (at least annually) of the GLBA initiatives. All of the components mentioned previously must be included in the report or presentation to the board. The other benefit of board awareness is that there can be no claim of "not aware" of security or privacy breaches in the institution. Thus, the board is equally liable for breaches of GLBA.

Presentation to the board is an important event to log as this brings each board member into liability if management support is not provided for GLBA compliance. You may consider using systems that track and audit board members' receipt of documentation relating to GLBA. A third-party content protection system cannot only deliver content in a predefined, restricted manner, but also track what the recipient did with that information (open it, read it, print it, etc....). This system would provide for proper audit trails if an organization were investigated for GLBA compliance and involvement of board members. These content systems use PKI to authenticate recipients and digitally sign audit trails.

Secure Wireless Communications under GLBA

Although GLBA does not explicitly refer to security and privacy of data over wireless networks, the implication of that protection is there. For firms providing data aggregation services to mobile devices or firms providing account information and the like via wireless networks, it is critical that the wireless networks are secured as adequately as wired networks. Furthermore, internal wireless networks are being used more and more to reduce the costs and time to roll out corporate networks. As a result, internal procedures and safeguards for wireless networks must be in place. Generally speaking, out-of-the-box, wireless networks are much easier to hack than wired networks; and as a result, they should be deployed only with proper security infrastructure, encryption and vulnerability testing.

Fair Credit Reporting Act

Given that in the United States, most activities center around debt and credit management, a consumer's credit report is perhaps one of his or her most important financial documents. The Fair Credit Reporting Act (FCRA) defines the procedures for managing credit reporting. It provides protection and guidelines for credit reporting agencies as well as users of credit reports.

There are a number of authentication services, including ones used by eBay (in conjunction with VeriSign), that verify the identity of a buyer using a combination of public and nonpublic information, including credit report information. Because a credit report gives authenticity not only to a consumer's identity but also to his or her credit worthiness, a rating can be assigned for the given application. Many of these services must comply with the FCRA. The PKI piece comes into play when, after authenticating the user, the user is given a digital certificate as proof of that authentication. This provides a persistent proof over a period of time of that user's validity. A user name and password can more easily be stolen, so a certificate tied with a personal identification number (PIN) provides the best method of authentication.

FCRA: THE FEDS VERSUS THE STATES ROUND I

When FCRA was written, a small clause was inserted that prevented state governments from preempting the federal government legislation. The intent was to simplify compliance through uniform rules. In addition, this would prevent the most stringent state from becoming the default common guideline for the country (especially for multistate financial institutions). This small clause is due to expire in early 2004. The expiration of the preemption of state legislation for FCRA means that we will see a flurry of activity near the end of 2003 and 2004. These activities could very well result in increased privacy and security standards and even a revisiting of the GLBA privacy provision. Companies should position themselves in the most secure and privacy-friendly manner possible to avoid further changes should state laws become even more stringent than federal laws.

Electronic Fund Transfer

The Electronic Funds Transfer Act (EFTA) provides that banks make disclosures at the time a consumer contracts for an electronic fund transfer service or for automated systems. This disclosure must happen before the first transaction is conducted. This allows consumers to have proper knowledge of the implications of certain transactions before being committed to them. PKI does not apply to the EFTA from a consumer perspective, but the ability to secure transactions on the back end remains the bank's responsibility. Thus, the banks will use PKI to secure transactions between systems.

In some sense, the EFTA is a model for PKI systems. If we consider a PKI as being a basis for electronic transactions, then a financial transaction should follow the same principles as a standard bank EFT. This would have implications of a liability limit of $50 if the private key is stolen (and if reported in a timely manner, as credit card companies have defined).

QUICK PKI: SWIFT

SWIFT is an industry-owned and -operated cooperative consisting of many financial institutions from around the world. SWIFT provides secure messaging services (for electronic financial transactions) and interface software for thousands of financial institutions. SWIFT has a product called SWIFTNet PKI that uses digital certificates to authenticate trading institutions and third parties. SWIFT's PKI (built on technology from Entrust) is a self-signed root that uses an X.500 database to track all members' certificates.

Online Mortgage and Loan Applications

According to the Mortgage Bankers Association, online mortgage originations are expected to grow to $250 billion by 2003 from $4 billion in 1999 (although more recent estimates put that number much lower due to the economic turmoil in the technology sectors).

A number of companies have developed solutions suitable for this space, validating the need for PKI as an infrastructure to support the growing demand for online real estate transactions. Companies such as eVincible, LLC have created XML-based solutions (using PKI) to provide a mechanism for online form creation and signing. The XML format allows for generic formats so that archiving and later validation becomes easy. Software solutions that store and sign forms in a specific format (like MS Word 6.0) will have trouble later validating and/or viewing the document if the original viewer (Word 6.0) is not available. Other companies have solutions tailored specifically to mortgages. For example, Ingeo, a Utah-based company, has solutions that allow for online mortgages to be prepared and recorded. It even has an offering that allows electronic interfacing with government recording offices — all based on using X.509 certificates.

MORTGAGES: ONLINE

Don't believe that PKI has been accepted in actual projects for the mortgage industry? Here are a few examples of how PKI trust solutions have been implemented in the financial subsector of real estate:

- ◆ **Riverside County, California, has more than 7,000 electronic recordings of tax liens that were completed using a PKI system set up for that purpose.**

- ◆ **Salt Lake County, Utah, has been using, in a production mode, electronic lien release documents since June 2000. Since the launch date, the county has processed several thousand documents using PKI.**

- ◆ **San Mateo County, California, has implemented (since July 2002) several hundred electronic recordings for the Franchise Tax Board using a PKI-based document system. The process reduced the previous method, which used to take several days, to only a few minutes.**

- ◆ **General Motors Acceptance Corporation Commercial Mortgage (GMACCM) uses a Silanis-based (a forms signing company in Canada) electronic signature solution for its commercial mortgages. GMACCM is one of the largest providers of commercial mortgages in North America.**

Since the federal e-sign legislation passed in 2000, online signatures were considered to have the same legal authority as ink-based signatures. One of the best areas in the financial industry for using PKI-based signatures is the mortgage industry. Experts guess about 15 to 20 touch points occur in a typical mortgage transaction (buyer, seller, escrow agent, notary public, banks, and more). As a result, the ability to authenticate users and then have them sign a digital mortgage application provides several advantages. The first key advantage is that the signatures and the document they sign can immediately be verified for authenticity. Second, the transaction can be automatically recorded and time-stamped. Finally, the archival (and subsequent retrieval) of the signed document becomes orders of magnitude easier (and cheaper) with digital signatures than a paper process.

The specific areas in which PKI can have a significant impact in the mortgage and loan process include the following:

- Loan origination
- Document processing and transfers (appraisals, for example)
- Loan closing (and creation of mortgage note)
- Loan recording

NOTE The first paperless mortgage was purchased in Broward County, Florida, in July 2000.

EZ MORTGAGES: THE EZESCROW STORY

BACKGROUND

Pen on paper is gone—or will soon be. That is the mantra of all the pioneers in the real estate industry. The long-awaited paperless real estate transaction is right around the corner, and there is a long list of visionaries—displaying the "arrows in the back" as proof—who now are able to see the light at the end of the tunnel. A little-known company, ezEscrow, Inc., has developed a patented process that allows the entire real estate transaction to be completed over the Internet—in a paperless, electronic environment—where consumers can now view, track, and sign their documents at their desktop, anytime or anyplace.

(continued)

EZ MORTGAGES: THE EZESCROW STORY *(continued)*

The single most important event that facilitated the course and speed of the paperless, electronic transaction was the E-Sign Act, a U.S. law signed in June 2000, which became effective on October 1, 2000. This single piece of legislation afforded digital, electronic signatures the same validity and legal standing as the more traditional "wet signatures." With the stroke of a digital signature, legal barriers were removed—opening up the ecommerce evolution—especially in the real estate industry.

THE OPPORTUNITY

With more than 5 million residential real estate transactions closing and changing hands each year in the United States—nearly 25,000 per day—the consumer has been waiting for (and demanding) a more streamlined, paperless approach that will eliminate much of the unnecessary stress that is all too common with today's traditional, antiquated processes.

THE APPROACH

ezEscrow,Inc., has leveraged more than 25 years of domain real estate and escrow experience, combined with its intellectual property and suite of services, and recently offered its first electronic real estate transaction. Using enhanced features of PKI technology, ezEscrow was able to confidently deliver secure real estate documents to a seller of a home in Southern California, a professional hockey player. While on the ice practicing for the upcoming Stanley Cup playoffs—using his laptop—he viewed, signed, and returned the documents electronically to ezEscrow in less than five minutes.

THE SOLUTION

To make certain that the digital signature technology met the standards provided in the E-Sign Act, ezEscrow, using public key cryptography, was able to maintain the integrity and encrypt the documents. This process involved wrapping a unique and complex mathematical algorithm around the document. In this manner, the document and digital signatures were unalterable if they were intercepted by someone other than the intended parties. The public key was used by the sender, the hockey player, to encrypt the electronic document, which was then sent to ezEscrow, which held the private key that was then used to decrypt and match the document back into a readable format. The client at all times was assured that no one other than the holder of the private key, ezEscrow (even if someone else intercepted it during transmission), could decrypt and read the contents of the electronic document. ezEscrow was confident that had the electronic document been intercepted or modified in any way during its transmission, the mathematical hash function and digest would reveal this and invalidate the digital signature.

Paperless real estate transaction, along with the PKI technology enabling this process, will be as common as using the soon-to-be archaic pen on paper. The cost savings, time savings, and efficiencies are leading local governments in the United Staets and around the world to move mundane paper processes to a digital solution.

One of the concrete rollouts in the mortgage industry is the implementation of the Real Estate Finance Trust Network, a service developed by industry participants. The REFTN is an architecture for PKI for the real estate industry, which, of course, includes mortgage applications. See Figure 6.1. The premise of creating an infrastructure for the industry would bring several key advantages, including the following:

- Faster loan processing (down to hours instead of weeks)

- Reduction in forgeries or altered documents (and, thus, reduction in checking for forgeries)

- Increased privacy for participants (because documents can be encrypted and delivered only to authenticated individuals and because audit trails can be put around access of the documents)

- Reduced overall loan costs, thus increasing the amount consumers can borrow

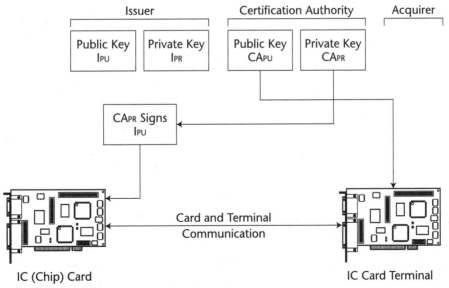

Figure 6.1 REFTN proposed architecture based on PKI.

Identrus

One of the significant milestones in the financial sector, as related to PKI, is the formation of Identrus. This section describes the purpose of Identrus, some applications, and a case study that shows an actual example of how Identrus is used. Although not required for PKI deployment, Identrus can greatly simplify the steps required for banks to deploy PKI-enabled transactions for their merchant customers.

What Is Identrus?

Identrus was formed in 1999 through a partnership of leading financial institutions, including ABN AMRO, Bank of America, Bankers Trust (since acquired by Deutsche Bank), Barclays, Chase Manhattan, Citigroup, Deutsche Bank, and Hypo Vereinsbank. The main purpose was to enable a trusted business-to-business (B2B) ecommerce marketplace with financial institutions as the key trust providers. The organization leverages financial institutions with a global reach that can still provide local presences. The organization provides identity validation and warranty protection for global B2B ecommerce. Identrus provides a vendor-neutral environment that has the legal backing of all that PKI brings.

Need for Identrus

The two biggest benefactors of Identrus are the trading partners that require nonrepudiatable identities of their counterparts and financial institutions that want to extend their banking online. These benefactors, among others, can also leverage a global standard, which would be difficult to do on their own. In addition, through a common standard, more banks are willing to use PKI-based technology because the cost of deployment is decreased with an increasing number of applications and trading partners.

IDENTRUS: A TIMELINE OF MILESTONES

- ◆ **April 1999: Identrus launched.**
- ◆ **Late 1999: Identrus received Federal Reserve/OCC approval.**
- ◆ **Early 2000: E-Sign Act brings the digital certificate into the mainstream in the United States in early 2000.**
- ◆ **Late 2000: Identrus completed its initial round of funding.**
- ◆ **Early 2001: Identrus acquires Eleanor payments project.**
- ◆ **Late 2001: Identrus gets EU approval; the tenth (of about 50 institutions at this time) begins its production implementation with Identrus.**
- ◆ **Early 2002: Identrus acquires Digital Signature Trust (DST).**

Architecture

The main components of the Identrus system are as follows:

- The digital certificates termed Identrus Global IDs
- Real-time validation infrastructure of the Identrus Global IDs
- Assurance (or warranties) for the Global IDs
- Globally recognized and enforceable contracts binding all members of the system
- An audit trail that can be used for dispute resolution

The Identrus model is built around the concept of "four corners." As shown in Figure 6.2, the main components in this model are these:

Identrus root. This root is run by Identrus's own private root. At this level Identrus maintains the trust relationship between the issuing and relying financial institutions.

CA for the subscribing (or issuing) member's financial institution. The root for this organization is signed by the Identrus root CA. The issuing institution generates certificates and issues them on smart cards to subscribing customers. The use of smart cards creates a higher level of protection for the issued certificates.

CA for the relying member's financial institution. The root for this organization is signed by the Identrus root CA. The relying institution, on behalf of its customers, checks the validity or status of the certificate being presented to the relying institution's client (via the Identrus OCSP responder).

Merchant/relying party. The relying party receives digitally secured and signed transaction messages from a subscribing party (in other words, the buyer). Software at the relying party's site allows it to receive the Identrus-enabled signatures from the subscribing party and forward the signatures to the relying party's financial institution for validation. Once the validation has occurred, the relying party can then act on the transaction message. One advantage of this four-corner model is that the relying party does not need to invest heavily in PKI or other systems as the relying party's financial institution performs those functions.

Buyer/subscribing party. This party is buying from the selling party.

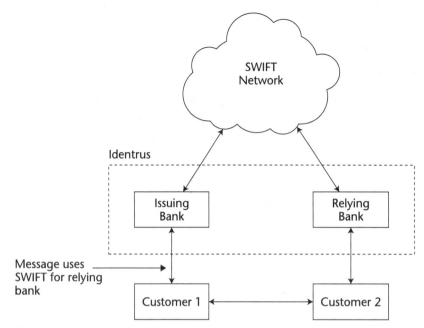

Figure 6.2   The Indentrus four-corner model.

As shown in Figure 6.2, there are three levels of organizations that must interact to complete a successful transaction in the Identrus model: the banks that issue Identrus-enabled certificates, the companies that participate in the process by using a bank's services, and employees that conduct the transactions. The banks that interface directly with Identrus are called Level One Financial Institutions (LOFIs). LOFIs can act, for their customers, as the subscribing or relying financial institution, depending on which merchant initiated the transaction. LOFIs have basic infrastructure that they must maintain in order to adequately conduct transactions, as shown in Figure 6.2. Typically, as far as PKI is concerned, LOFIs issue or revoke Identrus-compliant certificates and smart cards. In addition to the actual issuance, the LOFIs also ensure that customers enforce proper control over the issued certificates and smart cards in order to provide warranties on transactions effectively. Warranty and liability management for their customers is a key role for the LOFIs, including Level Two Identrus banks (which do not connect directly with Identrus).

IDENTRUS: PKI IN THE FAST LANE

The Royal Bank of Scotland is a member of the Identrus network providing a service called TrustAssured. This service utilizes Identrus Global Certificates to provide encryption, nonrepudiation, authentication, and trust through the form of warranties as provided in the Identrus model. This case study looks at how the Royal Bank of Scotland solved one specific problem with the Identrus model, based on PKI.

THE PROBLEM

Sixt Kenning is a multinational vehicle rental company with a significant leasing division in the United Kingdom. With its fleet of more than 12,000 vehicles, it regularly carries out leasing transactions with Lombard, the asset finance arm of RBS. The number of vehicles financed can vary from 30 to 500 per month, and a contract has to be signed by both parties for every deal. This used to mean a Lombard relationship manager traveling to and from customers' offices with the paperwork or the documents being sent by courier, fax, or post. Therefore, there was a considerable time lag between the company's receiving the contracts, signing them, and getting access to the financing from Lombard. This could create cash flow problems in the case of multimillion pound deals involving thousands of vans or lorries.

THE SOLUTION

TrustAssured from the Royal Bank of Scotland (RBS) helps companies manage risk and improve efficiency by speeding up deals to gain competitive advantage and yet giving their ecommerce transactions the same risk profile as traditional paper-based transactions. The TrustAssured service enables businesses to facilitate the electronic signing, exchange, and storing of documents and files online.

The basic advantages of the TrustAssured services are these:

- Reduced costs of doing business by migrating paper-based processes onto the Internet
- Reduced complexity of building trust relationships with counterparts around the world

The Sixt Kenning leasing division is now using TrustAssured Sign and Store to do these transactions online with Lombard. The purchasing executives authenticate and sign the contracts online through a "hack-proof" Web site using their own unique digital signatures, which are held on their smart cards. Additional security (should their smart cards or laptops get into the wrong hands) is a private PIN number and secure encryption. The documents are also time and date stamped, giving a protected audit trail.

Stuart Gordon, finance director at Sixt Kenning, deals with other leasing companies that still fax or post legally binding documents: "With Lombard a document can arrive at nine o'clock and can be checked and signed by ten o'clock. In the meantime, this allows us to set the wheels in motion much more quickly to authorize payment. With other companies it's cumbersome. By post, it can take up to a week. There has been a huge reduction in the time wasted. Now it takes a matter of minutes to check a document and seconds to sign, instead of a couple of days due to the traveling and waiting for faxes or postal deliveries," he added.

RBS customers need to be confident that as a trust service provider, RBS will deliver the services it claims to offer honestly and expertly. tScheme is the industry-led body set up to approve these services and provide that confidence. RBS was the first bank to be awarded with this quality mark.

Applications

Some recent examples (in the last few years) of usage of Identrus-enabled applications have included the following:

- Cisco Systems Capital group used Bank of America as its provider for Identrus-enabled applications so that Cisco could process leasing transactions online. Costs savings were seen in the reduction of paperwork and increased speed with which leasing arrangements could be accomplished.
- Allianz AG, one of the largest insurance companies in Europe, created an application to offer life insurance contracts for the employees of its corporate customers.

Other applications could include these:

- Corporate purchasing
- Letters of credit
- Financial statement delivery
- Online auction markets
- Electronic content delivery
- Insurance sales and contracts
- Securities trading
- Government filings, procurement, and more

Future of Identrus

As Identrus continues to grow and link up with other financial processing and trust institutions (such as SWIFT; see Figure 6.3), online commerce in general will benefit. By making solutions enabling corporate customers to trade more quickly, more cheaply, and with more confidence, Identrus will remain a big driver in the world of PKI and trust solutions.

Identrus Alternatives

Although Identrus is clearly the leader in the financial space, some other organizations have been created to address trust in the financial space. A number of these organizations have regional expertise or a more focused approach.

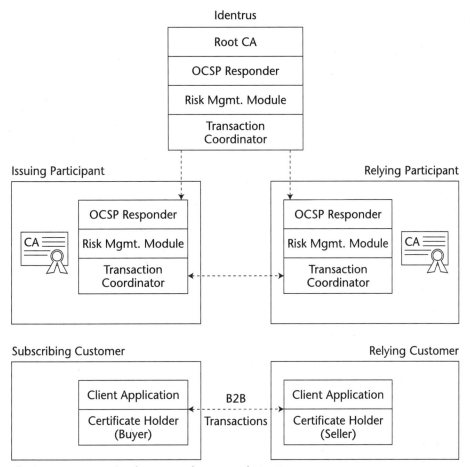

Figure 6.3 Interaction between Identrus and SWIFT.

Global Trust Authority

The Global Trust Authority (GTA) is a European-based organization that effectively provides similar services as Identrus: warranty protection and security infrastructure. These trust services are applied among its member banks, which reside in several countries including: Belgium, France, Italy, Netherlands, Portugal, and Spain.

The GTA offers several basic trust services including the following:

- A secure root CA for the GTA participants
- Issuing/revocation service to GTA's primary members, called the Master Trust Authorities (MTAs)

- Management of the revocation services associated with revoked GTA certificates
- Liability and warranty services for GTA members
- Guidelines for security and infrastructure for GTA members

The concept is that the GTA root sets up an infrastructure with a number of MTAs. The MTAs, in turn, issue certificates for their members called the Scheme Trust Authorities (STAs) and provide warranty and liability services for their members.

ABAecom

ABAecom is part of the American Bankers Association (ABA) and provides electronic banking and commerce trust services over the Internet. ABAecom's infrastructure was built on services provided by Digital Signature Trust (DST), a former competitor of Identrus. (Note that Identrus bought DST in mid-2002.) ABAecom brought its products to the level the average consumer could recognize. One product ABAecom produces is SiteCertain, a Web site trust seal. This is a competing concept to VeriSign's trust seal (VeriSign Secure Site) with similar functionality. The SiteCertain product identifies and validates the site owner and the URL to ensure that the user of the site can be confident of the identity and affiliation of the site. SiteCertain provided a feature-rich authentication and identification much earlier than VeriSign's SSL certificate and Secure Site campaign. VeriSign, however, had the dominant market presence, and, thus, SiteCertain is not as widely seen on Web sites today.

ABAecom also developed the concept of a *portable cert*. A portable cert, as it was envisioned, could be issued by any member bank after a series of authentications. The certificate could then be used on any computer to provide strong authentication of the user.

EMV Solutions

EMV (Europay, Mastercard, and Visa) is a standard created by some of the largest financial payment firms in the world. The concept, which was initiated in 1993, was to provide a method for digital payment based on smart cards that would be very similar to the method in which credit cards are used today.

The concept of using digital cash or smart cards has proven successful in key areas, especially Europe and parts of Asia. North America, as a whole, still relies on traditional credit cards and cash payments.

The EMV standards (originally issued in 1996) covered the following basic areas:

Card specifications. These specifications basically covered the common platform and software that would be required to use a universal EMV smart card. Included in this section of the specifications are the relevant PKI components (such as the RSA algorithm). Given that the issued card could be used for multiple applications, such as cash and loyalty, the card and the reader would need to synchronize on what applications are available per the card and the merchant's reader terminal. A microprocessor-based smart card (or payment card) would be universally accepted.

Terminal specifications. This section covers the physical terminal that accepts the cards defined in the previous section. Again, the goal was to provide a common terminal approach for wide acceptance. The device could run applications with minimum standards that could provide risk management and security.

Application specifications. Because the smart cards could also store applications (in addition to payment transactions), it was important to define standards on how these applications can be written to provide cross-compatibility. Common applications included loyalty applications (such as storing frequent flier miles, for example).

Although most EMV standards' core offerings center around the use of smart cards, these standards and applications provide yet another platform for the promotion and use of digital certificates. There are many complexities in implementing a mass-market smart card solution, most of which are outside the scope of this book. As a result, we will focus on those relevant areas that intersect with our understanding of how trust solutions are implemented in the area of EMV cards.

EMVCo is an organization created to manage and promote these EMV standards. EMVCo sets approval levels to ensure that companies are compatible with the previously mentioned specifications. A Level 1 approval applies to the physical, electromechanical aspects of the system (the cards and terminals). A Level 2 approval applies to all application software used in the process.

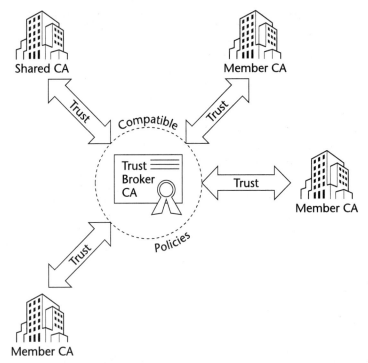

Figure 6.4   Example of static authentication in EMV standard (based on EMV specs 4.x).

EMV provides for a few different authentication modes for offline authentication:

Static data.   Static data authentication allows for the storage of the digital signature of the identity issued by a CA and for the CA certificate for verification. Up to six CAs per application can be provided. See Figure 6.4 for an example.

Dynamic data with and without a generated application cryptogram message (also known as standard dynamic data authentication and combined data authentication).   These options prevent cloning and counterfeiting of the card, something that static data does not do.

EU Directives

EU directives are laws adopted by the Council of the Europe Union (EU). These laws apply to all member EU states, which make them very powerful and useful by the standards they set. EU directives cover all manner of security issues ranging from digital signature law to specific privacy laws. In general, non-EU countries tend to have less strict laws in the area of privacy and security. As a result, EU directives serve as a model for many countries and companies.

EMV STANDARD TIDBITS

Here are some interesting items that the EMV specification requires, as relevant to digital certificates and PKI:

- ◆ All CA root keys expire on a December 31 date. New roots will be valid starting July 1 of a given year. (This makes certificate renewal/updates easier because it will occur fewer times a year in a well-controlled plan.)

- ◆ New root keys will be introduced on a regular basis, unless an emergency issue is involved. (Again, fewer changes at fewer times make the public key management life cycle much easier.)

- ◆ Smart cards using the EMV standard cannot expire beyond the validity of the CA root key's validity date. (This makes updates and transitions easier because once all the CA roots have expired, so does the card. At that point the user gets the card updated or replaced along with the new certificates.)

- ◆ EMV standards refer to the Payment System as the relying party for detecting and acting on root certificate compromise. (This puts all legal and financial liabilities on the CA for the payment system vendor, and as a result, the certificate practice statements and other legal components are very important.)

- ◆ Standards allow for up to six months for full revocation from all terminals, in the event of a CA certificate revocation. (This poses a problem for CAs as six months is a long exposure time. As a result, many root certificates tend to expire more quickly in the EMV standard than, say, in a desktop computer's browser.)

Directive 1999/93/EC

The European Union has defined specific directives to guide the development of digital signatures called the Directive 1999/93/EC of the European Parliament and of the Council of 13 December 1999 on a Community Framework for Electronic Signatures (or just EU directives for short). The thrust of the directives is to guide a process in implementing, supporting, and encouraging the use of digital signatures. The key articles (relevant to PKI and related trust solutions) are these:

Article 5. This article ensures that electronic signatures based on the EU qualified certificates have the same legal force as handwritten signatures and are admissible as proof in a court of law. This ensures the continuity and flow of business practices regardless of whether the transaction is done digitally or physically. The article gives some leeway in terms of the ability to not reject the use of electronic signatures based solely on noncompliance with specific EU directive initiatives, such as qualified certificates. In other words, it will be more difficult to prove a digital transaction if it does not follow the EU directives, but not following the EU directives should not disqualify that transaction from legal enforceability.

Article 6. This article provides that certificates will carry some level of liability for the certificate issuer based on some specific criteria. Liability protection is important because mistakes in the certificate issuance process can result in real losses with a forged or falsely obtained certificate. This is similar to the function that companies such as Visa or MasterCard serve in credit card transactions.

Article 7. This article defines the conditions under which non-EU countries can qualify under the EU directive as accredited certification providers. The article was designed to allow for a lowest-common-denominator concept where non-EU countries would have to come into compliance with the EU directives to do business in and out of the EU. Specific countries can contest regulations on a country-by-country basis should the requirements be inappropriate for those markets. Most companies that want to achieve a global dominance in trust solutions based on PKI will, as a result, attempt to achieve EU directive compliance.

Article 8. This article determines specific guidelines for the privacy and protection of the individual's rights as per the use of the individual's information, especially in conjunction with the data appearing in the certificate. Directive 95/46/EC of the European Parliament and of the Council of 24 October 1995 on the protection of individuals are the two key directives that certification service providers must follow to maintain protection of the data and the individual's privacy.

Directive 2000/31/EC

The June 2000 directive that was to be in force by January 17, 2002, laid out additional requirements over the previous 1999 directive. Essentially this directive added the following features:

- Requirements regarding the role of national authorities
- Guidance related to executing contracts online
- Liability caps of Internet intermediaries (like ISPs)
- Disclosure requirements of codes of conduct that bind a service provider

The most important, relevant pieces for trust are the additional guidelines for contract execution, which essentially enforce the legally binding nature of online transactions.

Safe Harbor Agreement

Given that business today is global and that the EU is a major player in trade and commerce, a method had to be developed to help non-EU companies come into reasonable standards to match EU-issued directives on security and

WHAT IS AN EU-QUALIFIED CERTIFICATE?

An EU-qualified certificate is a certificate that conforms to guidelines set in the EU directive standards. Some specific criteria for the EU-qualified certificate include the following:

- Identification of the certificate as a qualified certificate, certification service provider, and state of issuance
- Name of the signatory (or pseudonyms)
- Validity period of the certificate
- A unique identity code identifying the certificate
- Scope and limitations on the use of the certificate
- Any transaction value limits for which the certificate is valid

Further details can be found in Annex I of the EU directives guidelines. There are also specific guidelines noted in Annex II that define what a certification service provider must have to issue an EU-qualified certificate (such as anti-forgery techniques). Annex III defines the signature-signing devices that create the certificates. Annex IV identifies the recommendations for secure signature verification.

Some key definitions that arise in the EU directives and other regional (within the EU) signature laws are the following:

- Electronic signature—Refers to data in an electronic format that is associated with other electronic data as a mechanism for authentication.
- Advanced electronic signatures—An electronic signature that also is unique to the signer, can identify the signer, can provide nonrepudiation, and provides evidence of the integrity of the data being signed (this is the closest definition to the generic concept of digital certificates).
- Qualified electronic signatures—An advanced electronic signature that also falls under the definition of a "qualified certificate" (as defined in the Annex section of the EU directives) and created with a secure signature creation device (as defined in the EU directives).

privacy. The European Union and the United States worked out an agreement called the Safe Harbor. The EU Directive on Data Protection (put into effect in October 1998) prevented personal data of EU members from being used by non-EU-compliant companies. Essentially, the Safe Harbor Agreement (SHA) established a minimal level of "adequacy" for U.S. companies to use EU members' personal data.

The SHA directly affects the use and issuance of digital certificates because, by definition, the certificate must be unique and prove as an authentication mechanism for an individual. After all, without querying and verifying the personal data of an individual, it will not be possible, for example, to issue an EU-qualified certificate.

Some of the specific benefits of the SHA include the following:

- Companies complying with the SHA can continue to do business with the EU community.
- Specific EU regional requirements of prior approval will be waived or automatically approved.
- Complaints against U.S. companies will, in a limited manner, be brought up in the U.S. legal system.

To obtain these benefits, U.S. companies must enroll in the SHA and fulfill the following requirements:

Notice.   Individuals must be notified about how and why information is being used.

Choice.   Consumers should have the ability to opt out if they do not want their information to be disclosed to a third party.

Transfer.   Third-party organizations also must comply with notice and choice directives.

Access.   Individuals must be able to access the personal information an organization holds about them. They also have the right to correct any information.

Security.   Organizations must take "reasonable" protection to electronically safeguard personal data.

Data integrity.   Organizations must take steps to ensure that data is applied to its intended use and is reasonably accurate.

Enforcement.   There must be reasonably accessible means for redress of grievances.

What Do All These Standards Mean for Me?

How can you take advantage of the EMV standards? Basically, by building a secure infrastructure, such as a PKI, with qualified certificates (more on this in the *EU Directives* section), you can establish ecommerce with a physical world extension through smart cards. In this manner, much of the global market can be available for your business. The EMV and EU directives help define good, secure, legally enforceable electronic transactions.

There are several things to consider before embarking on creating this infrastructure:

Is your business heavily focused in the Western markets (Europe and Middle East/North America)?   If so, then the EU directives and U.S. privacy laws are critical and need to be followed carefully. Asian countries vary greatly in their implementations and, in general, have lower per-capita online purchase rates as a result of lower per-capita computer use. If you plan to attack all markets, including Asian markets, ensure that you have a three-pronged approach: North America, Europe, and Asia with respect to your privacy and security standards. Adjust the security and privacy parameters based on local and regional laws and business needs.

Consider hiring compliance officers.   It is difficult to keep up with changing regional legislation in the digital signature space. Given that some laws, like U.S. laws, have strong penalties for violations, it could even be considered an investment or cost avoidance strategy. Look for people with specific financial vertical expertise. It most likely will be necessary to hire several officers, based on regional presence.

Be involved in the industry.   If your company produces or consumes products that are affected by international and regional security and privacy laws, it is important to be involved in standards bodies and other international organizations.

Think globally, hire locally.   It is important to hire people with local knowledge of the regional laws. For example, even though the EU directive establishes guidelines for the EU, specific countries execute the directive slightly differently. As a result, it may be necessary to have very specific knowledge.

Summary: Money Talks

Given the high value of transactions the financial community must manage on a regular basis, there are a number of regulations to ensure the safety of consumers and financial institutions alike. As a result of these regulations, financial companies must use technology like PKI to ensure compliance with these regulations. Without PKI, compliance becomes very difficult and expensive by using more manual and audit-intensive methods. Various consortiums and standards have been developed to ease the pain of launching a complex technology like PKI to meet these regulatory challenges.

CHAPTER 7

Government Solutions

This chapter examines some of the government-level, PKI-based projects throughout the world. We will discuss the basic concepts of the types and requirements for government-level trust infrastructure projects. After explaining the concept, we will explore several examples. In the examples, the initial focus will be on the U.S. initiatives along with the specific legal drivers that have accelerated PKI adoption. Following a U.S.-centric discussion, we will examine a sample of international efforts to implement PKI on the scale of a national level. It is, of course, not feasible to cover the efforts of every country; however, the sample discussed here serves as an example of different methods of using PKI to create more accessible and efficient government.

Types of Government Solutions

There are effectively three main types of PKI efforts that cover the scope of an entire country (see Figure 7.1 for a visual representation):

National identity projects (NIPs). NIPs serve to create unique, digital methods of identifying all citizens for the purpose of identification. Additional applications, such as government services and communication, may also be leveraged based on this universal identification.

    Government regulations around the development of PKI in the private sector. Some countries have established direct government regulations while others have created accreditation bodies. In either case, the countries have realized the importance of the PKI infrastructure and created protection to ensure the smooth operation and continuity of the national PKI infrastructure.

    E-government projects. Some PKI implementations have been designed to give the citizen population greater and more access to government services. Some countries have established timelines in which a certain amount of services are required to move to an electronic method.

National Identity Projects

Increasingly there is a need to identify a state's citizens in a secure, consolidated manner. In some countries a citizen card is issued as proof of residency. Other countries, like the United States, are debating developing a national identity card concept. The benefit of such systems is that they can uniquely and quickly identify each resident of a country regardless of where and when they need services. Contrast this need for centralized information to the need for privacy and security of a government's citizens.

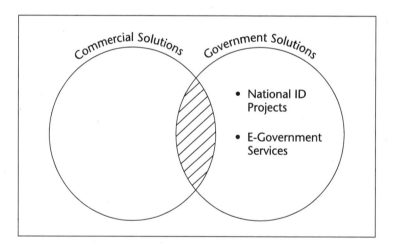

 Government regulations on commercial solutions used in government level projects (note as more governments rely on commercial solutions, the greater the overlay and regulations)

Figure 7.1 Overview of types of government solutions.

How would a successful national identity card system work? Consider that a number of countries already have "citizen identification" cards. Whereas in the United States, other than a passport or birth certificate, citizens do not have proof of residency. The "green card" (or resident alien card) applies only to U.S. residents who are not citizens. The closest the United States can consider to having a "citizen identification" system is the use of the social security card as it identifies every eligible worker in the United States.

With recent geo-political events, the rumblings in the United States for such a national undertaking have taken on new momentum. Some other countries are looking to modernize their systems from paper- or card-based identification to electronic systems. China, for example, is looking for a method to identify citizens and eligible voters, without the need for physical signatures (due to the relatively high illiteracy rates in rural areas).

Most proponents of NIPs focus on using technologies such as smart cards as the medium for carrying information to identify people and conduct transactions. In much of Europe and parts of Asia, smart cards are already widely adopted for everything from public telephone calls to currency-less cash systems.

Technology Challenges

From a technology perspective, a system has to be designed not only to store the credentials and applications that will be required for a multiuse national identity token or card, but also for the infrastructure to read and verify those tokens or cards.

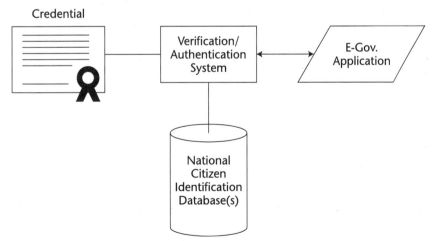

Figure 7.2 High-level architecture of a national ID system.

The basic elements of a national ID system include the following (see Figure 7.2 for a high-level view of such a system):

An identity verification system.   This system determines, through some method of authentication, the holder of a claimed identity with a high degree of confidence.

A database.   A database is required to track authentications for data analysis or for template matching or comparison. In some systems there is a central database, while in others a microdatabase is created and information relevant to an individual is stored on the same device that identifies that individual.

A token or card identification.   This device provides the actual identification. Generally, it is accepted that biometric-only identification for a large number of people (as in the population base of a country) is not quite ready for implementation at this time.

A token or card verification system.   This is required to read and understand the information stored in the token or card identification device.

Policy framework.   This includes how and when appropriate use of the system should take place. This includes the oversight and management of government use of data (which, in theory, could track citizen movements and every transaction). This is perhaps where most NIPs have failed by not being able to develop a good policy framework with the appropriate checks and balances to prevent misuse by insiders to data about citizens.

Scalability and multiapplication use.   As with any large project, the convergence of differing requirements and evolving needs will force evolution of the system that is finally implemented. As a result, the solution implemented must be able to update applications and uses dynamically. In addition, for sustainable value, the system must be able to serve multiple purposes. The ideal system would replace all credit, debit, and identification cards a person normally carries with a single identification device.

The Trust Factor

If NIP systems were created just for a convenient method of replacing hard currency (that is, physical cash), there would still need to be a strong element of trust between consumer and merchant that transactions are legally binding. When such a national system is also used for immigration, voting, and other citizen services, trust between consumer and government is also needed.

Although the ethical and privacy concerns are beyond the scope of this book, they do make up a large piece of why certain parts of the world have embraced this concept while others fear an Orwelian society. Perhaps the concept of being "not in the system," as highlighted in a number of science fiction movies, will be a future form of identity avoidance, replacing today's concern about identity theft.

Citizen Identification Device

Given that we need a device that can store information, allow updates to information, and do all this with relatively high levels of security, smart cards are the only practical technology out there. Why not just use biometrics? The challenge with biometrics is that there must be a central repository that holds valid biometric templates. If the repository is centralized, then this increases risks such as fraud and identity theft because all of the information is stored in one place. In addition, the technology for reliable biometric authentication for millions of users is not yet at a level where it can be universally deployed and accepted in a range of environmental and cultural areas.

Smart cards can combine biometric data with other authentication information. In this manner, the matching biometric template is stored on the card itself. For those locations and transactions that absolutely require biometric authentication, it can be done. For other locations or less valuable transactions, that information is simply ignored.

GIN AND TONIC, HOLD THE COUPONS

As a micro case study of the ethics of a national identification system, consider a March 2002 article published in the *New York Times* ("Welcome to the Database Lounge," *New York Times*, March 21, 2002). The article revealed that a bar called *The Rack* was doing a little bit of creative marketing. That bar took a patron's driver's license, used extensively as an age verification tool in the United States, and scanned the card, supposedly to determine its validity, into a scanning machine. Unbeknown to some of the patrons, the scanning device also recorded information about each patron that was accessible via the driver's license magnetic stripe including name, address, height, and weight. For The Rack, this would provide valuable marketing information. No explicit consent was sought from the patrons, and no privacy or security policy was stated on how the data may be used. The information could then potentially be resold to marketers who would get valuable information about a person's entire profile, right down to eye color!

Terminal Readers

In order for identification devices to work, readers are required at every location where the devices must be used. In the 2002 movie *Minority Report*, all citizens' irises were scanned as a means of identification. Such a system assumes an awesome amount of resources that are implemented to created readers all over a country. Currently, other than magnetic strip readers, smart card readers are probably the only (relatively) widespread readers (with the exception of North America).

Government Regulations

The majority of government regulations in the area of digital signatures around the world have been initiated by laws that have supported the legal effectiveness of digital signatures. The bulk of these laws give digital signatures the same legal weight as paper-based signatures. Other government regulations focus on existing organizations in the commercial sectors that support a PKI for that country. Some have taken direct government control regulations while others have no regulations at all.

A number of standards or consortium-based initiatives already exist for vendors in the world of trust solutions; however, without government regulations or laws to support these efforts, customers run the risk of relying on critical infrastructure that may fail. For example, most banking infrastructure in most countries is backed and protected by the government in case of failure. PKI and similar trust infrastructures that require such critical dependence must also, to be truly successful, be treated with such necessity.

E-Government Projects

The ultimate service a government can provide is the ability for its citizens to access government services 24 hours a day, 7 days a week. Services from tax filings to voting are all necessary services that require a high degree of security. Challenges faced in this process of moving to electronic government services include the ability to scale this solution in a friendly, easy-to-use manner for such a large audience (the country's populace). Other challenges include balancing the need for authentication of citizens and the ability to maintain privacy (such as in electronic voting).

Generally, most e-government solutions focus on converting basic functions such as tax filings or form submissions into electronic formats. More advanced applications, such as universal identification and e-voting (see Figure 7.3 for a theoretical example of an e-voting architecture), have not been implemented in most of the world.

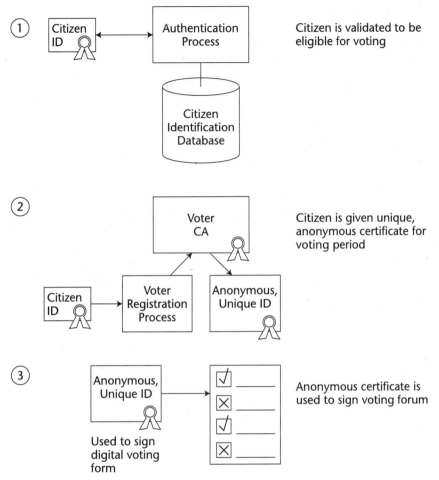

① Citizen is validated to be eligible for voting

② Citizen is given unique, anonymous certificate for voting period

③ Anonymous certificate is used to sign voting forum

Figure 7.3 E-voting theoretical architecture.

U.S. Government Initiatives

There are numerous government initiatives based on PKI and related trust solutions. This section describes some of the high-profile projects for the U.S. government. Government projects truly show scalability and reliability under extreme conditions, such as high security and large populations. As a result, private enterprises can look to these projects as a model for a robust architecture.

Common Access Card

One of the largest government PKI-based security projects in the United States is the Department of Defense's (DoD) Common Access Card (CAC) project. The CAC replaces the former mode of identification, the DD Form 2 Identification Card. The CAC contains specific identification information, along with PKI certificates and custom applications per specific departmental needs. From the perspective of PKI, a CAC-issued smart card contains up to three certificates in addition to personnel information. Figure 7.4 shows a high-level architecture diagram. CACs are issued to all active-duty military, selected reserves, DoD civilians, eligible foreign military, and eligible contractors. Supporting infrastructure includes the Defense Enrollment Eligibility Reporting System (DEERS) and the Real-time Automated Personnel Identification System (RAPIDS), which provide additional authentication mechanisms.

> **NOTE** A few million CAC cards and even more certificates have been issued during the CAC deployment. Each card costs approximately U.S. $7. Each certificate on the CAC has a validity period of three years, unless otherwise revoked.

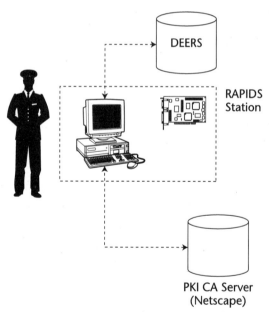

Figure 7.4 CAC architecture.

The CAC contains the following:

- An integrated circuit chip (ICC) that holds the data to be read or stored
- A magnetic stripe that serves as a form of reading the data, in case an ICC reader is not available
- A photo ID that serves as a physical identification device (for other humans)
- Certificates for multiple applications (see more on this in the text that follows)
- Biometric information for strong authentication
- Noncontact RF transmitter for access to buildings without the magnetic stripe or ICC reader

The three certificates stored on the CAC include the following:

An authentication certificate.   This certificate is reserved for nonrepudiation for transactions. Specifically, this certificate will be used to sign DoD documents and act as proof of identity for accessing secure Web portals.

A signing certificate.   This certificate is used to sign email.

An encryption certificate.   This certificate is used by others to send encrypted email to the CAC card owner. Separating the signing and encryption certificates allows the encryption certificate to be escrowed but not break the claim of nonrepudiation that can be substantiated with the signing certificate.

One advantage of the CAC implementation is that it uses a combination of biometrics and PIN to protect access to the card. In the event the PIN is lost or forgotten, the user can go to an authorized CAC station. At that station, if the biometric data from the user matches the information stored on the card, the station officer then can allow the user to create a new PIN. Without such a feature, loss of the PIN would be loss of the use of the entire card. In order to manage these various functions, the smart card vendors have packaged middleware software to manage issues like installing and updating certificates on the CAC (see Table 7.1 for CAC middleware requirements). Relying on biometric authentication alone would increase the cost of the project substantially as all access points would then have to be outfitted with biometric devices.

NOTE The deadline for CAC issuance to all DoD departments was extended to October 2003 from October 2002.

Given that PKI may not be enabled for all applications, especially custom applications designed for military purposes, it is important to have the flexibility to PKI-enable applications. In this regard, a developer's kit, produced by DMDC-West, has been created for the CAC program to PKI-enable applications.

One immediate PKI-enabled application for the CAC is for the Navy Marine Corps Intranet (NMCI) to sign email electronically and facilitate secure login to computer terminals. In addition, the certificates on the card will be used to access secure Web portals.

In order to be issued a CAC, the following are required for authentication:

- For those personnel not enrolled in the Defense Eligibility Reporting System (DEERS), two official identification credentials issued by a federal, state, or foreign country government agency, at least one of which must be a picture ID. For those already enrolled in DEERS, only one photo identification is required.

- A government email account. (If contractor employees do not have one, then the CAC may still be issued without the email certificate.)

- A completed DD Form 1172-2 (application for the DOD CAC — DEERS enrollment).

The backbone of the CAC is the PKI infrastructure that the DoD has set up for this purpose. It is a Netscape certificate server with a private hierarchy.

Table 7.1   Some CAC Smart Card Middleware Requirements

REQUIREMENT	COMMENTS
Use systems resources specified by the resource manager.	Middleware software must manage system resources to control security and memory conservation issues.
Hardware (cryptographic devices) must be able to generate, verify, and initiate certificate requests and generation.	Essentially, the hardware must perform the basic functions of a secure cryptographic device.
Maximum disk space required for software does not exceed 30MM for client workstations.	This limit is extended to 100MB for server-based code.
Perform session management.	This requirement allows multiple applications to function on the client machine and not create errors when running with other programs.
Software must be able to read and manage all elements of the CAC, not just the crypto pieces.	This requirement ensures that the DoD does not have to install a myriad of applications to read and manage the CAC.

GUNS, SMOKES, AND CERTIFICATES?

The U.S. Department of Treasury has a wide range of responsibilities, from protecting the President to minting U.S. currency to overseeing financial institutions. In order to support a growing need for common identification and increased security, the Treasury looked to smart cards that contain PKI elements to solve this challenge. Specifically, the Treasury had three main goals (relevant to PKI):

 ◆ Issue certificates to all Treasury employees

 ◆ Promote business use of PKI via smart cards

 ◆ Set standards around PKI and smart card deployment

 Here is the status of a few of those initial deployments in the various bureaus that make up the Treasury (the final project will be completed sometime in 2003):

 ◆ Alcohol, Tobacco, and Firearms (ATF): 50 users with PKI-enabled SSO.

 ◆ Bureau of Printing and Engraving: 50 users with PKI-enabled smart cards.

 ◆ Secret Service: 3,300 users with PKI-enabled SSO.

 ◆ Departmental offices: 3,500 users with PKI-enabled smart cards.

NOTE The CAC certificates are used by the DoD to address three legal drivers: information protected by the Privacy Act, information classified as "For Official Use Only," and sensitive but unclassified data and/or information protected by HIPAA.

ACES

The Access Certificates for Electronic Services (ACES) project is a U.S. government digital certification program that provides PKI technology to allow U.S. government employees to use digital certificates for e-government and ecommerce transactions (see Figure 7.5 for sample architecture). The project is a joint offering between industry (with corporations such as AT&T) and the General Services Administration. Other participants in the program include PKI vendor VeriSign, fraud protection services from Trans Union, and Eccelerate.com (a division of Dun and Bradstreet), which provides a unique business identification number for all government vendors (called a DUNS number). The project meets the following key goals:

 ■ Paperwork Reduction Act and Government Paperwork Reduction Act compliance. Because paperwork can be moved online and digital certificates can be used to authorize transactions, the PKI technology helps government agencies and departments come into compliance with the act.

■ Support for the Presidential Directive under the National Partnership for Reinventing Government to leverage Internet technologies for their efficiencies in lowering the cost of governmental services.

The government sponsors have identified several key applications for the ATT ACES certificates:

■ Application for and transfer of benefits

■ Application for and administration of government grants

■ Submission of reporting or filing requirements

■ Secure communication exchanges

■ Procurement transactions

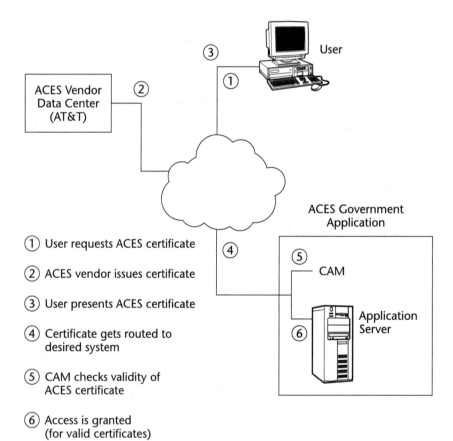

① User requests ACES certificate

② ACES vendor issues certificate

③ User presents ACES certificate

④ Certificate gets routed to desired system

⑤ CAM checks validity of ACES certificate

⑥ Access is granted (for valid certificates)

Figure 7.5 ACES sample architecture.

Essentially, the ACES certificates are client-side certificates that are used for validation and encryption of transactions. Costs, while not inexpensive, are reasonable: They range from $12 to $18 per certificate (per year), and validations (proof that a certificate has not been revoked) range from $1.20 down to about $.40 per transaction. The life of an ACES certificate is usually two years, and generally there is no cost to renew them. Note that most commercially available, outsourced PKI models issue client certificates only on a yearly basis. In fact, VeriSign started issuing multiyear certificates (SSL) only about a year ago. In the end, users have deemed that the risk of having a long validity period does not outweigh the inconvenience of yearly renewals.

Getting a certificate is only half the story. Validating certificates is also essential because in that two-year validity period, the ACES certificate may have to be revoked. The Computer Arbitrator Module (CAM) acts as a broker by validating ACES certificates, checking them against the various CAs to see which certificates have been revoked.

What is interesting is that in order to obtain an ACES certificate, quite a bit of information must be given and validated. For example, individuals must provide the following:

- First and last name (former last name if changed within the last 12 months)
- Address
- Social security number
- Date of birth
- A valid driver's license or state ID number
- Email address
- Work and home phone numbers
- A credit card issued to the same name and address provided in the application

Although all this information does not appear in the certificate, it is required for the authentication process. Similarly, business organizations that require an ACES certificate must provide personal information about the representative of that organization that can be authenticated (and proof that the person is indeed authorized to represent that organization). In addition, the business must provide organization name, address, type of organization, state of organization registration, and DBA and DUNS numbers (if available).

What actually appears in an ACES certificate is the following:

- Name of the certificate issuer
- Validity period
- Name of the certified subject (person or server)

- Organization name (ACES business representative and qualified relying party certificates)
- The public key of the certified subject

Basically, private information is not revealed in the certificate itself.

Legal Drivers

Numerous legal drivers have spurred the use of PKI in governmental applications. We will discuss a few here. The appendix contains an overall survey of various states and uses of PKI around the world. In this section, we will highlight some of the U.S. dominant drivers and some EU-driven directives.

Paperwork Reduction Act (E-Paper Act)

The Paperwork Reduction Act (Reduction Act) was designed to reduce the burden to citizens in interacting with the government. When the Reduction Act was implemented in 1980, the concept and infrastructure for PKI was not in widespread use. With the ability to tap into trust infrastructure such as PKI, the Reduction Act is more easily followed at a lower cost. Some of the highlights and relevant portions of the act are as follows (quoted excerpts are from Paperwork Reduction Act of 1995 legislation):

- "Minimize the cost to the Federal Government of the creation, collection, maintenance, use, dissemination, and disposition of information." Clearly moving into a digital format is the most effective way to accomplish this goal.
- "Security of information, including the Computer Security Act of 1987 (Public Law 100-235)...." The strength of digital certificates and PKI is that they allow strong security and privacy to be maintained.
- "Provide for the dissemination of public information on a timely basis...makes effective use of information technology." Clearly, the use of PKI can speed up the process of information delivery as the integrity of documents can be verified. In addition, the use of information technology to improve efficiencies is clearly followed.

Privacy Act

The Privacy Act, initially proposed in the 1970s, had several amendments to the act, which most recently afforded protection of electronic information regarding individuals' private information. In order to protect the privacy of individuals from being breached by various federal agencies, each agency must maintain security on individually identifiable information. (Note that in late 2002, Homeland Security initiatives have sought to revert many of the privacy laws either directly or indirectly by giving U.S. government agencies increased surveillance powers of its citizens, residents, and visitors.)

Federal Agency Protection of Privacy Act

The Privacy Act was proposed in October 2002 as H.R. 4561 (as of this writing it has not yet become law) and sought to introduce the concept of a privacy impact analysis. The act included provisions to ensure that users of data that may be deemed private must provide for the security of that data. In the digital world, privacy and security for electronic documents are very difficult to ensure without some form of encryption, and thus trust solutions like digital certificates become the ideal technology to use to comply with such a law.

Government Paperwork Elimination Act

The Government Paperwork Elimination Act (GPEA) requires all federal executive agencies to provide entities that deal with agencies the option of electronic management of information (as a substitute for paper), including the ability to support electronic signatures where practicable. The act specifically requires agencies to guard the privacy of the document contents (and owners) as well as protect against the alteration of those documents (after being executed). The Electronic Signatures in Global and National Commerce Act enforces the GPEA by giving full legal authority to documents executed digitally, equal to paper documents with physical signatures. In addition, adherence to the GPEA also supports the president's memorandum of December 17, 1999, "Electronic Government," in which the president directed the Office of Management and Budget (OMB) to guide federal agencies to become more "customer" friendly by providing electronic mechanisms for communicating information with citizens while still retaining security and privacy.

Almost equal to the emphasis on digital signatures is the emphasis by the OMB on the need for security policies and a policy framework. As we have discussed elsewhere in this book, a security policy is as important as the technology used.

Some of the guidelines the OMB provides can be applied to a range of government projects and not just for U.S.-centric governments. The basic policy framework guidance covers the following highlights:

- Establish a clear security policy that shows liability and risk assurance levels. Indicate the terms and agreements that users of the infrastructure should expect.

- Reduce the chance of repudiation of a transaction. Indicate the user's responsibility to protect the end certificate.

- Control access to information in a repository. Digital hashes and physical and logical security are necessary to ensure that integrity is maintained.

- Establish a reliable chain of custody. This will ensure that no repudiation can be made during the process of generating the private key or otherwise in the process of a digital signature. A digital receipt or some type of notarization post transaction would help in this process.

- Rely on legal counsel during the policy development phase. In the end, the law is what will be used to resolve disputes, so get good advice early on.

NOTE October 21, 2003, is the deadline for government agencies to become compliant with GPEA.

To help agencies meet this compliance deadline, the OMB proposed the following key steps that U.S. government agencies would need to take to execute on the GPEA:

- Provide a secure computing environment to protect against fraud and theft of information

- Plan electronic networks for the ability to use electronic methods for document management

SAMPLE REGULATIONS PASSED (BY AGENCY) ON THE VALIDITY OF DIGITAL SIGNATURES AND ELECTRONIC SUBMISSIONS

- ◆ Administrative Committee of the Federal Register (1 C.F.R. Part 18.7), electronic signatures on documents submitted for publication in the Federal Register.

- ◆ Commodity Futures Trading Commission (17 C.F.R. Part 1.4 and Part 1.3), electronic signatures for filings.

- ◆ Environmental Protection Agency (55 Fed. Reg. 31,030 (1990)), policy on electronic reporting.

- ◆ Food and Drug Administration (21 C.F.R. Part 11), electronic signatures and records.

- ◆ Federal Acquisition Regulation (48 C.F.R. Parts 2 and 4), electronic contracts.

- ◆ Federal Property Management Regulations (41 C.F.R. Part 101-41), electronic bills of lading.

- ◆ General Services Acquisition Regulation (48 C.F.R. Part 552.216-73), electronic orders.

- ◆ Internal Revenue Service (Treasury Reg. 301.6061-1), signature alternatives for tax filings.

- ◆ Securities and Exchange Commission (17 C.F.R. Part 232), electronic regulatory filings.

All of these compliance steps require a PKI infrastructure. Most importantly, PKI can help keep the costs of these implementations (relatively) low. Agencies can still use email (with PKI) without having to invest in dedicated workflow management systems. Hence, the only cost is in deployment and maintenance. Because most government agencies have contracted with industry partners to run the CA functionality, costs are generally found to be in the low single-dollar ranges per person (per year). The OMB does not specifically indicate the exact technology to use, but it does advise consideration of electronic signatures (that is, digital certificates).

NOTE The OMB specifically states in *Report to the Ranking Minority Member, Committee on Governmental Affairs, U.S. Senate* that an "important element of security will be wider implementation of public key cryptography" (p. 26 of the report).

Electronic Signatures in Global and National Commerce (E-Sign) Act

This area of the act moves it into a strong, legally enforceable method for the government to quickly and efficiently do business with its citizens.

The key aspects of the act are as follows:

Consent to electronic records.   This act essentially allows the government to use electronic methods for delivering required information given the knowledge and consent of the citizen receiving the information. This includes any hardware or software requirements necessary for conducting the task.

Confirmation of consent.   The act also clarifies that the legality of a transaction is not immediately invalidated if the user did not give consent to an electronic transaction (versus a paper-based one). Given that intent can be shown in different ways and that when the law was written, it was not clear how the technology would develop to support this, the legislators ensured that there would be no loopholes for acceptance of this law.

Prospective effect.   The revocation of consent post-transaction does not solely invalidate the electronic transaction. Again, the intent was that technology evolution would eventually be able to solve this issue (with, for example, digital receipts and time stamping).

Oral communications.   Verbal communications would not satisfy an electronic contract (for example, over an electronic device like the phone).

Retention of contracts and records.   Retention of executed transactions may require retention of information. In case a law for a specific type of transaction (mortgages, for example) required a minimum retention period, the contract would be valid only if the documents could be retained in electronic form *and* retrieved over the life of the period required for retention. In other words, if the document could not be retained electronically for later verification, the contract would be nullified.

The act effectively describes a technology that must be electronically applicable to digital documents, must provide for nonrepudiation, must maintain document integrity over a specified period of time, and can be used by the average consumer. This describes the core function of a PKI system. By using digital certificates, all of the provisions of the act are satisfied. Given that a number of applications are already PKI-enabled or simple tools can be used to enact digital transactions, it is feasible that PKI can be used by an organization to conduct legally binding transactions.

Federal Bridge Certification Authority

The Federal Bridge Certification Authority (FBCA) is an attempt to merge all of the various PKI CAs across the U.S. government into a single mesh of trust. The FBCA acts as a trusted meta-CA and uses its root to sign principal CAs from other hierarchies. The FBCA defines four levels of assurance through its model:

- Rudimentary
- Basic
- Medium
- High

Generally, the higher the confidence in the identity of the certificate holder (or CA in this case), the higher the assurance level.

One key point to make is that the FBCA is *not* a hierarchical model (see Figure 7.6). The idea of a single federal PKI root is not feasible in the near future. Due to changing technology, huge costs for implementation, and concerns about privacy, the FBCA provides the flexibility for individual agencies to serve their audience as needed without the concern of a master authority. The architecture and process consist of the FBCA cross-certifying member agencies providing for a seamless, transitive trust among member agencies to the FBCA project. FBCA root CAs are kept offline and used only when a cross-certification is required. This is similar to commercial CAs that keep their root CA keys offline to mitigate security risks. The entire operation is run by the General Services Administration and encourages departments to use commercial off-the-shelf tools (COTs).

NOTE September 19, 2002 was the date of the first cross-certification (in production) under the FBCA framework. The initial departments involved in this signing ceremony included the Department of Defense, the Agriculture Department's National Finance Center, NASA, and the Treasury Department. The platform was based on Entrust PKI. On November 21, 2002, the General Services Administration (GSA) validated interoperability with the outsourced PKI vendor VeriSign.

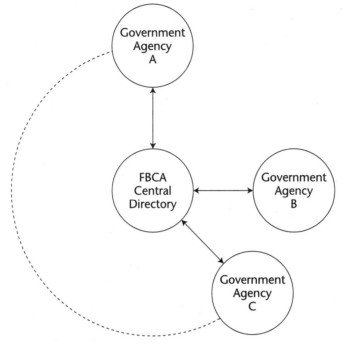

Agency C and Agency A communicate
via the FBCA Central Directory

Figure 7.6 Example of FBCA architecture.

The initial set of agencies involved in the FBCA included the DoD, Department of Justice (DoJ), Department of Commerce (DoC), Treasury, GSA, and OMB. Essentially, all disparate commercial CA products are cross-certified to ensure compatibility with different products among the different agencies. FBCA cross-certified certificates are stored in an X.500 directory with an LDAP interface, which allows almost any application to query for a certificate.

FBCA guidelines are compatible with IETF RFC 2527, which defines the certificate policy and certification practice statement framework. The difference between the FBCA and a private industry CA is that FBCA does not bear liability; it just makes claims on levels of assurance. A private-industry CA also backs up those claims of assurance with insurance, in the event that the CA makes a mistake on the level of assurance.

Meaning of Assurance

The levels of assurance in the FBCA are as follows:

Test. This level indicates technical interoperability between the FBCA and government agency infrastructure and makes no claims about assurance. Identification requirements for the CA administrator, the revocation time period, and the frequency of CRL updates will be established in the service level agreement.

Rudimentary. This level indicates the lowest level of assurance. At this level, risk of malicious activity is considered low; transactions that require confidentially and authentication are not recommended. No identification is required for the CA administrator (only a valid email address is necessary). No revocation is required. CRL updates are not required.

Basic. This level provides a base level of assurance where the risks of data compromise are not considered major. This level may require the use of private data during the authentication process, but there is a low degree of confidence that the data will not be compromised or impacted by a potential compromise. This level requires in-person identification before a trust agent or before an RA. Information presented will be verified against a trust database. A notarized claim of identity from an appropriate agency via mail will also be accepted. Revocation must occur within 6 hours. CRL updates must occur every 24 hours.

Medium. At this level, data is exposed to a high risk of compromise. In addition, the transactions being protected have high value or risk of fraud. Exposure of private data is considered to be a significant risk if compromised. This level requires in-person identity verification before a trust agent, RA, or a state or federal government–certified entity authorized to verify identities (such as a notary public). Credentials for proof of identity include a federal ID or at least two forms of nonfederal IDs, including at least one with a photo ID. Revocation must occur within 2 hours. CRL updates must occur every 18 hours.

High. This level is used to address data that needs to be protected in high-risk situations and where the consequences for compromise of data security are severe. This level requires in-person verification of identity in front of a trusted agent or RA and cannot be done via any other method. Credentials for proof of identity include a federal ID or at least two forms of nonfederal IDs, including at least one with a photo ID. All information will be verified. Revocation must occur within 30 minutes. CRL updates must occur every 6 hours.

The biggest step in working with different government agencies on their PKI systems is the mapping of the different certificate levels with a consistent assurance level that the FBCA uses. This is effectively established through policy via a Memorandum of Agreement between the government agency and the FBCA.

International Efforts

Thus far, we have discussed U.S-based PKI initiatives as a model and representative example for understanding other countries' systems. This next section will cover some key international government-level PKI initiatives. While we do not seek to include or exclude any specific government, some additional trust-related projects are listed in the Appendix, along with some resources to provide an even greater scope of the international efforts behind PKI.

Australia

Australia has taken on the model described as the gatekeeper model (see Figure 7.7). The gatekeeper model establishes a government-level advisory committee called the Gatekeeper Policy Advisory Committee (GPAC). The GPAC advises the National Office for Information Economy (NOIE) to provide technical guidance to the government lawmakers on the intricacies of overseeing PKI CAs. The NOIE directly accredits commercial CAs and RAs to ensure their reliability and security. Other countries have followed this concept of accreditation. Interestingly enough, the United States does not have any regulations for or concept of accreditation of CAs and RAs for universal use. The U.S. government does have specific projects that require certain parameters and testing to be performed, but it has nothing at the government level to regulate the quality and security of CAs for the commercial sector. The gatekeeper concept is that the GPAC advises on the technical standards and processes on which the NOIE makes a decision for accreditation.

In this model, no laws specifically enforce the gatekeeper model, although laws do exist for the enforceability of digital signatures. Specifically, the Electronic Transactions Act 1999 (ETA) provides that contracts executed in whole or in part electronically are not necessarily void. In order to enforce a digital signature, the following requirements must be met:

- Method must be established to identify the person and to indicate the person's approval of the information communicated.

- Method must be established to require that the reliability should be on par with the purposes for which the information was communicated.

- For transactions dealing with the Australian government, the method established must be implemented and used in compliance with the government's technology requirements. Any government agency must use the gatekeeper model when an electronic signature is used.

This model allows the NOIE and the GPAC to change recommendations and accreditation guidelines quickly to respond to changes in technology. If legislation was required, then changes would invariably be years behind actual technological capability.

The gatekeeper model specifies two types of certificates, each having three grades with varying degrees of authentication and confidence:

- Type 1: Certificates attributed to individuals. These certificates are bound to the unique identity of a single person.

- Type 2: Certificates attributed to an organization. These certificates represent an organization via an individual representative. For example, in signing contracts or dealing with third-party vendors, employees of one company are actually representatives making decisions on behalf of that company. This certificate also lets multiple individuals authorized to represent that company use the same certificate.

A third type of certificate, not specifically covered by the gatekeeper model is the Type 3 certificate, which can be viewed as gatekeeper "compliant." The Type 1 or Type 2 certificates are actually considered gatekeeper certificates. Organizations that issue Type 3 certificates must still seek accreditation from the gatekeeper model. Type 3 certificates are attributed to devices (not to individuals). This would include certificates for routers, VPNs, cable modems, and so on.

To assist in authenticating commercial entities, the gatekeeper model created the Australian Business Number Digital Signature Certificate (ABN-DSC). These certificates, using something similar to the U.S.'s DUNS number, help strongly bind the identity of an organization to the certificate. In fact, since March 2001, Australian banks with a valid ABN-DSC could conduct business with the Australian government electronically using those certificates.

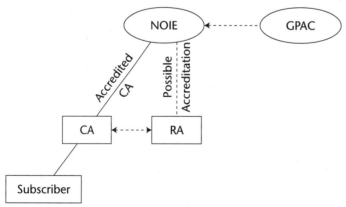

Figure 7.7 Australia's gatekeeper model.

United Kingdom

The United Kingdom has a mandate to provide all government services electronically by 2005 through its e-government strategy. (Note that this date was originally 2008 and was moved forward in an aggressive approach to making government more accessible and efficient!) It is quite a tall order that must take into account the complexity of back-office systems, usability across millions of people, and providing the necessary privacy and security to make citizens comfortable using e-government services. See Figure 7.8.

The U.K. government provides the "Government Gateway," which allows citizens and businesses to register for access to government services, including the ability to obtain digital certificates. Initially deployed services have included the following:

- The Integrated Administration and Control System (IACS) Area Aid Application from the Department for the Environment, Food, and Rural Affairs (DEFRA)

- Department of Trade and Industry (DTI) Export License Application

- Duty Deferment Electronic Statements (DDES) from Her Majesty's Customs & Excise (HMCE)

- Pay As You Earn (PAYE) from Inland Revenue (IR), including year-end submissions

- Self-Assessment from IR

- Value Added Tax (VAT) returns from HMCE

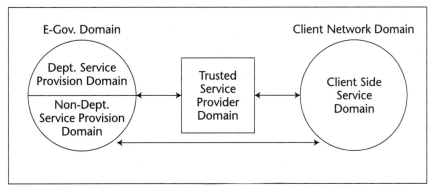

Note: Domain outside of E-Gov., trusted provider, and client network is considered the public domain (and thus the highest risk domain).

Figure 7.8 Security domains in the U.K. e-government initiative.

The security framework that has been built to support the U.K. e-government initiatives requires a PKI. Certain types of transactions have been flagged as necessary for higher forms of authentication and, thus, require digital certificates. Generally, these transactions are referred to as Level 3 transactions that explicitly require the use of digital certificates as authentication tools. Some key elements noted in regards to digital certificates in this initiative are as follows:

- The highest level of security will require a smart card or similar device to hold the private key associated with a digital certificate securely.

- The government will use third-party registration services (for digital certificates) that are aligned with the tScheme (an initiative that aligns the needs from the banking and retail sectors). By leveraging commercial mechanisms for registration and issuance of digital certificates, the government can obtain the latest technology at all times.

Some unique features (relative to other similar government initiatives) of the U.K.'s approach are the following:

- Delegate authorities are allowed to conduct business with the government. This implies a scheme for allowing the use of digital certificates for a primary beneficiary and a delegate. Delegates are identified as organizations conducting on behalf of an individual (for example, for tax services, legal services, and so on). To mitigate misuse, the designated party authorized to conduct delegate functions must be identified during the registration process of a certificate by the individual.

- Citizens are able to obtain anonymous certificates. These certificates would identify a unique individual but not identify that person. Possible cases for anonymous access are in anonymous medical screening, for example.

- Deregistration from the e-government gateway portal (that allows for access to e-government services) can be done online. Recommendations have been made, however, to have deregistration occur via physical, postal mail. This would prevent a denial-of-service attack.

- To prevent denial of service in another manner, revocations are held in suspension for up to 120 days pending any appeals. This also has the risk that a legitimate user may request revocation and then a hacker may request reinstatement. Again, recommendations for the use of postal, physical mail to mitigate these types of risks have been made.

India

As India increasingly takes center stage with its involvement in worldwide IT infrastructure services, it has taken a lead in adopting a good policy framework for a national PKI-based infrastructure.

In 2000, the Indian government passed the Information Technology Act that effectively granted the same power as physical signatures to electronic signatures. This allowed ecommerce transactions to bear the same legal standing as paper documents. Part of this act includes the establishment of the Controller of Certifying Authorities (CCA). The CCA was charged with the task of supervising and accrediting organizations within India to become CAs (certificate authorities). Although similar to the Australian gatekeeper model, the Indian act directly was mandated by the government and regulated the activities of CAs via the CCA.

NOTE IDC, a marketing research firm, reported in 2002 that nearly 15 percent of India's Internet users are online banking users as well. This creates a strong need for increased security for financial transactions.

Based on CCA regulation, a CA must meet the following criteria to be licensed as a CA:

- Consistently utilizes accepted technologies of accepted technological standards
- Utilizes appropriate computer security systems
- Utilizes hardware, software, and procedures that are reasonably secure from intrusion and misuse
- Provides a reasonable level of reliability in its services, which are reasonably suited for performing the intended functions
- Adheres to security procedures to ensure that the secrecy and privacy of the digital signature are assured
- Operations satisfy such other standards as may be prescribed by the Indian government (to account for future changes in technologies and regulations)

NOTE SafeScrypt Ltd., a technology company based in India, was the first CA to be certified by the CCA.

Here are some examples of how digital certificates are being used in commercial sectors of India under CAs within the new CCA guidelines:

- Two companies in the Hinduja Group, Ashok Leyland and Ashok Leyand Finance, are leading the way with secure email. Ashok Leyland uses digital certificates with its vendors and agents. Ashok Leyand Finance will use them with agents and loan processing, mainly to provide secure communication.

- L&T Group is using digitally signed construction documents that are sent electronically instead of physically being mailed. The signature indicates proper verification and integrity of the documents.

- The technology company Infosys is using secure email solutions with digital certificates among its executives.

- Each CA must provide a bank guarantee of up to five years that will be used in case the CA fails and all certificates must be transferred to another CA. This effectively treats CAs as critical institutions, much like banks. This makes CAs a critical component in the national infrastructure.

One key difference in India's approach to a national PKI infrastructure is that it has a government-owned CA as well as commercially available ones. The Reserve Bank of India (RBI)'s technology arm, called the Institute of Development and Research in Banking Technology (IDRBT), received a license from the CCA to become a CA. The main focus of the IDRBT is to provide a secure infrastructure, through PKI, for banking transactions. In addition, for government banking transactions, efficiencies and costs could be improved. Applications to be implemented include e-checks and similar digital payment schemes.

Summary: Citizen Certificate

From the sample of government initiatives we have discussed in this chapter, it is clear that trust solution technologies like PKI are critical for efficient governing. The ability to tie all of the benefits seen in the commercial sector to the government sectors is evident throughout the world. Technology vendors should take heart that their local government is most likely already looking at future purchases in the area of PKI and related authentication technologies.

The classic debate between the need for national security and the rights of the individual will continue to influence the structure and use of this technology. Size and the culture of a country define how PKI technology is implemented. Nonetheless, PKI proves it can scale and serve a large audience in a secure and reliable fashion.

CHAPTER 8

Communications Solutions

Just as trust solutions have had a big impact on enterprise customers, solutions that affect or are targeted to a wide audience have also generated waves in the marketplace. Many of the solutions in this chapter can also be used for the business customer, so it is not to say that these are consumer-only solutions. Rather, the focus of these solutions is the occasional user, small numbers of users, or the small- to medium-sized business market users.

Secure Messaging

Secure messaging is, by far, not just a mass-market or consumer solution. Significant revenue can be derived from messaging from the enterprise space. Given the mass audience for email, however, messaging is listed as a consumer solution due to its wide prevalence. Messaging, in its broadest definition, includes not only asynchronous messages, such as email, but also instant messaging (IM), which is real-time communication. Many solutions in the security market target messaging, especially email, because that is still the most frequently deployed application over the Internet.

The challenge with messaging is that usually backend infrastructure is required along with some type of messaging client. In some cases, the client may be a browser, but the browser serves as a client nonetheless. New approaches to solving this problem include the ability to access messages on mobile devices, which effectively remove the need for a dedicated terminal with a dedicated client.

There is also the problem of communicating with someone who might not have, or need to have, an existing relationship with another party. FedEx and UPS have built businesses around shipping goods from party to party even if doing so becomes just a one-time transaction. Likewise, in the messaging world, there is a growing need for an equivalent "electronic FedEx" system. This would eliminate the physical shipping of legal forms and allow them to be sent electronically, with the full assurance that the transaction would still be legally enforceable and auditable.

Methods of Secure Communications

There are several methods for establishing secure communications, in both asynchronous and synchronous communications. For the more common, asynchronous solutions, we will examine the following methods:

Encryption from point–to point (sender to recipient). This describes the ideal scenario in which only the sender and recipient can examine the contents of the communication.

Encryption from client to message server (sender to message server), with insecure pickup. For remote users, this refers to accessing messages via a Web server, but not providing security for the message once it leaves the message server at the sender's infrastructure.

Encryption from client to message server, with secure pickup. This describes the best alternative to the ideal scenario. The client uses a Web browser to send the message, and then the recipient receives a pickup message that establishes a secure connection with his or her Web browser connection.

Encryption Point–to Point

The ideal scenario in secure messaging is to encrypt all messages from sender to recipient. This leaves no chance that even internal administrators could intercept or read these messages. For email, this is a bit easier said than done due to the necessity that both sender and recipient must agree to a common solution. The only viable solution for complete point-to-point encryption is the use of digital certificates. Digital certificates not only authenticate the sender, but also allow the use of encryption as a result of the public keys contained in the certificates.

PGP: PRETTY GOOD PRIVACY

For completeness, it is important to mention that Pretty Good Privacy (PGP), is still a common method of securing communications from person to person. PGP originally started out as a hardcore privacy tool that was typically not supported by any corporate-level entity. The technology was eventually bought by Network Associates a number of years ago and repackaged for the corporate world. PGP during that time was also given the ability to use certificates to distribute the public encryption keys that users needed to send encrypted messages. Then Network Associates stopped development of PGP in early 2002. Nonetheless, PGP continues to have a wide installed base and strong usage, especially among individuals.

How does encryption work? Actually, with modern email clients, such as Microsoft Outlook or Outlook Express, it is quite easy. Figure 8.1 shows a diagram of the flow of an encrypted email message. The sender must enable digital encryption (to keep the message secret) and as an option to allow for digital signature (to authenticate the sender) on the email client. In Outlook the encryption and digital signature options can be accessed by just two small buttons. In the case of digital encryption, Outlook works in the background to find the digital certificate associated with the recipient, extract the public key, and then encrypt the message and its attachments using the public key. The recipient, in theory, should be the only holder of the private key that can decrypt the sender's encrypted message. Outlook does the encryption and decryption automatically for the user. For digitally signing a message, Outlook uses the certificate from the sender and encrypts the message with the sender's private key, then relies on the recipient's email client to verify and decode the message with the sender's public key. Digitally signing allows only sender authentication, not message privacy. In important cases, it may be necessary to do both.

The challenge with this method is that both parties need each other's digital certificates for messages that are encrypted and signed. As long as the parties are part of the same organization (such as two employees of the same company), exchanging certificates is relatively straightforward; however, when parties reside outside an organization or do not have any previous relationship, the task becomes more problematic.

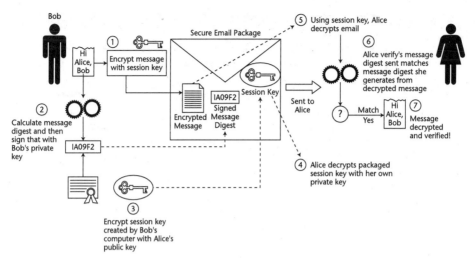

Figure 8.1 Diagram of the flow of an encrypted email message.

There are a number of solutions to this problem. For internal, affiliated members, a number of PKI vendors provide backend plug-ins for software like Microsoft Exchange or Lotus Notes. These plug-ins allow users to log in and associate their certificates with their name in the address book. In this manner, choosing a person's name from the address book also chooses that user's certificate. Again, this happens seamlessly for the end user in a number of email clients. The assumption here is that the user has already applied for and received a digital certificate. This could happen as a natural process of setting up a new employee or trading partner, for example, to minimize the initial costs of setting up an employee.

For external or nonaffiliated users, a common directory can be configured to locate and retrieve certificates. One company in the transaction could set up a restricted, externally accessible LDAP server that contains all the relevant certificates. Alternatively, many outsourced PKI providers give the option to their customers to publish their certificates in a global, publicly accessible database (which is, of course, not the best approach if security and privacy are a concern). Finally, a feature in some email systems that assists in certificate exchange is the ability to send a signed email with the sender's digital certificate automatically attached to the message. In this manner, the recipient gets not only the message but also the certificate. Future communications can be encrypted now that the user has the other party's digital certificate.

Encryption with Insecure Pickup

The simplest pseudo-security solution is encryption in transport on the sender's side with an insecure pickup model on the recipient's side. In this model, the sender logs on to the email system via a browser and SSL connection. This keeps communication from the client to the sender's message server private. Besides the limitations of using a Web-only interface, security is a bit dicey because only part of the transportation of the message is secured. When the recipient gets the message, he or she will not know how the message was sent, and it will not be secured. The recipient could minimize the risk by using an SSL Web browser connection on his or her end, but the risk between the respective organizations' message servers (between which the message would be transmitted without security) would still remain. Furthermore, no digital signature guarantee could be asserted because an SSL connection and user name/password combination are not sufficient to uniquely identify and maintain nonrepudiation of a message.

If security is not very good with this model, why use it? Generally, this model works best for a public-access situation. For example, a traveler needs access to view and send email at a public place, like an airport. Given the number of risks with using an unencrypted session, this model works well as nothing more than a Web browser is needed. Furthermore, if the browser on the kiosk machine is set properly, SSL pages will not be cached during the session, leaving no trace of anyone having used the service.

There are some tools on the market, although not widely used, that do allow for digital certificates to be used with Web-only solutions (like Outlook for Web Access). Given the complexity and lack of portability of these solutions, they are not recommended for Web use as a means of easy and portable access to email.

Encryption with Secure Pickup

This delivery model provides the best compromise in terms of security and mobility. In this model, the sender uses an SSL-enabled Web browser session to send an email message. The recipient is then automatically sent a note and a URL to which he or she must go to see the message. Thus, the nonsecure message sent to the recipient is just a URL point to an SSL Web page showing the message. The access to this page is protected by a digital certificate or by a user name and password.

The challenges with this model mainly rest with the fact that this is not truly seamless. The sender must upload the files to a particular location. File size transfer rates and limits can put a cap on how many files can be uploaded or how large the files can be. As a result, sending a message and/or attachment is not trivial. The recipient also must change his or her method of working. Messages must be manually downloaded and cannot be automatically synchronized with PDAs or local copies of email. In addition, this model generally will not allow claims of nonrepudiation.

Some variances to this model using digital certificates could be created. By using a certificate to authenticate the user to access the system (either to place the message into the secured upload area or to retrieve the message securely), a model can be constructed to provide nonrepudiation. The message then could be encrypted with some additional key to protect it in transit (such as an organizational certificate belonging to the ASP providing such a service).

THE WORKS: EMAIL, PKI, AND OUTSOURCING

Most providers of secure messaging in an outsourced model usually work with an outsourced PKI vendor or with an organization's internal vendor. One company based in Ireland, called Post.Trust, actually provides the whole package: secure email with the digital certificate infrastructure as well. How does this company pull it off? Well, it requires its users to download a root certificate in order for transactions to be trusted. This provides an interesting dilemma as the burden of this extra step can be problematic for large numbers of users; however, this also provides an additional security feature as email can then be delivered to a closed group of members (who trust the root certificate from Post.Trust).

The key advantage of this model is that the overhead cost of the PKI becomes very small as Post.Trust uses an internal PKI without the need for an external party's certificate services. Companies can use PKI as a point solution to solve the problem of securing the email messaging environment.

Eventually your organization must decide on the convenience (of using a public CA to avoid having users download the root certificate) or the cost savings (by using a low-cost approach to PKI as Post.Trust has done).

Instant Messaging

Instant messaging (IM), perhaps best known in the consumer sector as the cool way to chat with friends, has become, although ever so slowly, a respectable method of communication for consumers and business people alike. IM can be thought of as extended hallway conversations, except the hallway is as big as the Internet. As IM becomes as necessary as email, so must the need for security.

Some solutions on the market can detect and distinguish between internal IM users and external ones. In fact, some can force policy decisions and keep internal employees from talking with external people. The challenge is not just policy enforcement, but rather privacy and confidentiality. After all, just because two members of the HR staff discuss an employee's salary information internally over an IM chat does not mean that it is secure. The local system administrator could easily sniff the connection and get that data. Messaging must be secure point to point.

One of the easiest methods to keep IM secret between clients is to use digital certificates. Certificates could be used to create an encrypted tunnel from point to point. In addition, using certificates gives both parties a measure of confidence in the other party. Other methods include special IM clients that use symmetric encryption from client to client to protect information. One example of this is a freeware (for consumers) IM client called Secure Shuttle Transport (SST). SST also has a paid enterprise version solution. Another solution, designed for consumers and corporate applications, is a security solution for IM by Endeavors Technology, a California-based company. Endeavors Technology has utilized an interesting approach to applying trust to IM, as shown in the case study that follows.

ENDEAVORS' IM SOLUTION

A challenge in PKI is the ability to tie existing applications into a managed security environment without expensive changes.

Magi, a product from Endeavors, accomplishes this through the installation of a transparent, client-side Web proxy to handle Web presence, events, access control, notifications, and security functions. The product transforms the Web into a trusted interaction layer that gives users instant interaction with any existing application, file, or resource as a secure Web service directly from the desktop.

During installation, a user provides a set of identifying information that is used to generate an X.509, RSA-compliant, 1024-bit public and private key pair. Keys are stored in a desktop PKCS#12 keystore and unlocked upon a user's sign-on, which can be tied to a corporate single-sign-on service (SSO) or any public sign-on like AOL, Passport, or Webex. The public key is registered with the Magi certificate authority, which establishes the namespace. Certificate revocations are downloaded at sign-on and at regular intervals. Cross-firewall capabilities are handled through a connection broker that welds together two outgoing SSL calls. The welding operation ensures that content is never stored unprotected on an intermediate server nor decrypted outside of either protected domain.

One example of securing existing clients is instant messaging (IM). AOL Instant Messenger, Microsoft Messenger, Yahoo! IM, and Lotus Sametime all have inherent support for HTTP and HTTPS gateways. These gateways typically are used to allow the clients to be used through a secure network firewall. Endeavors Technology takes advantage of this fact to configure an existing IM client to speak with a credentialed desktop gateway, which is tied to the individual's user identity.

Using this approach, corporations can now use their traditional PKI policies and procedures to grant and revoke IM privileges, secure and reroute existing traffic over an SSL connection directly point to point, transparently capture traffic for auditing and tracking, and, most importantly, look up and tie public IM identities to corporate-controlled, strongly authenticated ones.

Peer to Peer

Peer to peer (P2P) is not too different from instant messaging, although the key difference is that instant messaging is a conscious communication mechanism, whereas P2P systems may exchange information without explicit interaction or authority. So far, security has not been a concern with P2P because organizations like (the now defunct) Napster have been doing the exact opposite, which is making it as easy to share (or steal, as some might view it) information. Newer software like KaZaa take this to the next level by allowing any type of media to be shared through a decentralized model (unlike Napster, which relied on a centralized swapping service).

> ### P2P: WE HAVE A GO ON A COUNTERSTRIKE
>
> A bill introduced in September 2002 (H.R. 5211) enabled copyright holders to initiate the ability for a copyright holder to "impair" illegally obtained software and media. Although the legislation does not give details about this, the implication of viruses, worms, and other mechanisms for hunting and destroying illegal works obtained through popular P2P tools remains. The attacker would not be held legally liable within certain parameters.
>
> Here is an excerpt from H.R. 5211, sponsored by Rep. Howard L. Berman (introduced originally on July 25, 2002, with subsequent updates):
>
> *a copyright owner shall not be liable in any criminal or civil action for disabling, interfering with, blocking, diverting, or otherwise impairing the unauthorized distribution, display, performance, or reproduction of his or her copyrighted work on a publicly accessible peer-to-peer file trading network, if such impairment does not, without authorization, alter, delete, or otherwise impair the integrity of any computer file or data residing on the computer of a file trader.*
>
> What does this mean for you? Well, if P2P is encrypted or otherwise secured, files cannot easily be detected nor counterattacked even if the bill were to become law. In the same way anti-virus software (at the servers) for firewalls and mail servers cannot detect malicious code in encrypted email; likewise it appears P2P will have to go to PKI for survival.

Guaranteed Delivery

Will email, IM, or P2P be sufficient in the critical moment? In most cases, these tools give us fairly high success rates with fairly quick and reliable service. When we deal with legal issues, however, almost is not good enough. For example, suppose an online mortgage company wanted to confirm a contract via email (or send a scanned copy of a contract), and legally the contract was not binding until delivered. In this case, a guaranteed delivery and auditing system must be in place. This is very much like an "e-FedEx" option where an electronic package can be guaranteed delivery (with insurance) and auditable milestones are given on its journey from source to destination.

Although this problem of a guaranteed, secured, and audible delivery system is very similar to that of email, the difference is that with a secure delivery system a third-party audit system must be set up for proving validity. One method of accomplishing this is to require the sender and recipient to use digital certificates to authenticate to the system. The sender then uploads the file to a central server. The server then automatically sends out a message to the recipient that a pickup is waiting. When the recipient clicks on the link sent in the email, he or she then authenticates himself or herself using a digital certificate. Then the file is downloaded to the recipient. The use of digital certificates allows the intermediary system to create a nonreputable audit trail.

A number of companies have jumped into this market as it represents a significant business opportunity that would take away business from some of the package and letter delivery companies. The approaches vary based on the company. Some key methods for providing such a service include these:

- Secure drop-off and pickup model
- Private Internet network

Secure Drop-Off and Pickup Model

This model is very similar to the email model described earlier as encryption with secure pickup. The main addition is that there are increased audit trail components. In addition, the servers for delivery are not messaging servers hosted by the customer, but rather hosted by a third party. In this manner the third party can achieve a 100 percent delivery rate because both sender and receiver have to come to the same infrastructure. Email interfaces can be made available (in other words, sending information through standard email versus posting to a Web page).

Authentication in this model, if it is to be legally binding, would have to be through a digital certificate, either through an outsourced model or through the provider's own private CA. The advantage of having the provider set up the PKI would be lower costs and easier use as everything can be managed together (account, delivery, and authentication certificate). Of course, authentication is required to access the audit trail itself or a digitally signed version of it. A digitally signed audit trail is simply a data log of sender and pickup activities, but signed with the provider's digital certificate. This will ensure that the audit log was not tampered with after it was created.

Private Internet Network

Another model, to provide maximum convenience, albeit at an increased cost, is a private Internet network. In this model, the customer places a provider's "pickup" box inside his or her firewall. This box then securely communicates with similar hosted boxes placed worldwide around the provider's host infrastructure. In this manner, messages can be tracked from point to point. Should something go wrong, the provider would know immediately between what two points the problem occurred and then set out to fix the problem. This is similar to the tracking ability for large shipping carriers.

COURT-SIDE SEATS: THE SLAM DUNK APPROACH

Among many companies attempting to solve the problem of secure document delivery, one interesting approach was taken by a company called Slam Dunk Networks (it is no longer in business — another victim of the dot-com era). Essentially, the system required adaptors that integrate with various applications that need to send messages or transactions. The adaptors then communicated with the hosted network to transport messages. A portal was provided for customer or administrator access and changes. Security was maintained because the adaptors used PKI technology to authenticate and encrypt data traffic.

This model, of course, requires additions to the customer's network, such as hardware required at each secure communication point. Thus, it is ideal for large numbers of transactions (and not just email messages). For example, a traditional electronic data interchange (EDI) network could be replaced with such a network, with even more reliability than newer value-added networks (VANs), as this model can provide more control over when and where messages are delivered within a specific timeframe. Thus, if a corporation has a high message volume, a small user community, and a communication security problem to address, the private Internet network may work best given its ability to handle robust security and message volume.

From a consumer perspective, this model is obviously not useful given that most consumers will not buy dedicated hardware for a point-to-point, limited security benefit. The previous model could be used, for example, in a mortgage or escrow service for the mass market. This model, though, is almost strictly reserved for high-volume, high-value transactions in a corporate environment.

Content Management

The other way to approach secure messaging is to secure just the content that needs to be protected, rather than an entire transaction or email stream. Today this is commonly known as content protection (but sometimes called digital rights management). In many ways, content management is more of a problem in the mass-market or consumer areas. After all, in business two parties can easily establish stronger relationships with stronger legal ties. In a typical mass-market scenario—for example, in dealing with one-time loan transactions or mortgage deals—the customer may be a party to a one-time transaction without previous or subsequent relationships with the other party.

Content management has always been difficult to execute well because it invariably affects the document (perhaps even altering it) to some degree. Solutions that do not affect the document affect the usability of the solution (in other words, the user has to perform some additional steps beyond sending a normal email). The trade-off, though, is worth it because the benefit of audit trails and targeted delivery of messages or documents means less fraud and lower exposure to IP (intellectual property) theft.

There are several methods to approaching content management (relative to messages and documents):

Policy methods.   Policies are tied to email servers that allow only certain activities (such as replies or forwarding to happen as per preset policy guidelines).

Secured delivery.   Policies restrict access to messages and documents through some type of secured pickup model.

Encapsulation.   This is a method in which the original document format is translated or encapsulated into another format to be read by a dedicated reader.

Secure space.   This method partitions a portion of the computer's memory or storage space and treats it as a secured area in which (based on policy) media can be placed and controlled.

Policy Methods

Policy methods essentially insert software at the mail server's backend to intercept, parse, and then apply security policies to the outgoing or incoming mail. Policies then can be created that allow email to be sent internally only, or both internally and externally, and to prevent forwarding and other such actions. The actual method to lock down messages can vary from solution to solution. One way to enforce policy is to encrypt a document and release the key to decrypt the document only after the policy criteria has been met. In this manner, the message can be sent but will be unintelligible until the policy is met. Another method of enforcing policy is to intercept the message and accept or reject it based on policy criteria. In other words, whether the message gets sent depends on whether the policy is met. The latter of the two methods is more secure because it is possible in the first method to use various hacking methods to break the encryption. While highly unlikely, decrypting the document is possible.

MICROSOFT'S PALLADIUM (ANOTHER MONOPOLY?)

Microsoft announced its Palladium initiative in August 2002. The concept of Palladium is that digital rights management (DRM) could be extended to any media on the computer by being built into the Operating system of that PC (its architecture is shown in Figure 8.2). This allows a PKI to encrypt and protect data and data stores with specific policies set by the publisher.

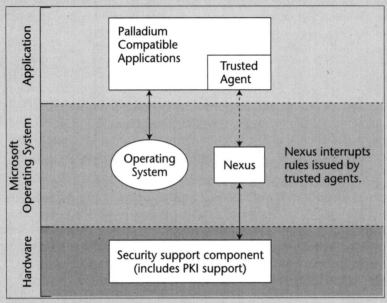

Figure 8.2 Palladium architecture overview.

It has a simple operation that relies on a public/private key pair called the Security Support Component. This component interacts with a "Nexus" that manages tasks like data encryption on the hardware or interaction with "Trusted Agents" that deal with DRM policy for software. These Agents would be embedded in each program that was Palladium-enabled and provide feedback into what the policies are for that media. The Agents would be preset by the publisher of that media.

Microsoft claims that this "feature" can be turned off either in software or in the PC's hardware. This allows an opt-out feature. It does seem a bit difficult to understand why this "feature" would actually exist in the final product. After all, if DRM was an option, then Napster-like companies would continue to thrive. The challenge will be that the consumer may not have a choice in the DRM solution (nor will the publisher of that media) if the solution is built into the operating system.

MICROSOFT'S PALLADIUM (ANOTHER MONOPOLY?) *(continued)*

Other challenges include a lack of privacy. Now that each medium can uniquely identify the user via Palladium, it is possible that the medium's "Trusted Agent" could relay back information (via the Internet) on usage patterns or even confidential information. This would be vaguely akin to Intel's attempt at uniquely branding each CPU and making that unique information known to any applications that queried it. In Intel's case the privacy concerns forced the company to retract that "feature."

Secured Delivery

In a similar concept of the secured pickup model in standard email messaging, as described previously, secured content delivery not only protects the document but also applies specific policies. Policy criteria can range from authentication requirements to temporal requirements so that the document expires after a certain period of time. Generally, these models require the use of a Web browser for all pickup. Then, from these portal or Web-based systems, users can retrieve messages or documents based on set policy.

For the sender, various methods of securing delivery, including integration, can be employed within the mail client being used either through Outlook forms, for example, or other mechanisms that work directly with the mail client to hide the background encryption and verification.

Encapsulation

It is possible to simply encapsulate every message or document into an encrypted package that becomes unencrypted only when certain policies are met. The Secure Multipurpose Internet Mail Extensions (S/MIME) standard does not allow for the encryption of the email headers. This can pose a problem because this means participants in the message cannot be kept private though the body of the message might be. In this case, a client is required on both the sender's and recipient's machines. It could be a small ActiveX or similarly lightweight client. Either asymmetric or symmetric encryption can be used. In the case of IM, a combination is usually used because IM has the advantage of always requiring a client.

Secure Space

Perhaps the most complex but effective method of securing content is to require a client for the sender and the recipient that creates a protected workspace (either in memory or in storage). This secure space, using digital certificates as one method, encrypts all data within its boundaries. When a request is made for content in that space, the policy of that data would be checked with a software agent, and, if allowed, the content would be released in the manner appropriate for that data. This concept is similar (generally) to what Microsoft has planned with its Palladium initiative. Other companies, such as Groove Networks, also have a concept of levels of secured space (although they treat secured space based on roles). One advantage of this secured space concept is that it allows group interactions by creating a common shared space on a network drive, for example.

Again, for the mass markets, this is not the easiest method due to the complexity of the configuration and the installation of client software. In addition, concepts like backup and disaster recovery (because the data is usually encrypted in the secured space) make it very difficult to plan for unlikely occurrences.

Time Stamping

One of the challenges with mass-market applications is that it is difficult to control the client's desktop or environment. As a result, it is a challenge to verify the date or time of a transaction in such a manner that it will hold up in a court of law. A physical letter or document sent by a carrier has a physical mark indicating the date and time the communication or transaction was executed. For communication and transaction applications that require accurate date/time stamps, it is important to have a digital time-stamping capability. The question, of course, is this: What is the right time? A number of companies make time servers that coordinate with a known, accurate source. These servers are built for accuracy and the ability to synchronize with these trusted time servers (usually atomic clocks). The servers then, in turn, provide the entire corporate network of a company with the ability to use NTP (network time protocol) to keep all machines in synch with the master time server.

Many time servers now come in an appliance model. An appliance model is a data-center-ready, rack-mountable device that contains all of the hardware and software needed to run the time server. This simplifies the setup of the server and ensures that it will be compatible with space requirements in a data center. The critical element the servers provide is an accurate date and time. The main application for these servers, beyond the obvious data logging and time stamping, is the ability to stamp digital transactions, such as digital form signing or digital Web page signing. This can allow, for example, a brokerage customer to execute a trade or even open an account online, with all the legally binding benefits of PKI. The time server makes it legally and (due to SEC regulations in some cases) necessarily beneficial.

The time-stamp server has its own certificate that it uses to sign transactions. Then a hash of that transaction log can be created and signed itself. The signed hash from the time-stamping server can then serve as a fingerprint or digital receipt for the transaction. Because the signed hash does not reveal the contents or what was signed, confidentiality can easily be maintained. To prove the validity of a particular log file, the file in question could be put through the same hash algorithm, and then the two hashes (the one generated from the log file and the one that was digitally signed) could be compared. If they match, then the log file is authentic and the transaction can be legally validated.

In terms of architecture (see Figure 8.3 for a visual example), one synchronizing time-stamping server must be kept so that it may access synchronization time sources outside of the company's infrastructure. Then a time-stamping server must be placed at each point a transaction needs to be stamped. An additional server can be provided so that with application plug-ins, users can themselves validate the stamp of a particular document directly (although this would be better suited for an enterprise than a mass-market or consumer scenario).

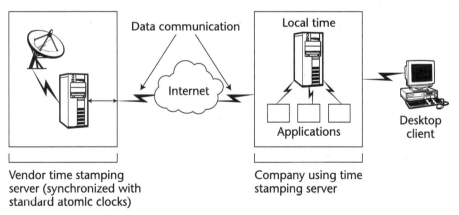

Vendor time stamping
server (synchronized with
standard atomic clocks)

Company using time
stamping server

Figure 8.3   Sample time-stamping server architecture.

SSL: The Old Standby

Secure Sockets Layer (SSL) is the biggest application for PKI that nearly every consumer has embraced. It is amazing that such a technology has taken on the characteristics of a brand for some Web sites. The appearance of the lock symbol in the browser, meaning that a sight is secured or trusted, is considered a distinguishing trait for a merchant. In a loose sense this can be considered a communication tool because data is being presented in a particular manner based on queries or transactions that the user has made. For certain communication tools, like Web-based email, SSL is the backbone of the security behind those types of communication applications. As a result, we will discuss SSL in the category of communications solutions.

For a mass-market or consumer scenario, SSL is by far the most basic and simplest method of providing base-level security. SSL, to be clear, provides two basic functions:

- Authentication of the merchant site being accessed
- Transport encryption (in other words, data between client and server is protected)

SSL does not claim to make any site or merchant more secure because all collected information resides in the merchant's databases, which may or may not be secure. Without SSL, all network traffic can easily be sniffed.

SSL can actually be used in many applications and not just for secure Web sites. Given that SSL certificates are just that—certificates—they can be used for site-to-site encryption as well as authentication. Some newer concepts have included the ability to identify an organization using an "organizational" certificate. This would allow anyone as part of that organization to use the certificate. This could, for example, allow the creation of transaction-based, temporary encryption tunnels, thereby avoiding the need for VPN or similar changes. One mainstream example is the use of SSL for securing communication of user name/password combinations for email POP/IMAP accounts and LDAP queries. In both cases, without SSL, important information could easily be sniffed, causing irreparable damage. With SSL, the connection to and from the email or database is secured. Usually, the email itself will not be passed through the SSL connection (just the initial exchange of user name and password).

One of the key reasons SSL is perfect for consumer or mass-market applications is that very little effort is required on the client's or recipient's side. If a publicly issued CA certificate is used, then the end user has to do very little to rely on the trust the certificate technology provides.

Challenges with SSL

There can be glitches in this process. For example, the certificate is tied to a specific URL (for example, www.securitypundit.com). Should that URL change (for example, link to a different aspect of the site, something like login .securitypundit.com), then the browser will flag a warning message (as shown in Figure 8.4). Generally, many users do not know the meaning of the warning and end up simply accepting and clicking through the warning without further investigation. This then brings up the issue of whether SSL certificates truly provide a trusted environment or just a moderate amount of safety. Given that the cost of SSL certificates has plummeted despite stronger authentication and more insurance for higher-priced certificates, it seems that the trust component of SSL—for example, the identity of the merchant or the merchant's ability to claim he or she really owns a URL—has been traded off for just plain security. This plain security allows data to be encrypted in transit but does not provide any measure of trust in regard to the merchant. Such trends will eventually see a rise in fraud as merchants get SSL certificates from cheaper agencies that may not perform any authentication at all. To avoid this trend, it is possible that consumers will demand some other type of trust assurance—for example, a trust assurance mark. A trust assurance mark appears on a Web site indicating that it has gone through some level of security or identity verification. Examples include the BBB (Better Business Bureau) mark and the TrustE mark, both of which give some level of trust assurance.

Other user issues include redirection between SSL and non-SSL enabled sites. As a result of the fact that SSL operations are CPU intensive, many sites limit the specific pages, or frames, that are SSL-enabled. This prevents having to slow down access to all pages (such as the home or information pages).

For the administrator, SSL has been something of a challenge in that the certificates, through some of the name brand providers, can take some time to obtain. Because SSL certificates are given only after authorization and verification of the identity of the certificate requestor (usually companies), it can take several days. The fine balance of proper and thorough authentication of a company's identity and the speed at which the certificate can be given has spawned several competing approaches in the marketplace. The other challenge for the administrator has been in applying for the certificate. In the past, the effort was a manual task, involving cutting and pasting of large cryptic data blocks to various Web sites. More recently, many Web server vendors have taken great strides in merging the certificate request process with specific certificate providers.

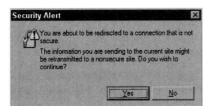

Figure 8.4 Example of an SSL warning.

Finally, we address the issue of multiple Web servers in the same domain, all of which need Web server certificates. For large companies, ISPs, or other users of large Web server farms, it becomes impossible to register each machine manually for a certificate. To resolve this issue, many vendors have come up with a range of solutions. Some solutions provide a single, master authentication of the company's domain (for example, www.securitypundit.com) and allow the trusted administrator at that company to issue future certificates to subdomains (like mail.securitypundit.com or new.securitypundit.com). Another approach is the concept of Shared SSL (or wildcard SSL), which usually allows any subdomain (one level) to be issued and used (see the section *Deployment Strategies* later in this chapter). Both of these methods will help a customer avoid having a warning message appear in the browser that claims that the URL the certificate contains does not match the URL the customer is trying to access.

Deployment Strategies

What is the best method for deploying SSL? Given the changes over the last several years, SSL has clearly become a valued commodity. For example, SSL certificates were selling for more than $500 or $600 several years ago. Now those same certificates are down to $150 or $200 each on average. With the growth of ecommerce came the need for server farms, load balancing, and SSL acceleration. Because SSL results in a big hit on CPU resources, many large Web sites use dedicated hardware SSL accelerators to improve site performance by offloading SSL encryption functions from the main CPU.

Essentially, there are several scenarios for SSL deployment:

- Classic dedicated SSL certificate
- Shared SSL
- Server appliance model

Dedicated SSL

In a classic dedicated SSL certificate scenario, each Web server required for serving pages to customers has a certificate. The certificate ties the specific URL on that Web server to that specific Web site. For the most part, this is the easiest and simplest approach for most small- to medium-sized Web sites. The key advantage of this approach is that the end user will be able to use the benefit of SSL without any problems. Because the URL associated with the certificate matches the URL the customer is going to, there will be no warning messages. See Figure 8.5.

Figure 8.5 Sample SSL certificate.

Shared SSL

In a shared SSL environment, the user is usually an ISP hosting a number of different customer Web sites. In this manner, each customer of the ISP essentially leverages the few certificates the ISP operator has set up. The one key challenge with this arrangement is that users who go to a merchant on the ISP's shared SSL site will not be specifically listed as the trusted party in the certificate. This will cause a warning message to pop up to the end customer saying that the site URL does not match the URL listed in the certificate.

Some outsourced providers, like VeriSign, have managed to mitigate some of the issues with shared SSL by extending the "VeriSign Secured Site" logo to the ISP's customers on the shared SSL system. Essentially, the logo can appear on the merchant's site to confirm that it is a trusted merchant of the ISP provider that holds the SSL certificate. The warning messages may still appear (as that is a "feature" of the browser), but at least the customer can see the trust brand.

Server Appliance Model

In the server appliance model, the merchant most likely has decided that enough encrypted traffic warrants a faster, more dedicated approach to providing smoother connections. In this model, a dedicated appliance is placed between the Web server farm and the perimeter router. An SSL certificate is then tied to the appliance rather than the individual Web server. Some outsourced CAs have license restrictions that may require one SSL certificate per Web server, in which case the appliance can be configured to handle this (usually up to 255 certificates per appliance for low-end systems). The certificates will then be stored on the appliance.

Alternative Approach: OpenSSL

An open-source project was kicked off to give organizations the ability to build their own SSL solutions. Essentially, this provides the cheapest method to enabling SSL. Given that self-signed certificates are not recognized by default setups in browsers, this approach is not suggested for mass-market audiences. This method may be good for a closed community (like employees using a VPN) or for internal, protected communications between, say, an LDAP database and a Web program. This project is based on the SSLeay libraries developed via an open source community and follows very liberal licensing schemes.

Code Signing

Nothing is more important to a business than ensuring that its customers get safe, reliable software (at least from this author's perspective!). Given the proliferation of software ranging from freeware to open source and the popularity of P2P networks, the reliability and authenticity of software are always in question. After all, when you download a new version of a program from a Web site, how do you know that it is the real software? And when legitimate software from a trusted source is downloaded, are you sure that the software did not get manipulated in transit?

Code signing is the concept of being able to authenticate software that was distributed (either physically on CDs or via the Internet) from the expected source and was not changed in transit. We can think of code signing as a secure email-type solution for software.

Code signing works in a similar fashion as SSL. The code publisher must request a third party to issue a certificate (as shown in Figure 8.6) that identifies that publisher as the rightful, authenticated owner of a particular company name. Then all code is signed with that digital certificate. When code is distributed to end users, they can choose to validate that the certificate and code used in the generation of the distribution kit of the software package are still valid and trustworthy.

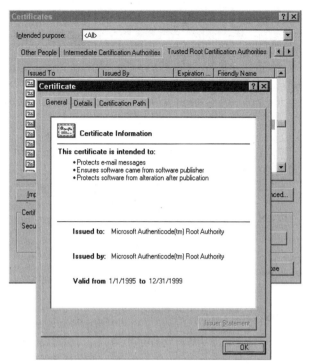

Figure 8.6 Sample code-signing certificate.

WHAT'S IN A NAME? THE BOGUS CODE-SIGNING CERTIFICATE

In March 2001, two companies made headlines news in the security world—VeriSign and Microsoft—for all of the wrong reasons. Somehow, a rogue hacker managed to spoof his identity sufficiently that he was issued a legitimate code-signing (also known as Class 3) certificate attributed to Microsoft. This hacker could then, in theory, sign any code, including Trojan horses and viruses, and that code would look legitimate because the certificate would match up to Microsoft's.

To compound the situation, although the certificate could be revoked as soon as the error was discovered at VeriSign, the Microsoft software did not automatically check the certificate revocation list (the list of all revoked code-signing certificates). Microsoft released an update to fix that problem, but that meant a manual and labor-intensive effort for many companies.

The bogus certificate was never used, but this incident did cause quite a stir. The theft of a certificate could be attributed to identity theft, and, in this case, the identity of an entire corporation. VeriSign has since put in audit controls to ensure that something similar does not occur again.

Table 8.1   Benefits of Hosted Secure eMessaging

BUSINESS NEED	VALUE
Achieve compliance with HIPAA, Paper Act	Regulatory compliance
Gain time savings: instantaneous versus waiting hours or days for confidential information	Workflow efficiencies
Achieve cost savings: reduce courier mail costs without adding hardware or software	Email security with ROI on any new investments
Guarantee electronic time stamp and authentication of sender	Eliminate paper
Reduce risk of legal breaches	Audit trail for sensitive information

Summary: Speaking Digitally

Table 8.2 highlights some applications that fall in the category of communications. In addition, the table discusses how PKI is used to provide security for the listed method of communication.

As we have seen in this chapter, a number of communications solutions utilize PKI. Whether we need PKI's extra security features depends on the specific communication and its content. Generally, it is recommended that all communications be kept secret because this will give the biggest obstacle to hackers in determining what to break and what to ignore. While traditional messaging like email will remain the driving force for most of PKI solutions, new, emerging technologies like P2P and IM will eventually dominate the need for security (see the summary in Table 8.2).

Table 8.2   Summary of Communication Methods and PKI Usage

COMMUNICATION METHODS	PKI USE
Instant messaging (IM)	Encryption between IM clients
Email	Encryption from sender to recipient, plus encryption of stored email
Peer to peer	Encryption between P2P clients
Web server/portal	Encryption between Web server and client
e-document delivery	Encryption between sender to recipient with audit trail

Other Solutions

Given the range of situations that require trust, many solutions at the operating-system and application levels exist for enforcing trust in transactions. Those solutions that were not specifically tied to a vertical are discussed here. It is possible that these solutions could be adapted to work more effectively for a specific area, like healthcare; however, we will discuss them generically here. The goal is to give you, the reader, an appreciation for the wide range of solutions and the pervasiveness of trust solutions based on PKI.

Virtual Private Networks

Perhaps the oldest and most widely deployed use of PKI-related solutions is the use of VPNs (virtual private networks). VPNs have become a staple in corporate IT infrastructure today. The fact that VPNs allow multiple offices and roaming employees to connect to their offices cheaply and easily has allowed business to become far more global than ever before.

What Is a VPN?

A VPN is a privately constructed, virtual communication tunnel that allows a user to create a secure connection between his or her computer and the trusted server at the user's corporate site. By adding security, VPNs allow public access methods, such as the Internet, to be used freely. This provides ubiquitous access at very cheap rates by replacing older methods of remote connections, including dial-up modem banks or dedicated or leased lines. The main thrust of the rise of VPNs has been in the cost savings they bring when a corporation migrates from modem banks and leased lines to a mode of cheaper access using the Internet. The fundamental link in the success of VPNs has been the security it affords users.

There are several types of VPN solutions:

Hardware-based solutions.   These solutions use a hardware appliance for increasing the efficiency and ease of administration. The trend favoring hardware appliances has prompted numerous companies to enter this space over the last few years. Generally, hardware solutions require client software to establish the secure tunnel from client to server.

Software-based solutions.   These solutions tend to be cheaper and more flexible than hardware-based solutions. The flexibility of the platform and the ease of deployment (because it is just software) makes software-based solutions attractive.

Firewall hybrid solutions.   Solutions in this space provide multipurpose advantages by providing firewall protection as well as standard VPN access and services. Depending on the bandwidth and traffic patterns, these solutions tend to be able to handle less throughput than dedicated VPN solutions.

Outsourced solutions.   The concept of managed services was very hot in the late 1990s. With the turn of fortunes came the demise of many managed services. There are still a few managed VPN services solutions on the market today. VPN managed solutions require a third party, an ISP, for example, to manage user administration and maintenance of the VPN solution.

Choosing a specific type of VPN solution depends on a number of factors, including user base, budgets, and numbers of remote sites to be linked in the VPN. In general, costs for VPN solutions have dropped dramatically as VPNs are effectively commodity solutions.

Why Do We Need Them?

Although today VPNs are a staple of the corporate IT arsenal, it was not too long ago that a case had to be made for why they were so useful. The success of VPNs eventually led to the need for a more scalable approach to them, which would rely on digital certificates (discussed later in this chapter). The types of users that require VPN technology could include mobile users who need to access corporate information securely as well as users who need to access sensitive information securely whether or not they are mobile.

TIP GLBA, HIPAA, and other international directives *require* secure communications over the Internet for most sensitive communications. VPNs are a very easy way to ensure that the employee base follows these guidelines.

Pros of VPNs

The main reason VPNs are useful is that they reduce costs dramatically for remote access to corporate networks (they are less expensive than modem banks or dedicated leased lines). Cost savings can be realized through reduced toll charges because the remote user uses a local dial-up access number to connect to the main office through the Internet. The hardware and IT support costs usually associated with modem banks and dedicated leased lines are also reduced.

Cons of VPNs

A key drawback with VPNs is setting them up can incur additional complexities and security risks. Given that an organization with a VPN exposes itself to security risks on the Internet, additional expertise is required for setting up and protecting a VPN properly. Additional drawbacks include the need for client software and related configurations. Finally, VPNs require an access control list, which adds to IT administration.

How Do They Work?

VPNs basically work in one of three modes:

Remote access client connections.   This is the common mode for mobile users, for example, who travel and need to access corporate resources while on the road.

Site-to-site connections (for connecting multiple offices).   This is usually set up to allow multiple office locations to communicate as if they were part of one large network. Site-to-site connections usually have dedicated hardware or software, or both, to increase the throughput.

Extranet access.   This is used for extranet relationships, for example, with vendors or suppliers. In this manner, access to specific information can be given and then removed after a period of time.

Three main protocols are used in VPNs (there are others, but these are most commonly discussed and used):

Point-to-Point Tunneling Protocol (PPTP).   PPTP allows the basic protocol of PPP to work by encapsulating PPP packets within IP packets.

Layer Two Tunneling Protocol (L2TP).   L2TP can be thought of as an extension to PPTP that allows the operation of a VPN over the Internet.

Internet Protocol Security (IPSec).   IPSec was developed by the IETF to provide secure solutions compatible with existing IP standards most commonly used on the Internet. IPSec has the advantage of supporting any network protocol, including UDP (stateless), TCP (stateful), and ICMP protocols. IPSec is considered the most flexible of the three options.

For the purposes of this section, we will focus on IPSec-based solutions as they are deemed to be the most secure of the three protocols. In addition, IPSec uses certificates (see Figure 9.1 for an example), which are directly relevant to showing how trust is enabled for VPNs. IPSec seeks to address the following issues:

- Authentication, which ensures that the identity of the entity (person or machine) is who he, she, or it claims to be. This is similar to all other applications of authentication using digital certificates: Prove the requestor's identity.

- Integrity, which ensures that any transmitted data packets have not been modified during transmission.

- Confidentiality, which ensures that data cannot be observed or read in transit. This, of course, is a key element of the need for VPNs.

- Protection from replay attacks to ensure that an attacker cannot intercept a packet and send it out again later, spoofing the original authentication session. Many attacks rely on sniffing a network connection and recording the packet transmissions. Without proper protection, an attacker could simulate, for example, the login sequence and initiate his or her own session.

- Automated management of cryptographic keys and security associations. This automation simplifies enforcement of a company's VPN policy. As VPN deployments grow, so does the need to create virtual tunnels between the various sites in the organization. Manual methods include emailing or otherwise making the shared secret available to all VPN sites. With IPSec, this process is much simpler and allows for more frequent updates.

Some major advantages of IPSec are the following:

- The requirement that the client and server understand the protocol, but the rest of the network only need to be able manage IP packets

- An edge over the older PPTP as IPSec uses public/private key pair technology, which allows it to make the network setup easier and allows for more frequent key exchanges (resulting in higher security)
- Its support by all major VPN vendors as well as its compatibility with Microsoft operating systems

The challenges with IPSec include the following:

- An inability to deal with some lesser-used protocols such as IPX (Novell)
- The need to perform additional steps at the client side to obtain and install certificates when using IPSec with digital certificates, which can add some cost

Internet Key Exchange

Internet Key Exchange (IKE) requires three pieces of information:

- A host identity represented by the IP address of the host
- The public key for the host through the host's IPSec certificates
- The CA's public key delivered by the CA root certificate

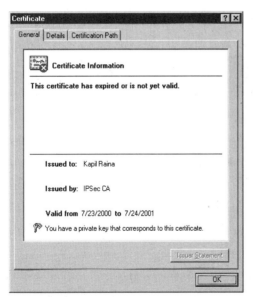

Figure 9.1   Example of an IPSec certificate.

In essence, the method for establishing a secure connection is similar to how SSL certificate exchanges work. A symmetric, or session, key is generated and transmitted securely by encrypting it with the host's public key. The host then decrypts the key using its corresponding private key, and future transmission is performed using the session, or symmetric, key. Because the symmetric key will enable faster communication, the key can be shared securely in an automated fashion. Without an IKE-type scenario, each VPN would have to share a symmetric key, but that key would still be delivered through some out-of-band communication for full security. IKE allows a VPN infrastructure to scale rapidly.

Two main encryption modes exist under the IPSec protocol: tunnel and transport. Tunnel mode encrypts both the header and payload data for each packet. Transport mode encrypts only the payload data and authenticates only the transport layer of the IP packet. Hence, the tunnel model is considered more secure because less information (such as the sender and recipient's identities) is revealed during transmission.

In some VPNs that have the option of not using digital certificates, but rather use only symmetric keys, the system would be vulnerable to a man-in-the-middle attack (that is, an attack in which an impersonator pretends to be both sender and recipient to fool each party into thinking it is communicating directly with each other). By using digital certificates (Diffie-Hellman exchanges), this attack is mitigated. Hash algorithms such as MD5 and SHA-1 can be used to verify the integrity of the certificate used (to ensure that the certificate itself was not modified by an attacker).

IKE provides two main methods for handling key distribution: automated and manual. Manual distribution is, of course, suitable for small sites with very few VPN access points. An automated method allows for distribution and exchange of keys across many different VPN access points. In addition, the automated method allows more frequent exchanges, reducing the chance that a key may have been somehow compromised. In this manner, the exposure to an attack for a particular set of keys is mitigated.

Some of the various communications IPSec can encrypt and protect include these:

- Router-to-router communication
- Firewall-to-router communication
- PC system-to-router communication
- PC-to-server communication (the end-user scenario)

Extensions

IPSec requires bidirectional authentication (between client and server) using either symmetric keys (preshared secrets) or digital certificates. In the first phase of the IPSec protocol both connections authenticate each other. This requires a PKI to already be in place for this initial connection. IKE does not support the use of user name/password combinations to avoid this scenario (by design because the user name/password method is much weaker).

Xauth is an extension to IKE that allows users to authenticate via legacy methods (such as SecurID) after the first phase of the IPSec protocol. The challenge with Xauth is that the remote user's IP address must already be known for this exchange to work. In addition, Xauth is susceptible to man-in-the-middle attacks.

A refinement of Xauth is Hybrid Auth, which allows two unidirectional authentications essentially to complete a mutually authenticated session. In Hybrid Auth, the VPN gateway is authenticated to the client (via a VPN gateway certificate). Then the gateway authenticates the remote user by some method (legacy or otherwise). It is far easier to implement digital certificates at the gateway in the first deployment of a VPN than to ensure that all end users have certificates to begin using IKE right away.

Alternatives to IPSec VPNs?

A number of solutions have arisen that address the VPN functionality market, without the need for the setup and expertise normally required for a full-featured VPN deployment. Various terms are used to describe this space, ranging from *instant VPNs* to *VPN alternatives*. In any case, these solutions leverage the browser connection and pipe data through the browser or over a browser initiated connection, and they present certain functions over this method. For the majority of users who may require email, Internet access, or access to internal resources, such functionality proves useful. The administrators favor such deployments for department-level or small-site deployments because this reduces deployment and administrative overhead.

> **WARNING** Many of these alternate solutions do not provide the appropriate levels of security for strong nonrepudiation. Look for solutions that require client certificates as part of the authentication process. Most legal drivers require the ability to show nonrepudiation.

Generally, certificates are used to create SSL connections, and in some solutions client certificates are required for additional authentication (over just user name/password). One example of a U.S.-based company in this space, Flatrock, Inc., demonstrates how it simplified the problem of remote user access without the overhead of a full-featured VPN (see the case study).

CASE STUDY: FLATROCK LEVELS THE IPSEC VPN SPACE

When Spectrian needed its outsourcing partner to access an internal application, it turned to Flatrock to solve its business-to-business extranet problem.

"Using Flatrock's products to integrate our overseas business partners, we are able to quickly get our partners online with our applications."

Lee Penning, CIO of Spectrian

Spectrian is a $100 million supplier of advanced radio frequency (RF) amplifiers to the wireless communications industry, headquartered in Sunnyvale, California. Spectrian focuses its core technology capabilities on RF product design and increases efficiency by contracting manufacturing to partners around the world. To create extranet connections with its contractors, Spectrian grants access to a variety of legacy and non-Web applications. Spectrian, however, has only a few applications to share and a network to secure. Spectrian determined that there was a prohibitively high cost to establishing VPN connections to their outsourcer's networks due to the effort required to coordinate and reconfigure multiple IT domains.

Spectrian, therefore, began using secure application routers from Flatrock, Inc. to provide secure, authenticated access to specific internal applications at its contractor sites in Taiwan and China. Flatrock "virtualizes" the required applications on the contractor networks as local resources providing full, unmodified operation, unlike a Web portal or SSL-based reverse proxy VPN. In addition, the virtualized applications can print invoices, shipping labels, and other critical documents to local printers because these resources are "reverse-deployed" back to Spectrian's network.

Flatrock provides greater security than an IPSec VPN on an application-specific basis while eliminating the headaches of using a VPN between companies: Address translation issues, private IP address overlaps, firewall rules, and unintended access are all handled or prevented automatically by the application routers.

Flatrock application routers exchange 2048-bit public keys to authenticate all site-to-site communication. Each application delivered to a subscriber site is managed independently, giving Spectrian unparalleled control over deployments. Each can be independently encrypted (with a variety of industry-standard encryption algorithms), throttled or compressed, and monitored.

Flatrock application routers also contain internal certificate authorities to control access to the delivered resources at a subscriber site (for example, Spectrian's contractors) and all management access. Users receive these certificates through their browser when they log in to their local subscriber or provider application router. In addition, Flatrock subscriber application routers control per-user access by integrating with external authentication servers at the provider site (for example, Spectrian). When a user at the subscriber site wishes to access an application delivered via Flatrock, he or she must first successfully authenticate against the provider server. After authenticating, he or she receives the necessary certificates to access applications delivered to the site.

Smart Cards

The use of additional authentication for applications such as VPNs or local computer access has, in parts of the world, been taken to the next level with smart cards. Smart cards provide features such as memory storage and, in the case of higher-end formats, the ability to store and update small applications (such as loyalty programs, as would be needed in a frequent-flier program).

Smart cards basically work as small computers and have the ability (at least the high-end ones do) to do things like generate private keys for certificates and run small programs. This ability allows the cards not only to create secure private key storage, but to increase their utility by providing applications to track things from frequent-flier miles to cash.

Although the details of smart-card technology are beyond the scope of this book, the intersection of smart cards and PKI is significant for geographic markets such as Europe where smart card adoption is higher than in other parts of the world. Essentially, the smart card acts as a container that holds the private key (which is associated with a particular digital certificate). In this manner, the private key is removed from the computer and can be physically secured separately from the computer. This allows additional security because a physical loss of the computer system does not necessarily result in access to services like VPNs that may be based on the use of certificates for access.

> **TIP** Smart cards will satisfy the minimum two-factor authentication that regulations like HIPAA require. Realize, though, that many healthcare organizations, especially in the United States, do not have the latest technology to support smart-card readers and relevant drivers.

PKI has seen some stimulus through the use of smart cards. In general, except for a few select geographic markets and vertical applications, adoption of smart cards with PKI has been relatively slow. Numerous factors have contributed to the slow adoption including the following:

Lack of consistent standards.   Most vendors have variations in their implementations. There are many types of cards, readers, and card standards that need to be matched up for each customer's applications. As a result, widespread adoption has been hindered.

Hacking exposures.   Along with vendor-specific implementations are vendor-specific exposures to hackers, especially from the cardholder to the issuer. Attacks can be physical (the card is stolen) or logical (interception of the PIN or other similar means). In the end, most smart cards are protected with a PIN, but at least the cards can be physically secured, unlike most computers.

Costs.   Costs are still higher for smart cards relative to other solutions, such as token FOBs and software-based authentication. If the cards are used for multiple applications, then the cost per application can drop below the cost of dedicated hardware like token FOBs.

Reader availability.   Smart cards require readers, but not enough momentum has been built, especially in North America, for these cards to be universally accepted. The technology needs to be promoted and made ubiquitous, but the catch is that people are waiting for the technology to become ubiquitous before using it.

Nonetheless, smart cards will become the de facto standard for digital credentialing. The only question that remains is when that will occur because the need for the convergence of so many digital IDs leads to this route. As costs decrease, smart cards will replace numerous expensive, dedicated credentials as a single platform for digital identity management.

Novell Architecture

Although Novell is not a widely used operating system, it is still prevalent in areas like healthcare organizations in the United States. As a result, it is worthwhile to note some of the basic features Novell provides for PKI. Novell has built its security (relevant to PKI) on the concept called Security Domain Infrastructure (SDI). The SDI consists of three key components:

Machine-unique CA and SDI key.   These keys, which are unique to each server, create the ability to sign the CA hierarchy created in the SDI system.

Server certificates.   These are the same as SSL certificates available from outsourced CAs, with the difference that they are created in a private hierarchy. This makes these SSL certificates most useful for intra-organization communication from server to server.

User certificates.   These are basically client certificates issued to end users on the network.

Given that Novell's approach (similar to Microsoft's) is to use a private PKI system, the root CA must be explicitly trusted by all users. If these roots are not trusted, certain applications will not work or (as in the case of browser-based applications in IE) will flash warning messages about insecure or untrusted connections. In addition, the server containing the root CA must be locked down, and proper audit trails must be maintained to ensure the integrity of the PKI.

Token FOB

With the rise of VPNs, security that used to be delegated to the user name and password has been deemed old and insufficient. Even if using certificates, the challenge is to protect access to the certificate that serves as a proof of identity—for example, a VPN connection request. The market today has answered that question with a range of small hardware tokens (also called key FOBs). These devices can also be considered hybrid SSO solutions, as they provide a single point of authentication regardless of physical location (see Chapter 11 for some example solutions in this space). Generally, these devices work with a USB connection and serve two main purposes:

Authentication devices.   They store some encrypted information that serves to provide authentication information when the token is connected. Some use digital certificates; others use a proprietary algorithm (like RSA's SecurID, which actually does not require a physical connection to the computer).

Storage devices.   They allow storage of information on tokens, letting a user roam with his or her certificate. By storing the certificate and private key in an encrypted fashion, the user can then move from computer to computer and perform certificate-enabled tasks freely. From a usability perspective, there are some issues with this approach because special drivers may be required on each computer where the token must be used. Nonetheless, in a closed environment (for example, a hospital or office complex), this might be an acceptable trade-off for the benefit of being able to roam.

The alternative to the hardware token FOB is what is called *soft roaming*. In soft roaming a certificate's private key is broken up into two or more pieces. Each piece is then stored at different servers (and ideally managed by different organizations). An authentication software prompts the user for identification, usually in the form of a password or passphrase. Once authenticated, the software makes a call to the two or more servers that host the private key. The certificate and associated private key are then reassembled at the location of the authentication software for the user to use. Once the user has completed using the certificate, the software then destroys all memory or drive copies of the assembled certificates.

TIP   Low-end key FOBs provide a good, cheap way to meet two-factor authentication requirements. Look for solutions that utilize Microsoft smart-card drivers. This will minimize the customization that will be needed on each system.

While this may appear to be a step above hardware tokens, the challenge is that it still relies on only a user name and password scheme in the end. In addition, the management and hosting of the dual private key servers make this an expensive solution. Many of the PKI vendors carry such a solution, but most have not seen a rush of users for such services.

Kerberos

Kerberos is an authentication protocol that provides SSO capability by performing an authentication once with the client and then using a ticket system to perform subsequent authentications. The system is akin to a corporate badge for a corporate campus. Once the authentication is performed an employee can use that badge as a form of authentication at various buildings and rooms. Each building or room access device confirms the level of authentication and grants access accordingly. Kerberos, an MIT-created protocol, has been mentioned in parts of this book because it has gone from being an academic protocol to a mainstream commercial protocol, thanks to the Microsoft machine. Microsoft uses Kerberos as part of its authentication scheme in Windows 2000 and later architectures to provide SSO authentication across various domains in a Microsoft-based network.

Currently Kerberos is used to create a model to allow easy hand-off of credentials from server to server. This creates the appearance of SSO for Microsoft product users. In fact, Microsoft is planning to use this security architecture for all its passport properties. SSO for Internet services is long held as the holy grail of customer service for many portal and Internet players. In addition, with the increasing fees of services, this SSO becomes almost a necessity.

To provide flexibility in authentication, Windows 2000 provides extensions to the standard Kerberos protocol based on certificates in addition to the symmetric keys used in the standard Kerberos protocol. The purpose of using certificates in the Microsoft Kerberos model is to allow clients to request an initial Kerberos ticket, signed with the client's private key. The Key Distribution Center (KDC) verifies this request by using the public key found in the client's certificate. The KDC accesses this certificate (see Figure 9.2) from the Active Directory, which stores the certificate. (Note that previous operating system versions used a special repository for certificates, and no applications could equally access the certificates. The use of Active Directory as a certificate repository makes the use and interoperability of certificates in the Microsoft environment much easier.) Following the initial certificate-signed communications, symmetric (or session) keys are used in communicating with the KDC for future session tickets.

KERBEROS: REARS ITS HEAD, AGAIN, AGAIN, AND AGAIN

A number of initiatives have been developed to formalize the merger of PKI and Kerberos. Given the strengths of both systems, a merger of these two systems would create an easy-to-use SSO concept that could scale to millions of users. One such active initiative is the Globus Project. The purpose of this effort, funded by the Grid Research Integration Development and Support (GRIDS) Center is to develop secure systems that can support the concept of grid computing (in other words, using computing services in a scalable fashion on demand).

The security elements of the Globus Project, which is outside the scope of this discussion, basically revolve around using the concepts of proxy credentials (in other words, certificates) to access the grid. These certificates then are used in conjunction with the Kerberos scheme to provide SSO capability and access to other resources.

One of the main reasons Kerberos cannot stand alone as an authentication mechanism for Internet-based resources is that it is not, nor was it, designed to scale to millions of users. PKI, on the other hand, was designed for the express purpose of communicating with large numbers of users over an insecure network. As a result, Microsoft saw the combination of these technologies as a natural fit.

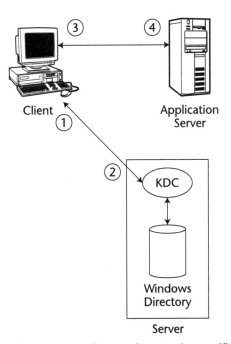

Client

Application
Server

1. Client authenticates with KDC

2. Session ticket presented by KDC back to client

3. Session ticket presented by client to application server

4. Session ticket verified by application server

KDC

Windows
Directory

Server

Figure 9.2 Kerberos scheme using certificates.

Tool Kits

Several vendors have tool kits that allow easier integration with PKI-related functions. Many tool kits are provided by the PKI vendor directly, while a few are provided by a third party. Generally, third-party tool kits are preferable only because they are more likely to integrate with various PKI vendor standards.

Microsoft

Microsoft has created a tool kit, called CAPICOM, that gives programmers a COM interface API for PKI-related tasks for Visual Basic, Active Server Pages, and other Microsoft-related environments. Designed as an ActiveX control (built on Microsoft's CryptoAPI), CAPICOM allows the following basic functions to be executed:

- Verify and digitally sign data with a certificate's private key
- Display certificate content
- Add or delete certificates from the system
- Use certificates to encrypt and decrypt data

CAPICOM greatly simplifies the use of digital certificates and will, we hope, make the use of digital certificates more prevalent to help mitigate security threats. Questions, of course, arise about the security of the CAPICOM tool kit itself. Nonetheless, this still offers more advantages that just relying on basic SSL for all the security needs of an Internet-based transaction.

Xetex

Xetex, a Texas-based company, has developed a series of tool kits built on its Java platform. The tool kits provide a simplified approach for programmers to use and verify digital certificates. One particular product called PKIT CRS from Xetex even has integration with VeriSign's Certificate Request Signing (CRS) protocol (used for creating requests for certificates). Although many PKI vendors provide APIs, very few have Java-based APIs that are standardized. Xetex has also developed products and services for the Identrus platform (which was discussed in the *Financial Solutions* section of Chapter 6).

Broadband

There are several projects underway by CableLabs, a Colorado-based company, which address security in the broadband industry. Some of these projects include the following:

- Data Over Cable Service Interface Specification (DOCSIS)
- PacketCable

- CableHome
- OpenCable

DOCSIS sets up the requirements for cable modems that transmit data over the standard cable television system network infrastructure (See Figures 9.3 and 9.4). DOCSIS has been more recently renamed as the CableLabs Certified Cable Modem project. The most common standard in use is DOCSIS 1.1, which provides the following security features:

- Data privacy
- Authentication
- Code signing (for cable modems)

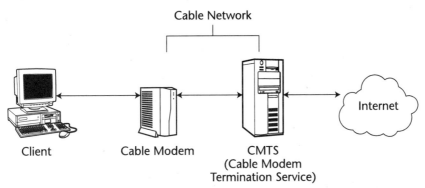

Figure 9.3 DOCSIS high-level architecture.

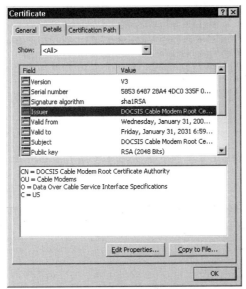

Figure 9.4 Example of a DOCSIS certificate (root CA issued by DOCSIS).

PacketCable specified the standards needed for using IP technology as a basis for real-time multimedia (as in the case of video conferencing). This data is designed to work over the existing television cable infrastructure. Packet-Cable standards support the following security elements:

- Integrity and secrecy using IPSec
- Use of X.509 v3 certificates for client-side authentication
- Nonrepudiation as a result of the support for client certificates

CableHome provides specifications that extend networking within the home environment. In this manner, an incoming broadband feed (for example, from a cable modem connected to the Internet) could then be shared with an internal network.

OpenCable was created to provide specifications for interactive services that cable operators may be able to provide over the existing cable infrastructure.

DOCSIS

There are several ways to adhere to the DOCSIS standards for creating a secure environment for communications over cable and broadband networks:

Control and own the DOCSIS components.   This involves using the DOCSIS security software directly in the cable modem provider's devices. In addition, the manufacturer will have to create and manage its own CA for issuing certificates to its devices, as per the DOCSIS standard. One key advantage to this is that there is greater control over the keys used to create the device certificates.

Outsource security to an external service provider.   In this model, an outsourced PKI vendor delivers the public and private key pairs and associated certificates to the cable modem manufacturer. Management of the certificate is minimal because device certificates are generally valid for a time period that will far exceed the useful life of the device itself.

Roll your own security.   A select few organizations may have the needed resources and expertise to develop their own security solutions based on the DOCSIS standards.

NOTE Many of the DOCSIS standards are designed to benefit the modem manufacturer. This should translate into cost savings for the end user as piracy of services can be mitigated. There is no legal driver for this move, but the use of an embedded certificate in a cable modem, for example, increases nonrepudiation claims.

DOCSIS REVIEW: AN INDUSTRY VETERAN'S PERSPECTIVE

INTRODUCTION

The cable industry has created specifications for data, voice, multimedia, video, and home networking through an industry sponsored consortium, Cable Television Laboratories (also known as CableLabs). The specifications are aligned into sets of documents for each project to describe technical interfaces. These interfaces support the cable operators' plan to bring consumer services over the cable infrastructure. Each of the projects has incorporated security into the architecture. CableLabs' specifications require digital certificates to provide authentication of the customer premise equipment (CPE) hardware, of the CPE code image, and for servers needing authentication in the cable operators' back office. The various specifications are as follows:

- Data specifications are called DOCSIS.
- Voice and multimedia specifications are called PacketCable.
- Video specifications are called OpenCable and OCAP.
- Home networking specifications are called CableHome.

This case study discusses the certificate usage in DOCSIS, PacketCable, and CableHome. DOCSIS, PacketCable, and CableHome specify the use of X.509- and RFC3280-compliant digital certificates (which are the most common type of certificates supported by most PKI-enabled solutions). The details for each of the certificate profiles are listed in the respective specifications available at www.cablelabs.com.

HISTORY

The broadband specifications were created in 1997 by CableLabs, beginning with DOCSIS, to provide the cable industry with an interoperable platform to roll out high-speed data service over the emerging technology provided by the cable modem. Leading the industry in this technology was Rouzbeh Yassini, Founder of LANCity, who successfully has built and marketed cable modems since 1988 and is well known as the Father of the Cable Modem. Rouzbeh Yassini is the Founder, CEO, and President of YAS Broadband Ventures, LLC. YAS has been engaged in a variety of worldwide activities in the cable and broadband industries, including providing consultants with 20+ years experience who specialize in broadband architectures. The security architect from YAS, Nancy Davoust, currently leading security for DOCSIS and CableHome, was a primary author for the PKI on the PacketCable and CableHome specifications and a contributor on the DOCSIS team.

(continued)

DOCSIS REVIEW: AN INDUSTRY VETERAN'S PERSPECTIVE *(continued)*

CERTIFICATES FOR DEVICE AUTHENTICATION

Device authentication is used to establish the secure identity of the CPE in the home. This identity ensures that devices are compliant with the specifications. The device certificates include the Media Access Control (MAC) address of the device, which is burned in at the factory. In addition, the device certificate is chained up to the certificate for the manufacturer of the device and in turn chained to a trusted root CA held by CableLabs. Some devices contain more than one MAC address, and, in that case, the specification requires that the certificate be tied to the device management MAC address. Once trust is established by validating and verifying the device certificate on boot-up (during the provisioning sequence), the device is then allowed to proceed with provisioning and operations. This provides the cable operator with a level playing field for interoperability. It can then be expected that a device will behave according to the specifications for device provisioning, management, and operations.

BENEFITS OF DEVICE AUTHENTICATION

Device certificates not only provide authentication but also support the trust infrastructure of the network. Each individual device and piece of software on the device in the home can be clearly identified, which greatly assists network management. Certificates help protect the cable industry from cloned devices and software. Certificates also help minimize theft of service for the cable operators because service can be clearly tied to an authenticated identity.

SOFTWARE AUTHENTICATION

Software authentication is used to establish the secure identity of the code image to ensure that the code came from a compliant manufacturer as well as to provide a guarantee that the image has not been changed since the manufacturer signed it. Additionally, CableLabs signs CableLabs Certified code images (with its code-signing certificate). In addition, the cable operator may chose to sign code images to ensure that only the code images it approves are provisioned into the devices in the home. The use of digital certificates for code images is termed secure software download, and the details are available in the DOCSIS and CableHome specifications. Essentially, the manufacturer (and optionally CableLabs and the cable operator) signs the code image with its Code Verification private key creating a Code Verification Signature (CVS) over the image. The Code Verification Certificate (CVC) is attached to the code image with the CVS so that the public key can be used to verify the signature and the CVC can be validated to be chained to a trusted CableLabs-owned root.

OTHER BENEFITS OF CERTIFICATES

Certificates are also specified to provide secure identity for some of the servers in the cable operator's back office. These servers were identified as needing a higher level of security to provide secure identification to the CPE for security information or to lawfully authorized law enforcement agencies for electronic surveillance.

Table 9.1 Contents of a DOCSIS Digital Certificate

HIGH-LEVEL REQUIREMENT	COMMENTS
Country	Mandatory
Organization	Mandatory
Organizational unit = DOCSIS	Mandatory
Common name = <company name>	Mandatory
Cable modem root CA	Mandatory
Validity date	Minimum 20 years

A DOCSIS-defined specification uses certificates (see Table 9.1 for details on the contents of a DOCSIS certificate) from the communication between the cable modem and the cable modem termination system (CMTS), which resides at the cable provider's site. Therefore, certificates provide authentication to prevent fraudulent use of the cable provider's resources in addition to adding a security tunnel for certain information.

Outsourced Security

One of the more popular models for managing security is to outsource the PKI components. Generally, outsourcing PKI has its own challenges despite the benefits. In the case of device certificates many of those issues are resolved because there is minimal certificate life cycle maintenance. Generally, when certificates are issued for cable modems, their validity period is usually well beyond the practical use of the device itself. In this manner, issues such as renewal of certificates are avoided.

The basic steps for the certificate issuance process in this model are as follows:

1. Cable modem sends lists of MAC addresses (which uniquely identify each device) to the PKI vendor.

2. The PKI vendor uses the MAC addresses as unique identifiers in the certificates and generates the public and private key pairs needed to create device certificates.

3. Generally, these certificates are produced in a batch form and then sent to the cable modem manufacturer in the form of an electronic file. To protect this file from interception, the entire file is usually encrypted using the cable modem manufacturer's own certificate.

4. The manufacturer then decrypts the received file from the PKI provider and then inserts the certificates and associated private keys into the cable modems at the time of manufacturing.

The key advantage of outsourcing is that the security can be implemented very quickly. Maintenance and the security of the CA-related functions lie with another party who will bear the risks and liability in the event of a security or process breach. The disadvantages are that an integral aspect of the cable modem manufacturer's business is dependent on a third party. In addition, third-party outsourcing can be (relatively) more expensive for smaller manufacturers due to the large volume commitments outsourced vendors usually require. The trade-off is between the speed and cost that result in working with outsourced vendors.

PacketCable

PacketCable specified the standards needed for using IP technology as a basis for real-time multimedia (for example, as in the case of video conferencing). This would allow the existing infrastructure to be used for more than just simple Web surfing, the most common application for cable modems today. Due to the requirements of performance (because the information must be seamlessly transmitted in real time), the security solution must accommodate this aspect of real-time communication.

Certificates have a key role in helping secure communication in the Packet-Cable specifications. PacketCable 1.2 specifications use IKE (as described previously in the VPN section earlier in this chapter) to exchange shared keys between the various components in the cable infrastructure.

The key uses of digital certificates in the PacketCable (see Table 9.2 for more details on the contents of the PacketCable certificate) standard include the following:

- Securing and verifying communication between the Operations Systems Support (OSS) and the Multimedia Terminal Adaptor (MTA). The MTA verifies the signature from the OSS to ensure that the device configuration information is not spoofed.

- SNMP messages sent from the MTA to the master SNMP manager are signed. The SNMP manager authenticates those messages that have verifiable signatures from the MTA Device certificate and MTA Manufacturer certificate.

- The MTA uses a Kerberos ticketing scheme to gain seamless access to application servers. The KDC distributes tickets to the MTA via a secured connection using digital certificates.

Table 9.2   Contents of a PacketCable Digital Certificate

HIGH-LEVEL REQUIREMENT	COMMENTS
Country	Mandatory
Organization	Mandatory
Organizational unit = PacketCable	Mandatory
Common name = PacketCable CA	Mandatory
Validity date	Minimum 30 years

CableHome

CableHome provides specifications to extend networking within the home environment. In this manner, an incoming broadband feed (for example, from a cable modem connected to the Internet) could then be shared with an internal network.

The use of certificates in the CableHome specification is required. There are a number of areas in which CableHome uses certificates with the security specification (see Figure 9.5 for a pictorial overview of CableHome security elements):

Secure management messaging.   This covers the SNMP and traffic control messaging between various components in the system.

Code signing.   When a CableModem device downloads new code from the provider, the device verifies the code for authenticity and integrity before installing. This prevents viruses or unauthorized modifications to the device.

Root CA verification.   By verifying the root CA (see Figure 9.6 for the CableHome certificate hierarchy), the device can ensure that it is a legitimate device produced in the proper format and processes under the auspices of the CableHome standards.

KDC operations.   Certificates are used to exchange KDC information between components. KDC tickets allow for a single authentication credential to be used across multiple resources and applications. This format is the same as specified in the PacketCable format.

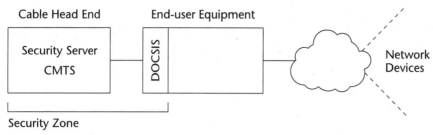

Security Zone

Figure 9.5 CableHome security elements overview.

OpenCable

OpenCable defines specifications for interactive services over broadband. This standard deals mainly with the ability for North American cable operators to provide additional services to increase revenue stream for the operators. OpenCable is outside the scope of this chapter and, thus, is not covered in depth here.

Euro-DOCSIS

To manage slightly different technology and standards in Europe, Euro-DOCSIS, a DOCSIS-based standard tweaked for the European markets, is managed by a company called TcomLabs, N.V. Some basic differences lie in the cable infrastructure and how the specifications must change to manage different equipment in Europe versus in the United States. A Euro-DOCSIS manufacturer certificate requires the minimum information shown in Table 9.3.

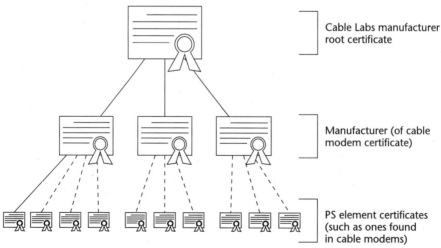

Figure 9.6 CableHome certificate hierarchy.

Table 9.3 Contents of a Euro-DOCSIS Digital Certificate

HIGH-LEVEL REQUIREMENT	COMMENTS
country = <Country of Manufacturer>	This is a mandatory field.
[stateOrProvinceName=<state/province>]	This is an optional field.
[localityName=<City>]	This is an optional field.
organizationName = <Company Name>	This is a mandatory field that must be shown in the certificate.
OrganizationalUnitName	This is a mandatory field and must have the value of "Euro-DOCSIS" or "DOCSIS" to indicate the specific standard and qualification the manufacturer underwent.
[organizationalUnitName=<Manufacturing Location>]	This is an optional field.
CommonName	Cable Modem Root Certificate Authority. This is a mandatory field and must be displayed in the certificate.

PKI on a Chip

While certificates can protect hardware like cable modems, other devices, like the PC, are also using hardware-based components to simplify security and administration of PKI. For example, a number of PC vendors are coming out with PKI-friendly solutions. One specific example is IBM's ThinkPad T30, which contains IBM's Embedded Security Subsystem 2.0. This subsystem allows for the creation and management of private keys for digital certificates to be handled by the hardware rather than in memory software.

IBM's security chip works through direction from software called IBM Client Security Software. The following sections discuss the key components of the security software. A visual representation of the interaction and architecture of the security components is shown in Figure 9.7.

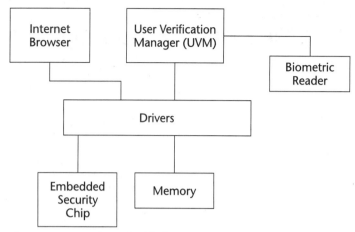

Figure 9.7 IBM's embedded security components (based on the Embedded Security Services data sheet).

Integrated Security Chip

This is a code support library that allows the software to interact with the hardware components. Some critical functions this piece performs are the code required to initiate 1024-bit and 512-bit RSA digital signatures as well as 256-bit symmetric key encryption and decryption.

User Verification Manager

This component is considered the central element in the client software. The User Verification Manager (UVM) provides configurable security mechanisms that can identify a user and determine that user's access rights. An interface is also provided that allows the administrator to manage multiple authentication software and hardware components as per the security policy.

The UVM acts as a middleware for authentication devices that may be used for additional authentication to the system, such as biometrics devices. In addition, the UVM can provide security policies that manage how and when authentication devices need to be used to enhance security for the local system. In theory, a user can be required to provide a biometric authentication, a passphrase, and a hardware authentication token, creating the highest level of authentication.

Other aspects of security are applied to the application layer. The UVM provides for screensaver password-locking systems or the Windows login-in function. As a default case, the UVM provides for a passphrase authentication if there are no other authentication devices or mechanisms available to authenticate the user.

A developer's tool kit has been provided for further enhancements.

PKI Standards Support

The client software interacts with the underlying security chip to provide public key infrastructure support by supporting Microsoft's Cryptographic Application Programming Interface (CAPI) and RSA's Public-Key Cryptography Standard (PKCS) #11. These are the basic standards required for generating the public and private key pairs needed for creating certificates. The client software gets downloaded by the end user without any keys or passwords. This maintains the highest level of security as only the end user has control of the keys required for maintaining nonrepudiation. In addition, because cryptographic functions are performed by the hardware, private keys are generated in the most secure manner because software threats are mitigated.

IBM claims to support Entrust certificate technology, have an ability to use IE and Netscape key generation mechanisms, and support Lotus Notes.

Administrator Utility

The administrator of the system can use this utility for initialization, configuration, and even archiving of the data created and stored as part of the client software interactions with the chip security system. Essentially, the software client allows the creation of an administrator certificate and associated password. This admin cert allows for control (archival and migration) of other user keys. This is perhaps the weakest aspect of the system because a compromise of the administrator certificate can result in a compromise of the entire system.

The other functions that the admin utility performs include the following:

- Creating the base hardware key pair.
- Resetting the fail counter for the hardware private key password. The counter prevents a brute-force attack attempting to guess the password. After the threshold is reached, the system locks up.
- Creating a key archive. This essentially creates a backup of the user keys and certificates.
- Restoring archived keys. This allows for the restoration of backed-up keys in the course, for example, of a disaster recovery plan.
- System board replacement. Because the admin cert resides on the hardware, it must be re-created when a new system board is used. This requires the admin utility to migrate security data from the old board to the new one.

File and Folder Protection

Protecting the local file system is accomplished by using a high-bit symmetric key algorithm (256-bit AES). The system prevents system-critical files from being encrypted to avoid accidental inoperability. An interesting aspect of performing file protection with a security chip is that only the logged-in user has access to the encrypted files, allowing a system to be shared with greater confidence. The symmetric keys used in the encryption are protected with the certificates tied to the hardware. This means that if the security chip is removed or if the files are copied on to a different hardware system, decryption will not be possible. The security advantage also creates a concern in terms of disaster recovery as planned backup strategies are more important when having to protect the data and the security keys with which they are encrypted.

> **NOTE** File protection is critical for many EU and Asian compliance laws. Should personally identifiable data be out of the control of the trusted party, the liable party will be the aggregator of that data.

(VPN) Authentication

Given that two-factor token authentication has become nearly ubiquitous for many corporate networks, IBM's security platform supports integration with RSA's SecurID authentication tokens. The system authorizes the VPN credentials to be released only after the use has been authenticated. This implies that a hacker could not even attempt to attack the VPN network credentials (as can be done without a hardware-based system) until he or she was able to break the hardware-based security platform.

Intel's Solution

A few years back, Intel attempted to release a CPU serial number scheme. This would uniquely identify each Intel CPU and, thus, could be tied to a host of applications, such as product registration and unique session identification. One interesting approach this would have offered to PKI is that the CPU serial number could be used to generate a certificate tied to that desktop machine. By tying the machine to the certificate, in addition to having a user-issued certificate, security could be increased because there would be two key data points for every transaction: the user certificate that is locked by a PIN or biometric device and the device certificate that identifies the specific device used. The drawback in the whole scheme has been that it removes a large amount of privacy because that machine is now uniquely identifiable in the entire Intel universe. Intel has since pulled the scheme from implementation, but most likely this will come up again with Microsoft's introduction of Palladium. Palladium is Microsoft's answer to digital rights management. By combining the Intel components with a software or OS-based system, a more robust security system can be created.

In November 2002, Intel created a partnership with VeriSign to embed VeriSign certificates into the processor of its Banias CPU line of chips. Again, the certificate, like the old CPU ID concept from Intel, uniquely identifies the person or the machine. There will be a fine balance between the user's privacy and the benefits the certificates provide. One advantage of such a system is the ability to revoke the certificate in the event of the loss of the computer. The revocation of the certificate would, in theory, render the computer useless. In actuality, however, the system has to be connected to the Internet to know that the certificate has been revoked. Another advantage is that this is a short-term strategy, pre-Palladium, which provides content protection of the local file system. The certificate, like IBM's security system, can encrypt files on the local file system until the proper authorization is provided.

Other Applications

Other applications that leverage the device certificate concept include the X-Bulk standard, which allows for a large number of device certificates to be loaded onto devices such as smart cards and even printers that carry secure connections to ensure that data to and from the printer is not intercepted using certificates.

X-Bulk

As we see an increase in the need for protecting devices with certificates, manufacturers increasingly need a standard that can allow for a bulk issuance of certificates. X-Bulk is a standard based on XML that specifies how bulk issuance of certificates using XML-based technology can be managed. The design of the X-Bulk standard is made up of the following key criteria:

- Be compatible with existing XKMS standards
- Manage key registration requests and responses for status updates in a batch-mode fashion
- Stay compatible with the PKCS #10,1 standards
- Manage both client- and server-side generation of keys

Some use scenarios for X-Bulk include the following:

- Smart cards
- Wireless devices
- Cable-modem applications
- Device factories in general

The X-bulk standard defines the basic process as follows:

1. A batch request for certificates is submitted to a CA. Each batch file contains a header identifying the batch. The batch header contains the batch ID, creation date, and process information for additional processing (to allow for later flexibility). A bulk registration process is then initiated upon receiving the batch request. The information then is used to generate the needed certificates and related information.

2. If the specific implementation of the standard supports it, a status can be given on the status of the processing of the batch file (via the header identification). Status updates require responders that listen for batch file status requests.

3. Finally, the last step is the registration result, which contains the batch header, the registration results, and a signature (for authenticity). This is what the end manufacturer will then use to embed the generated certificates into the device.

Printers

HP JetDirect print servers use digital certificates to validate and authenticate printer requests and secure administrative commands and traffic to the print server. The JetDirect server has a certificate that allows it to be identified to network printer clients and network authentication servers. Up to 3K is reserved for certificate storage (and usually this is more than sufficient for a single certificate, which usually is 1.5K–2.5K, depending on the type and content). A cold reset of the system still preserves the device certificate, but not additional CA certificates used for verification of a certificate's issuer.

TIP   Privacy and security can be compromised by intercepting the stream of data sent to a printer. This may violate certain privacy and security regulations as per the corporate policy.

The JetDirect gives administrators the ability to perform the following certificate-related functions:

- Create a self-signed certificate
- Request a certificate
- Install a certificate
- Use an existing certificate

- Disable SSL/TLS
- Install a CA certificate
- Delete CA certificate

Summary: PKI Is Far and Wide

As we have seen in this chapter, from the most common PKI trust applications, such as VPNs, to the less well-known but very large use, broadband, PKI is pervasive in our daily lives. Some of these solutions help solve specific business issues for consumers, while others solve problems for the vendor by helping keep costs low. Even the acceptance of PKI by Microsoft as a critical component in security validates the need for the technology. As we look to the future, we will definitely see PKI more and more as an embedded, behind-the-scenes technology that provides more security and helps minimize costs.

Trust Solutions Guide

CHAPTER

10

Overview of Trust Solutions

We have seen a number of different areas where trust solutions might be applied across various industry verticals. It is important to highlight that the trust solutions presented thus far are only a sample of the many options organizations have. This chapter highlights more solutions you can take as examples of possible configurations and usage scenarios for your specific trust solution needs. In fact, you may already know or use some of these solutions without realizing they are built on secure trust technology like PKI.

It is important to point out that we have no intention of including or excluding solutions from this chapter. These are only some of the various types of trust solutions that exist. The intent of this chapter is simply to point to different methods of achieving a secure and trustworthy infrastructure. No endorsement of a particular solution is implicitly or explicitly given.

Consultant's Corner

The challenge in presenting a myriad of options is that it will be difficult to choose one and justify it. In addition to the points made in Chapter 3 (in the *Vendor/Technology Selection* section), this section will cover best practices specifically aimed at consultants or those professionals who are in a position to recommend solutions to their clients.

Challenges

One of the biggest challenges in being a consultant, also known as a *domain expert*, is that the client will expect complete knowledge of not only the domain for which the consultant was brought in to service, but also related ones. For example, many people will go to see a medical doctor for a particular ailment, and while with the doctor they ask about other health-related issues. Although the doctor might be a generalist, patients expect answers to their questions, even if they are referred to a specialist. Likewise, technology consultants are expected to know not only the basics of their field, but specific solutions, issues, and trends. In the computer security field this means that if a company is looking to be HIPAA compliant, the consultant should be ready to speak not only to HIPAA regulations, but also virtual private networks (VPNs), secure email technologies, biometrics, form signing and workflow products, and the basics of security technologies and networking.

Another area in which trust solutions pose a challenge is the task of keeping up with the ever-changing technology landscape. In a typical, secured public key infrastructure, you will use VPNs, firewalls, physical security, PKI-enabled applications, and other components. Changes in any one of these components can affect the overall system design. As a result, it is important to keep system planning and architecture down to a minimum. This will help reduce the impact of advancing technology. In addition, it may be necessary for clients to upgrade to standard, current systems before even considering a trust solution. For example, it is common in the healthcare industry to have firms using Novell as their primary network architecture. Unfortunately, many PKI systems do not take Novell into account for all their applications and support. As a result, the deployment of such a project is already at risk before the project even gets started.

Another issue that challenges many consultants is whether the trust infrastructure can be outsourced. Whether it is outsourcing a VPN service or an entire PKI deployment, many companies are nervous about outsourcing, yet may not be able to manage an in-house deployment. By using return on investment (ROI) tools, consultants can provide clear, quantitative reasons for making a decision. In addition, service level agreements (SLAs) and other customer references can help clients rest assured with the recommendation made by the consultant.

It's the Law!

Consultants dealing with PKI-related trust solutions must understand the various legal aspects in a typical usage and deployment scenario. PKI, in many ways, is more of a legally driven technology because it was designed to be commercially viable in transactions between unknown parties. In addition, many of the chapters we have presented already cover specific legal requirements that companies must comply with. As a result, understanding legal aspects of the compliance laws as well as the liability and risk issues with PKI is essential, even if you are dealing with "just" technology implementation.

Staying Current

It is interesting that many resellers, consultants, and value-added resellers do not fully leverage vendors to learn more about the new features and benefits of various solutions. It is critical that consultants keep up-to-date on emerging trends because many times clients start planning based on the new or latest technology. It is advisable to set up weekly vendor presentations in various core competency areas that can allow consultants to have both a theoretical and practical knowledge of various solutions.

It is quite common, especially for the large consulting organizations, to have template summaries for current engagements. The danger in relying on this is that the market solutions may have changed and may affect system design. For example, as SSL accelerators and load balances became more common, the concept of shared SSL arose. Suddenly, consultants had to design a PKI-enabled Web server that could also load balance and share an SSL connection. Solutions hit the market and evolved rapidly over a period of less than six months. Such changes can affect not only implementations, but even the pre-sales process. With responses to requests for proposals (RFPs), which are usually delivered based on preexisting responses, information may not take into account more recent technology changes.

Guide to Commercial Solutions by Category

Although there are many categories of trust solutions on the market today, I have highlighted just a few of them here. (See Figure 10.1.)The lack of a category or the inclusion of a category does not necessarily imply its importance, but rather my experience in what solutions appear to be the most frequently discussed by enterprises today. Geography, industry segment, and corporation size, among other factors, can change the interest and priority in the solution category and the specific solution that is best for a particular organization.

VPN Solutions

The most common PKI application today is clearly for the VPN space. VPNs provide cost-efficient, secure tunnels to allow remote users to communicate with a secured infrastructure. Using PKI in a VPN solution allows more efficient and scalable use of a VPN (although it is not necessary for all VPN scenarios).

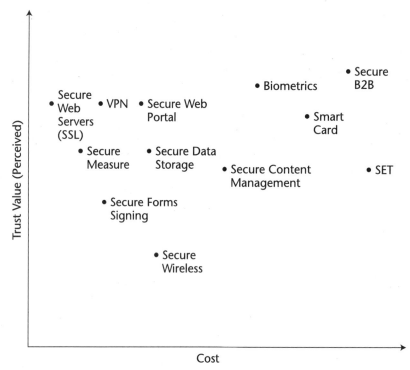

Figure 10.1   Relative cost of trust solutions.

The key differentiator in the VPN space is how well the client aspect is managed. Given that VPNs require clients on the remote machines, user management is central to how easily a particular solution is accomplished. For example, does the IT staff have to install the client manually on every desktop? Can the software be pushed out to the machine while it is on a LAN? Although later versions of most VPN clients resolve these issues, will the VPN client work behind a firewall or allow multiple systems to communicate via a single network access point?

A newer, transitional technology space has arisen to fill the gap between full-blown VPN solutions and point solutions, such as security for just one application, like email (for example, through the Outlook for Web Access solution from Microsoft). This area is called Instant Virtual Extranets (IVEs). Although IVEs position themselves as cheaper VPN solutions, in reality they fill the gap for the small- to medium-sized enterprise markets (or department-level needs in large corporations) that do not wish to implement all of the features of a VPN. Generally, IVEs focus on providing secure, remote access to specific applications such as email, network file servers, or corporate intranets.

Checkpoint

Checkpoint is one of the oldest and strongest leaders in the firewall/VPN space. Since its inception, the company has evolved into a broader security company, including solutions in security policy and performance acceleration components. Checkpoint partnered with Entrust to produce a certificate-based authentication system for users to access a VPN protected by Checkpoint's Firewall-1 software. In this manner, Checkpoint's client software (which resides on the computer of each user wanting access to a protected resource), can be loaded with a certificate issued by the customer. This certificate proves the validity of the user to the VPN/firewall software.

Nokia

As one of the leading vendors in the VPN appliance market, Nokia has targeted larger enterprises with its solutions. Nokia creates a remote user client with Checkpoint's VPN client and different types of gateways for managing different types of VPN connections. Given that the VPN client bundled with Nokia's solution is preconfigured for remote access with Nokia's VPN solution, this makes it cost-efficient as minimal configuration, and desktop support is required.

Netscreen

Netscreen took a more simplistic approach to VPN software by making a single appliance. This appliance concept propelled the VPN technologies into becoming much easier to set up and manage. Netscreen also worked to make the use of certificates much easier, by providing a GUI for loading and installing certificates within the administrator console of the Netscreen box. Certificates can be loaded into the machine as gateway certificates. One important distinction Netscreen has over similar competitors is that it will reject connections if a CRL cannot be updated. This is important because a network faces a serious security breach if a revoked certificate is allowed in, even if the event is alarmed or logged, (because, after all, the certificate was revoked for a good reason). In addition, Netscreen advertises compatibility with multiple CAs.

SonicWall

Perhaps a very close competitor to Netscreen, SonicWall has done well to provide solutions to ISPs to help them manage VPNs for their small business customers. SonicWall has done a tight integration with a VeriSign CA, allowing clients to use VeriSign certificates in a seamless fashion. One key area of difference is that the products are generally geared to small- and medium-sized businesses. Some aspects, including a lack of a server load-balancing solution, no traffic shaping, or virtual LAN (VLAN) tags, make it a less likely competitor for the large enterprise markets.

Biometric Solutions

There are numerous solutions in this space, ranging from device vendors to complex authentication management software suites. A range of solutions is presented here, focusing on the most common biometric approaches in the industry today.

Device Vendors

These solutions provide a single biometric device that can be used for authentication. Some solutions integrate with the operating system, and others are tied directly to a particular application. In general, most biometrics (device) vendors today do not have direct integration with any PKI systems. The few that are listed here are given as a snapshot of the types of devices that exist, not necessarily only those with PKI trust solutions capability.

Digital Persona

Digital Persona's U.are.U line of products is geared to a range of applications. The focus of these products is the fingerprint scanner Digital Persona produces, which uses an optical scanner method. The products can be used for security, including accessing the system. In addition, the products can be used for convenience—for example, switching from one user to another (in Windows XP), just by presenting the proper fingerprint.

Digital Persona has products that have integrations with the Personal Trust Agent (PTA) from VeriSign, Inc. This allows the fingerprint scanner to access the PTA profile, which, in turns, allows access to a digital certificate. Although Digital Persona does not provide direct PKI functionality, it does provide this ready-made integration for VeriSign customers. Additional tool kits are available for other systems and configurations.

Visionics/Identix

Visionics and Identix merged in 2002 to allow a broader range of biometrics across multiple verticals. Currently the solutions are not compatible with PKI (out of the box), but they do include integration tools that allow tying biometric components with digital certificates. Applications for this type of biometric include the ability to provide a quick, nonintrusive method of authentication for in-person transactions.

Iridian

Known for its iris-scanning technologies, Iridian does not directly provide integration with PKI. It does have integrations with several SSO or middleware companies, which, in turn, integrate with PKI. These systems are used for moderate levels of security and convenience. Further integration directly with PKI systems would be extremely useful for end users, especially for kiosk use (for example, performing digitally signed transactions at an ATM).

Middleware Vendors

These solutions aggregate multiple biometric devices into a single programmatic interface, which allows the end user to choose from a range of devices, without having to enable each biometric device with a particular application. In addition, these vendors provide additional integration with various authorization middleware to determine, for example, which biometric devices are required for a particular application. For example, a company's CFO may require a fingerprint scan and voice authentication, whereas a clerk may require only a fingerprint scan.

Bionetrix

Bionetrix, a Vienna, Virginia–based company, takes an interesting approach to biometrics data management issues. By acting as a device aggregator, its product suite allows the end user to choose from a range of device vendors without worrying about device compatibility. Bionetrix uses a concept called *connectors* to develop integration with device vendors. As a result, for devices that do not fall into the Bionetrix pre-integrated set of devices, users can add integration.

In addition to device aggregation, Bionetrix provides for single-sign-on (SSO) integration. With this feature, a device can authenticate a user based on rule sets programmed into the product suite. SSO decision criteria may also come from external software like Netegrity. PKI integration for the Bionetrix suite is provided through a connector that was developed to use VeriSign certificates. In this manner, a device can be used that would allow access to a particular certificate, as per the rule set defined in the Bionetrix software. This would allow biometric lockdown of a certificate.

Form-Signing Solutions

One of the more common uses of PKI is for form-signing applications. Form signing can be viewed in two ways:

- Signing individual forms and routing those forms through traditional methods, such as email
- As a component of a workflow model in which signing the form triggers an event in the workflow

There are good solutions in both categories, although most solutions have a hybrid approach, either focusing on stand-alone form signing but including some elements of workflow or being a workflow product that includes form signing. In choosing a form-signing solution, it is critical to determine if the solution is meant for internal processes (employees only) or for hybrid processes (including vendors and customers). Internal-only processes can be managed using self-signed certificates (although there are issues with legally binding aspects to self-signed certificates). Hybrid solutions will almost always require a public CA certificate, and therefore each use must have a certificate prior to being able to use the application (unlike self-signed certificates that can be generated within the application).

Generally, form-signing solutions have two main goals:

- Simplify and increase efficiencies for processes
- Increase the legally binding defense aspect of a digitally signed form

Stand-Alone Form Signing

In cases where form signing needs to be accomplished without a live Internet connection, stand-alone form-signing solutions work well. Other aspects of stand-alone form-signing solutions include their requirement for software at the client to manage the signing process. Generally, these solutions work well for intranet or other internal uses of form signing.

Adobe

Adobe has been well known for its portable document format (PDF). What is perhaps not known as extensively is Adobe's form-signing and security features. Adobe offers (through its various products) the ability to create a PDF form and then allow the end user to digitally sign this form after it is filled out. Some of this functionality was obtained through Adobe's acquisition of Accelio, a workflow company, in 2002.

Adobe allows the user to use a self-signed certificate (in other words, the program creates a certificate with its own built-in certificate authority) or to specify another CA's certificate. Depending on the application, either may be effective.

Silanis

Silanis, a Canadian company, provides various form-signing solutions for the enterprise. Its products range from internal processes to business-to-business and business-to-consumer products. Basically, Silanis offers a desktop client plug-in for major software packages such as Microsoft's Word or Autodesk's

AutoCAD. With this plug-in, a user can digitally sign a document and also create an embedded audit trail (which can then be viewed later to see who signed the document). Silanis also offers a plug-in for Adobe, but that would have been more useful if Adobe had not already improved its security and signing features for forms.

Silanis also offers a Web-based, business-to-consumer solution. This solution allows users without the Silanis plug-in to sign forms on a Web page. This is, of course, very useful for any application outside of internal processes.

Hybrid

Hybrid form-signing solutions attempt to merge the benefit of being able to avoid dedicated client software yet allowing a robust set of features without this client. Generally, these solutions require a small downloadable client (such as ActiveX or similar control) during the form-signing session.

Evincible

Evincible provides four main products: Secure Forms, Ink, Privacy, and Access. In summary, the combination of these products allows users to use digital certificates as the basis for many trust-related transactions. For example, users can digitally sign documents, create receipts, and validate the authenticity of documents by combining the offered products. As a result of Evincible's partnerships with leading PKI vendors such as VeriSign and Baltimore, the company's products can offer a range of compatible digital certificates.

One key aspect of Evincible's technology is that it uses XKMS, a forward-looking standard, to minimize the impact of PKI on the end user. As a result of XKMS, users can validate certificates with real-time information, without the hassle of propriety toolkits or delays by using alternate technologies such as CRLs. In addition, some workflow capability is built into its products, making this more flexible than a pure form-signing solution.

The key focus areas for this line of products are legislation-prompted activities, such as HIPAA, GPEA, and others. Sample customers include companies like Exostar.

Lexsign

Lexsign positions itself as a multiapplication forms-signing technology with products that also provide workflow capability. Its Prosigner product suite offers add-ins for popular applications (very similar to the Silanis plug-in concept) to allow signing in the native application. Lexsign provides the utilization of certificates from various PKI vendors and, in addition, provides authentication through a PIN concept (useful when deploying a PKI infrastructure as this allows the immediate use of the application as the PKI is rolled out). Lexsign also offers an interesting feature that allows a physically digitized signature to be associated with a digital signature (same as Silanis). Lexsign provides a separate reader for the recipient of a signed document to read the document and associated audit trail and verification of the associated digital signature. The key verticals Lexsign focuses on include finance, public sector (government), and healthcare.

iLumin

As a provider of what it calls secure ebusiness, iLumin falls into the hybrid category as it provides form-signing solutions and Web-based workflow and secure storage solutions. Part of its product line includes a form designer tool that provides the ability to create custom forms. Most form-signing vendors provide the ability to create self-signed certificates — that is, certificates that use a privately created root (in other words, a public CA is not used to create the certificate). Likewise, iLumin has a product line called the Digital Credential Authority to provide this very concept.

Core Technology

This category provides examples of companies that provide development libraries or prepackaged software kits that allow an end user to develop customer software-signing applications more easily.

InfoMosaic

As a relatively new company, InfoMosaic provides XML-based digital signature solutions. Its product suites, called Secure XML, provide a range of XML-based solutions from client-side form signing to server-side (clientless) form signing. XML-based solutions are not in themselves unique, as many of the vendors listed in the form-signing solution section are also XML-based. By InfoMosaic's providing software libraries, however, customers can customize and build a very specific form-signing application.

Xetex

Xetex provides a range of products for the PKI-related space. One specific tool it provides is an ActiveX control for form signing. It also provides various tool kits to interface with specific CAs (like the PKIT CRS product that works with VeriSign's CRS protocol for requesting certificates) or work with your own CA components. In addition to products, it also provides integration and consulting services for these products and technologies. For more information go to www.xetex.com.

XKMS

One area of PKI that will influence many different solutions and improve the ease of PKI deployments is the development of a technology called XML Key Management Specification (XKMS).

In order to remove the complexity of PKI from the application and solution vendors as well as the customers, one key technology has emerged to ease the pain of PKI integration. XKMS provides the following:

◆ The ability for developers to leverage nonproprietary tool kits, which are the primary method of PKI development today

◆ Simple deployment because most of the PKI operations are done on a server back-end, versus the client, which is the current method most PKI systems use

◆ Simplified utility on mobile platforms because XKMS removes the burden on the client of most PKI functions

◆ Industry-wide standards because leading vendors in this space have supported and/or contributed, including Microsoft, webMethods, VeriSign, and Entrust

Secure Messaging

The killer application of the Internet could also be the killer application of the security world. Email technology has progressed quite a bit since it was first introduced. Email systems can now integrate with other systems, including contact management software and wireless devices. Many solutions have attempted to address this area by addressing one of two markets: the enterprise market and the mass market. In any product line, the mass market tends to be more difficult to implement and develop as a business model. A number of initial services for securing messages for the average consumer have come and gone. For example, Yahoo!'s free secure email service based on Zixit technology disappeared from its offerings sometime ago.

Solutions in this category can be broken into two main types: solutions requiring end-user clients and solutions without a (dedicated) client that use the Web browser. Solutions with end-user clients can provide more robust and feature-rich services, such as integrating the certificate request and other life cycle management features directly into the client. Solutions without the need for dedicated end-user clients have the advantage of being very mobile, cheap, and easier to deploy. Each has its place, depending on the needs of the organization.

Another category that could be loosely lumped into this one is secure document delivery. A variance on simply sending email messages and attachments is to send a document sometimes on a one-time basis. In addition, this category may involve single, one-time communications with a previously unknown party. Most of these types of solutions utilize a Web interface and have some type of limitation on the size of documents.

Most of the nonclient solutions usually have an option to have the back-end infrastructure hosted (in other words, an Application Service Provider model).

Solutions with End-User Clients

This section covers a few of the most widely used email clients (on PC platforms) with digital certificate support.

Microsoft

Microsoft has dominated the market with its Outlook and Outlook Express products, both of which are fully integrated with digital certificates. Outlook allows users to send messages unencrypted, encrypted, or signed (or a combination of encrypted and signed). In Outlook, buttons are presented on a message interface to allow the user to manually select the type of trust service to be applied to a particular message (or default options can also be configured). Outlook Express can associate certificates with particular user addresses or profiles.

One interesting feature of Outlook is that it supports dual key formats. This means that two certificates can be used: one for encryption and one for signing. This is important because if an organization wants to escrow its employees' certificates, it needs to escrow only the encryption certificate. In this manner, nonrepudiation can be maintained because the signing certificate never has to be escrowed.

Qualcomm

Eudora, by Qualcomm, is another popular email client package. It comes with SSL certificate compatibility out of the box. This means messages to and from a mail server are encrypted. It does not encrypt a particular message or allow for signing of messages. To achieve this feature, a third-party plug-in is necessary. For example, DST (Digital Signature Trust, which is now part of Identrus) creates the WorldSecure Client plug-in for Eudora to allow client certificate functions such as message encryption and signing.

Solutions without End-User Clients

A dedicated end-user client can be burdensome to manage as a result of the fact that mobility is restricted because the client needs to be carried with the user. A number of solutions that are Web based and, therefore, do not require dedicated clients allow easy access to secure email solutions even while mobile.

USA.net

USA.net provides an ASP model in which companies have the ability to use either client-based systems (for example, with Outlook) or purely Web-based systems. In either case, the back-end infrastructure can be hosted at their data centers. What is interesting is that USA.net now provides Web-based mail and digital certificates. This makes it very easy and convenient because the same vendor can provide both components.

Zixit

Zixit provides a hybrid model and does not provide complete clientless operation. Essentially, the various components in the Zixit product line allow users to use standard email clients (with Zixit plug-ins) and send encrypted email. The recipient, however, does not need any special software and can use Zixit's Web service for the pickup and reply of those emails (a link for the secure pickup of that message gets sent to the end user's regular email inbox). Zixit essentially removes the complexity of requiring each user to hold a digital certificate, but this also decreases the strength of nonrepudiation.

HushMail

HushMail aims to be a completely Web-based, secure email provider. Built on OpenPGP, each mail message is uniquely encrypted from sender to receiver. The way the system works is by taking a message composed on the Web portal and then using the PGP software, encrypting the message. The system does require an applet download in the form of a windows CAB file and is a multi-step process for the recipient because the recipient has to decode the PGP message. The key aspects are that the service can be made fairly mobile and clientless (if you ignore the small applet download).

ZipLip

ZipLip has elements of both a client-based system (by making back-end software for the enterprise) and a clientless hybrid version. Similar to the way Zixit works, the sender uploads a file that is then stored securely. The recipient is then notified to pick up the message through the security provided by SSL (versus client certificates). With ZipLip's APIs other possibilities can be created such as biometric integration.

Miscellaneous Solutions

For certain applications, high-end solutions can provide more customization and control over how and when encryption is implemented during the email session. These solutions are generally fit for corporatewide deployments for large numbers of users.

Tumbleweed

Tumbleweed offers a range of products that provide secure messaging and secure document delivery. Although (secure) email could serve as a method of secure document delivery, there are a few cases in which audit trails, guaranteed delivery, and other features may be necessary for the needs of some enterprises. Generally, its solution works like many other solutions in this category: the pickup model. To provide secure messaging without digital certificates, the sender receives a secure Web site link to pick up the message. In this manner Tumbleweed can offer the ability to provide a solution with standard SSL certificates (versus client certificates). Tumbleweed also offers a server-based S/MIME solution. The challenge of encrypted messaging is that virus scanners at the mail server cannot read the message to scan for viruses. The burden then gets put on the end user to ensure that the received message, after unencryption, is scanned and checked for viruses. A server-based solution essentially decrypts the message, performs the scanning, and then (possibly) encrypts the message again before delivering it to the end recipient. This approach, of course, decreases the nonrepudiation of a secure message.

Sendmail

Sendmail has been most commonly associated with the beginnings of the Internet and its pioneering approach in providing email systems for so many early Internet companies. Sendmail has evolved into a company that can provide a full-featured set of services and products. One particular module, called Sendmail MailStream Manager, provides the ability for SMTP traffic to utilize SSL encryption. This keeps mail protected in transit from server to server. This technology is based on the IETF RFC 2487.

Secure Wireless Solutions

Wireless PKI has always sounded like an oxymoron. When dealing with the wireless space, PKI has been a challenge to implement for a number of different reasons. The most critical is the limited processing power and memory on many wireless devices. This section covers some of the approaches developed to overcome these limitations. Two of the main approaches to enabling trust solutions on mobile devices are as follows:

Wireless Transport Layer Security (WTLS) certificates.   WTLS certificates are modified X.509 certificates that allow for smaller (relative to standard desktops) CPU and memory requirements to accommodate small, mobile devices.

Wireless Public Key Infrastructure (WPKI).   Currently mobile devices solve the problem of trust through a WPKI. WPKI consists of the same elements of standard PKI such as a CA, RA, and end-entity; however, a WPKI also uses a PKI portal that can translate interactions between the WAP client on the mobile device and the wired Internet CA.

Certicom

Certicom is a leader in elliptical curve cryptography (ECC), which is a specialized cryptography standard for small devices with little processing and/or memory power. Certicom has a range of solutions in the wireless space, spanning from WLAN solutions to PKI for wireless devices. Certicom offers its own PKI CA server and WPKI portal for issuing digital certificates to devices, such as PDAs and mobile phones. In addition, Certicom offers its mobile VPN line of products called movianVPN for mobile devices. The solution also works with the industry-standard Internet Key Exchange (IKE) protocol for establishing a VPN session. This solution provides a VPN for mobile devices that also works with popular two-factor authentication devices.

Openwave

One of the leaders in the wireless application space, Openwave has created a number of products compatible with various trust services. The most notable is the microbrowser (Openwave Mobile Browser) that supports WTLS certificates (a variation on regular digital certificates adapted to the constraints of the small wireless device). From Openwave's perspective, security has been established by various standards, including WAP (wireless application protocol), and, thus, its applications and tool kits must be compliant.

Diversinet

Diversinet provides secure, wireless VPN solutions through its Passport Wireless product line. This wireless VPN fully supports the use of client-side digital certificates as authentication criteria. The product works with a range of wireless networks including GPRS, CDMA, and GSM (the most common wireless protocols in use). A key feature includes the ability to roam between multiple types of networks and still maintain a secured, authenticated session (for example, through an airport). Generally, a customer of a Passport Wireless system would need the mobile authentication server along with a certificate server (which Diversinet can also provide), and possibly a Passport VPN Mobile Session server to maintain a seamless transition in a mobile environment that switches from network to network and suffers lags.

Single Sign-On Solutions

SSO solutions are perhaps the highest of all holy grails in the security industry. Broadly defined, SSO solutions allow a user to identify himself or herself once and then use that authentication to access a range of resources, as per the security policy that has been defined. Today, there is a range of solutions to help achieve some semblance of SSO. Without an SSO solution, users will need to identify themselves periodically at various, disjointed systems. Repeated authentication creates a major inconvenience as well as security risks because many users will choose easy-to-guess passwords across several systems.

There are two main types of SSO solutions, both of which are rather expensive:

Integrated solutions.   Integrated solutions provide sign-on integration within a particular operating system, so as to leverage the operating system security with additional authentication and authorization information being provided by a third-party system.

Hybrid tacked-on solutions.   These solutions refer to the fact that there is a combination of technologies, including hardware tokens, that allows for the SSO to be achieved by mimicking the user input on a user name and password challenge. These solutions will generally store credentials (passwords, pins, or certificates) on software wallets or hardware tokens, and users can identify which credential to apply to which resource. These are clearly transitional technology niches; as integrated or add-on solutions become more sophisticated, the need for tacked-on solutions will disappear.

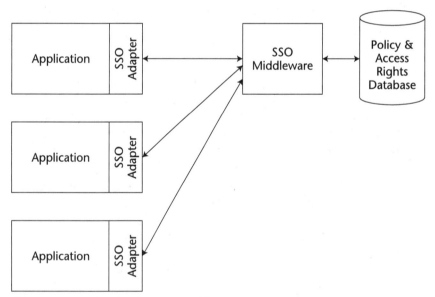

Figure 10.2   Example of an SSO architecture.

Integrated Solutions

Most integrated systems are sold by larger companies in which the software has built-in hooks and during implementation is integrated into various aspects of a corporation's IT infrastructure. In addition, most integrated solutions have seamless logon ability, with integration into the operating system security system. For example, the ability to sign on to a desktop via Windows 2000 or XP allows the user to use that authentication seamlessly for other resources (such as file systems or application server access).

Computer Associates

As a large company, Computer Associates has the benefit of tying together multiple aspects of an enterprise's security infrastructure. One key product line that helps customers address the need for trust solutions is the eTrust PKI. This product essentially allows a customer to set up all aspects of a PKI at the customer's data center. This model is similar to that of other PKI vendors such as Entrust or Baltimore.

One key advantage a Computer Associates customer will have with the eTrust PKI solution is that it will integrate well with the other eTrust products such as the single-sign-on and Web access control products. Because most customers will not use a PKI without some sort of integration, this suite can provide a one-stop shop, which appears to be the trend in the industry today.

IBM

IBM has improved its strength in the security market through acquisitions and key alliances throughout 2002. Alliances and acquisitions with companies like Kroll, Access360, VeriSign, and PriceWaterhouse Consulting have bolstered IBM's formidable presence in the world of computer security. Through its various product lines, IBM can offer entitlements, provisioning, and security services to build applications on top of a PKI-based infrastructure. IBM effectively exited the PKI business when it created a marketing agreement with VeriSign; IBM in effect gave its PKI business to VeriSign. Most of the products related to IBM's support of PKI solutions center around its Tivoli product line. The Tivoli line manages access, intrusion response, and identity management, among other security-related tasks. IBM has other extensive offerings in the enterprise security space.

Netegrity

Netegrity became a success initially because of its SiteMinder product. This product was positioned to be a mid-level entitlement management solution for the enterprise. With SiteMinder, an organization could achieve SSO-like capabilities, authenticate users, and dictate entitlements (in other words, what a user is authorized to do for a particular resource). Netegrity created the ability to authenticate users with a digital certificate and use that as the proof of authentication for the other pieces of the system. Since the initial product launch, Netegrity has launched many other products including a proxy server to proxy Web connections, such as SSL and HTTPS. Based on its price point and feature set, this solution would be considered mid-level. Like many other solutions in this space, a fair amount of consulting is required to set up and integrate the various pieces of an organization's systems with the Netegrity solutions.

Oblix

Oblix positioned itself in the entitlements space as a feature-rich, but cheaper solution (in terms of overall cost, including software and consulting). In addition, Oblix integrated with PKI vendors several years ago to ensure the use of digital certificates and created a seamless solution (or as seamless as the technology can be). In this manner, a certificate, once presented to the Oblix Netpoint software, can serve as the authentication mechanism on which the Netpoint product can make decisions regarding the access levels and resource availability tied to that certificate. Further integration with third-party products allow for increased identity management and federated identification systems.

Hybrid Solutions

Effectively, hybrid solutions are software that provide a stop-gap solution to mimic an integrated solution. The advantage of these solutions is that their price points are much more favorable as they are more easily scalable and their deployment issues are simplified.

ActivCard

ActivCard built its reputation on competing solutions to RSA's SecureID token (the market leader for dual-factor remote access solutions). Through a slightly different method than its competitors, ActivCard was able to realize cost savings and increased technical efficiencies. ActivCard supports a range of products from VPN access solutions to smart cards. ActivCard's involvement with smart cards makes it easy to work with digital certificates. Typically digital certificates (among other information) are stored on the smart card. This card then acts as a universal, all-in-one component for authentication. Given that it is difficult to integrate the use of smart cards in most applications across the enterprise, this company's set of solutions can be positioned as additional technology to help achieve SSO and other security efficiencies through add-on components. Integration, for most applications (other than remote access and user logins), needs to be done with their smart-card APIs.

Symantec (Axent)

Symantec, although known mostly for virus-fighting solutions, also offers SSO solutions, as a result of its acquisition of Axent a number of years ago. The solution, referred to as PassGo, essentially works by using a central authentication server with various agents deployed for specific applications that need to leverage the SSO solution. Symantec has created a number of agents for common software and has provided a developer's tool kit for other types of applications. The central authentication server also can tie in with a management server such as IBM's Tivoli product.

Alladin

Alladin offers its hardware token product called eToken, which serves as a USB-based key device that is small enough to be portable. This device contains memory and some amount of processing capability to allow it to work with PKI-enabled applications. The token can generate RSA 1024-bit keys, which are sufficient for basic encryption applications (although, for very serious applications, 2048-bit for RSA or the use of the new Advanced Encryption Standard [AES] would be more appropriate). This token was designed as a dual-factor and supplement authentication for end users. An important factor is that it has been designed for security, including tamper-evident cases and ITSEC-LE4 certification.

Content Management Solutions

Perhaps the next holy solution (next to a true single-sign-on solution) is a perfect content management solution. Content management in the context of security refers to the ability to restrict any digital content per the attributes assigned by the content's creator. Much ado has been made during the last several years about the protection of digital music and related content. In reality, most of the solutions for the enterprise will focus on the security of documents.

The difficulty in architecting a secure content management solution centers on the fact that the recipient most likely does not need or want the solution, while the sender, on the other hand, wants to protect the content. As a result, solutions fall into two main areas based on the needs and flexibility the sender is looking to bear:

Clientless solutions.   Generally, these solutions revolve around using an Internet Web browser to deliver the content directly in the browser or deliver a hybrid model giving a link to the actual content. These solutions are ideal for scenarios in which a member outside of an organization, such as a customer, needs access to information.

Client solutions.   These solutions require a client that can decode the original document and release specific content as per the security policy.

In terms of architecture, some solutions have hosted (outsourced) models, while others require a central server at the organization to manage the central policy server. The more advanced systems use PKI for authentication and creating (legally enforceable) audit trails. Given the mixed rate of adoption of digital certificates by many organizations, many of these solutions offer certificates in addition to using user names and passwords. The issue with using only a user name and password is that should a violation or breach of security occur with a document, it is difficult to substantiate nonrepudiation (because, after all, multiple copies of that user name and password may exist). Solutions listed here describe a sample of those solutions that work with PKI to create a higher level of trust:

Probix

Probix accomplishes something that is difficult to do in the world of enterprise content management: a client as close to a zero footprint as possible. By using a combination of Web technologies and encryption techniques, content can be locked down as specified by the sender and then sent off to someone who may or may not have used Probix's system. Essentially, this model is designed to be a pickup model, with the end user going to a Web link that allows him or her to retrieve the content. This system works well because it makes some fundamental assumptions: End users may have only a Web browser as the common software, a firewall may reside between sender and recipient, and speed is an issue for the user.

Certificates are used as authentication mechanisms (versus user name and password combinations, although they are also an option) to access the hosted system for pushing content or retrieving content. Later versions of the system have the ability to use a standard email client such as Outlook to email content directly to an end user rather than having to upload content manually to the hosted system.

Alchemedia

Alchemedia (now part of Finjan Software via an acquisition in December 2002) takes a unique approach to content protection by setting up a server at the customer's site. This server, called the Mirage Server, provides the functionality required to manage data, flag content to be protected, and otherwise apply policies to data leaving the corporate site. In addition, a desktop client is required to use the protection system. The system is supposedly compatible with PKI through interfaces that allow certificates to provide the basis of encryption keys for protecting content data.

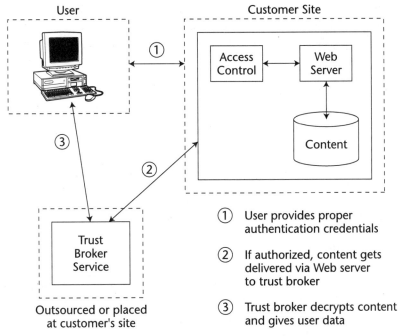

Figure 10.3 Example of a content management architecture.

Web Servers

Naturally, Web servers are a clear use for trust-based applications. Most e-commerce today is conducted via a number of secure methods, but nearly all rely on using Secure Socket Layer (SSL) certificates. SSL certificates were one of the earliest uses of PKI technology. SSL certificates allow creation of a secure tunnel between the client browser and the organization's Web server.

One of the main reasons SSL certificates took off as a key application for trust is that in order for companies to get an SSL certificate from a third-party PKI vendor, they must do authentication. This allows for not only stronger authentication of the vendor, but also user convenience because the PKI vendor's root is already in most browsers.

An interesting trend, however, is emerging among the PKI vendors in the area of SSL certificates. SSL certificates are quickly becoming commodities, as evidenced by price wars in the industry. As of the end of 2002, VeriSign, while still the market leader, suffered immense price erosion through companies like Geotrust. Geotrust offered SSL certificates at a fraction of the cost of VeriSign certificates. End users did not perceive the value in the VeriSign brand sufficiently enough to stop from defecting. Furthermore, late in the third quarter and early fourth quarter of 2002, Entrust also started attacking VeriSign SSL certificates specifically on price. It appeared that the value of stronger authentication through VeriSign's rigorous procedures was not as important as price to the marketplace.

There are two types of Web servers today, much like firewalls and VPNs: software- and hardware- (appliance-) based systems. Related technologies, like SSL accelerators, have become increasingly important as a result of the heavy use of encrypted traffic for commerce. SSL accelerators perform the cryptographic functions needed to establish an SSL connection with a requesting client. By using dedicated hardware, the server's main CPU is spared the drain on resources, and more SSL connections can be handled at the same time. Another increasing trend, as related to these accelerators, is the concept of shared SSL certificates. This idea is that the SSL connection is from the accelerator (or load balancer) to the client. But internal to the network on the Web server side, the accelerator sits in front of the Web server (for dedicated boxes). This avoids the need for point- (client) to-point (Web server) SSL connections. Challenges to this have been mainly for the SSL certificate vendors because now an entire farm of Web servers can be served with a only a few certificates. This trend, too, has reduced the revenue streams for PKI merchants.

Software Web Servers

Web servers can be implemented as software applications on existing hardware. Adding security is fairly simple as most of the Web servers have easy-to-install processes and tools for adding SSL certificates.

Figure 10.4 Example of an SSL certificate.

Apache

By far, Apache is the leader of the free Web server market, with close to 65 percent of the market. Apache's dominance was created in large part because, with a zero-cost software option and compatibility across major platforms, it provided a very easy way for small companies (and now larger companies) to become Web-enabled. Apache, with an add-on module, is able to manage SSL connections. Generally, administrators of Apache require highly technical skills as most certificate-related operations are command-line operations (although there are vendors providing variations on this with a GUI, but the original software does not have a GUI built in).

Microsoft IIS

Microsoft's IIS Web server trails Apache with about 20 percent of the Web server market. It is vastly different from Apache in its approach because, unlike the mass contributions and evolution of Apache, updates constantly are available because there are enough bugs and security issues to warrant them (or as determined by Microsoft). One key advantage IIS has had since its earliest versions is that it has a (relatively) nice GUI interface. This makes some functions, such as installing server certificates, a little easier.

Hardware (Appliance) Web Servers

The popularity of these servers, even for large corporations, is that they are built to fit into data centers and simplify the job of configuration. According to Dataquest ("Forecast and Analysis of the Appliance Server Market, 2000–2005," IDC, 2001) nearly 37 percent of medium-sized to large businesses are using appliance servers (generically, not just Web servers). Nearly 55 percent of companies surveyed said that they use appliances for Web server functions.

Sun Cobalt

Sun Microsystems got a jump on the low-end server appliance market through its purchase of Cobalt Networks. Essentially a hardened box based on Linux, the server provides standard Web functionality including the ability to use FrontPage extensions. As for security, the box accepts SSL connections and provides various security user name/password combinations for user and administrator access.

Net Integrator

Net Integrator uses the Mark server line of products to provide an all-in-one solution combining features such as VPNs and Web servers in one box. SSL support for 128-bit certificates is provided, along with additional modules that can supply virus-scanning features. It also includes a CA generator to use self-signed certificates for testing or to create a private hierarchy.

UVNetworks WebBox

One of the few appliances based on something other than Intel, the UVNetworks WebBox appliance has a Sun Microsystems–based hardware platform. Like other appliances, it provides SSL support (up to 128 bits). In addition, the box features a mail server and FTP servers. Generally, the target audience for this box is ISPs/ASPs because this machine was built for bandwidth and scalability.

Smart Cards

Smart cards are computer chips in a credit card–like form. Applications for smart cards can range from simple data storage (like a certificate) to complex transactions involving cashless financial transactions. There are quite a number of players in this space, with a number of complex pieces to make the use of smart cards possible.

In this section, we will focus on those vendors that can provide smart cards in relation to a specific trust-related transaction (as opposed to just card manufacturers). In some sense, for low-end smart cards, we are basically looking at the storage of key data as similar to the private key for a digital certificate. This can then serve two main purposes:

- Increased security because the smart card (and thus the private key) can be physically removed and locked separately from the computer

- Increased mobility for the private key, which would allow some roaming capability for the user

In addition, there are many types of smart cards, which will determine the functionality and applications for which the card could be used. For the purposes of brevity, we cover companies that can provide a range of features and applications, without going into the specifics.

Here are the key features to look for when researching smart-card solutions (there are many more parameters, but these are the highlights):

Price.   Costs range from less than $1 for memory-type smart cards (in other words, they just hold data) to $15 for more sophisticated cards. Readers and software applications will be extra.

Storage capacity.   Depending on the type of smart cards, the low-end cards can hold, for example, two or three digital certificates, whereas the high-end cards can hold more than 128K of data.

Security.   Some readers have PIN keyboards built into them, which prevents any software Trojan program from reading the user's PIN as he or she enters it to unlock the smart card to access the information. Low-end memory cards and readers usually do not have this level of security. Almost all cards are tamper evident.

Gemplus

One of the largest smart-card vendors, Gemplus, offers a range of cards and readers. Gemplus has integrated with the Computer Associates eTrust PKI system to allow multiple uses and stronger authentication from a single card.

Schlumberger

Schlumberger targets PKI applications with its CryptoFlex card line of products. The cards can hold up to 32K of information, with the ability to generate up to 2048 bits for an RSA public/private key pair generation. Commands to the card can be restricted as per the security policy set by the user. The card is FIPS 140-1 Level 2 certified, making it useful for most secure applications.

Data Storage Protection

With the rise of storage area networks and other forms of electronic archiving, data needs to be stored in a safe, protected manner. This applies not only to the corporate servers and infrastructure, but also to the client desktop. If a laptop, for example, is stolen, the loss is mitigated if the entire hard drive remains encrypted without the presentation of some type of external authentication device. Likewise for the enterprise, a storage area network (SAN) is more secure, especially during the backup process (where data may be sent to a third party off-site).

There are two key areas in which PKI trust solutions can be applied to SANs:

Fabric-to-fabric security.   This refers to authenticating the switch's identity before allowing it into a SAN.

Management-to-fabric security.   This refers to protecting data from an administrator's console to the SAN components. PKI technology is used to provide encryption as well as authentication of the management console commands.

Brocade

An industry leader, Brocade has designed security into many of its platforms through what it calls a Secure Fabric OS. Security solutions are built around the ability of each component in the SAN to be able to communicate securely with each other and provide sufficient authentication to avoid rogue components from joining the system. The key areas of this security concept include switch connection controls. This allows the administration device to determine when a valid member of the SAN is brought online. Each switch is given a digital certificate at the time of manufacture, and it is this certificate that the SAN administration hardware and software check to determine if that switch is authorized (based on access control lists) to be part of the network. By using digital certificates, the switch name can also be authenticated, and the name maintains integrity.

In addition, through what is called "secure management communications," certificates can be used to encrypt (administrative) data traffic between components. For example, administrator logins can be secured over the network. Interestingly enough, Brocade is one of the few companies that emphasize security to the extent it has, relative to other leaders like Veritas.

Veritas

Veritas holds the majority share for the market in the SAN arena so it had to be mentioned here, but it is far from providing a trusted solution. Interestingly, security does not seem to play a (visible) role in its solutions. One specific component, called Netbackup Encryption, claims to use only 40-bit or 56-bit DES for encryption. Obviously, this is inadequate security because most security applications now use Triple Data Encryption Standard (3DES) or Advanced Encryption Standard (AES). Furthermore, digital certificates are not directly used; therefore, Veritas cannot leverage scalable solutions. Veritas does contain a number of security features, but most rely either on text access files or the operating system's own security features. Kerberos can be used for some of the product lines, but not without specific, additional steps (in other words, this is not built directly into the products). A trusted environment could possibly be added to make up this gap by relying on internal VPN security (in other words, set up internal VPN connections from key components).

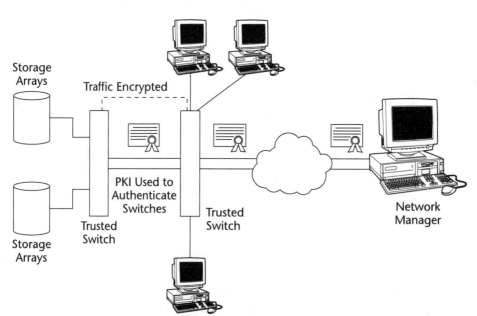

Figure 10.5   Example of the SAN security architecture.

Web Portals

Portals are becoming quite popular as a method of consolidating disparate information. Whether they are intranet, extranet, or Internet portals, security is a big factor in determining how useful a portal becomes. Portal creation and management usually happens (at least in most large enterprises) through portal management software.

Generally, the two areas of trust solution applications are the authentication of the individual users accessing the portal and the encryption of the data that flows from the server to the client. These applications are very similar to standard SSL and client authentication mechanisms for other applications. The main difference is that the portal system must be able to display customized information based on the certificate contents. This requires the portal vendor to authenticate the certificate and then extract information.

One important note is that many PKI vendors are providing secure portals or similar concepts. In reality, this is just a pre-integration with portal vendors. Whether the solution is purchased from the PKI vendor or the portal vendor, PKI becomes an integral factor in improving efficiencies and security.

Plumtree

Plumtree has focused on the portal market with variances for various verticals. By working with RSA Data Security, Inc. Plumtree provides access to SSO capability through RSA's ClearTrust software suite. Essentially users are authenticated with digital certificates, and information about the user's access is stored in an LDAP directory that is accessed securely (via SSL). Other PKI trust solution partners include Netegrity, which can also be integrated with Plumtree to provide even more robust and scalable SSO capability.

Hummingbird

As another major player in the Web portal space, Hummingbird's security is primarily focused on SSL protection (as relevant to trust solutions). Client-based PKI is not emphasized in the base product, although it could be integrated into its systems. Security is based on role-based access control and document-level (revision) control so that internal users can see various revisions, but end users can see only the final version. Some basic content protection can be extended to protect the document on the end-user side.

B2B

The death of business-to-business (B2B) commerce has been greatly exaggerated. Although dynamic hubs of commerce are no longer being created through simple Internet-based models, there is a clear need for B2B solutions.

Security is perhaps a central aspect of these solutions, given that these systems allow the trade of physical goods or initiate large financial transactions.

Cyclone Commerce

Cyclone Commerce essentially provides solutions for what it calls trading communities. Essentially, this concept is similar to a supply chain management community or a value chain vendor management concept. By providing a vehicle for document exchange, customers can migrate from legacy systems, like EDI, to leverage the advantages of the Internet or use multiple systems and formats in parallel. One of the early adopters of XKMS, Cyclone Commerce has developed support for digital certificates as an embedded concept in its suite of products. Certificates are used to authenticate the parties of transactions and to maintain security throughout the transactions. In addition, its solutions provide the ability to track specific documents with a digital receipt/audit trail concept to create a nonrepuditable log of transactions.

webMethods

webMethods started as a Web services company that created solutions for Web services applications. One of the applications is an adaptor to its base integration suite that allows EDI and similar B2B transactions. Security is managed via XKMS, which webMethods helped create as a standard. As with other vendors in this field, security is a key element in a successful solution.

SET

Secure Electronic Transaction (SET) is a protocol designed in collaboration with a number of different companies, including Visa and MasterCard. SET was designed to create a transactional model in which electronic transactions using secure payment cards could be conducted over the Internet. SET relies on digital certificates to create a chain of trust between merchants, the banks, and the consumer.

IBM

Given that IBM contributed to the SET protocol design, it has a number of SET-enabled solutions. These solutions include a consumer wallet, a payment registry, a payment (gateway) server, and a payment manager. Each component in IBM's SET product line adds the ability to leverage the SET protocol. Through the combination of these products, customers can process payments through the ACH (automated clearing house), integrate with CRP and ERP applications, and capture certain buyer payment information for financial routing.

VeriFone

VeriFone, a division of Hewlett-Packard, has been long involved in payment processing and related businesses. It offers its "vPOS" product suite, which has been designed to provide merchants with (among other things) a SET-enabled transaction platform. The system works directly with the merchant's bank to provide transaction information. In addition, the software platform also provides interoperability with SSL for transport security.

Summary: The Answer Is ... Solutions!

In this chapter we have seen a wide range of PKI-enabled trust solutions. Some of these solutions are an absolute necessity for production functions, while others improve business efficiencies and allow us to offer new services. Although it may be perceived that PKI is a complex, unusable technology, we have shown many areas that currently continue to utilize PKI as an underlying infrastructure to build trust. When you think about PKI, most likely you are thinking about a particular solution that uses PKI. Pick the solution first, and the rest will fall into place.

CHAPTER 11

The Future of PKI

Will security go the way of Enterprise Resource Planning (ERP)? Although security services and products have become increasingly sophisticated, the need for security has been clearly established through numerous, highly visible security incidents. Furthermore, many studies support the importance of security and show that organizations are going to continue to spend money on security. Even during the economic and geo-political turmoil of the past year (2002), a J.P. Morgan/*Computerworld* survey found that IT security would be expected to grow to more than 10 percent of the overall enterprise IT spending for 2002. In addition, a 2002 Ernst and Young study showed that 51 percent of survey respondents found that IT security was a top priority relative to other IT projects. It also showed that 70 percent found that the complexity and challenge of more sophisticated threats increased the need and awareness for IT security in an enterprise. Overall, J.P. Morgan believes that IT security will grow to a $38 billion business by 2006.

PKI will clearly benefit from the increased spending in security as it is a significant subset of the overall security market. In addition to playing a vital role in defending enterprises from security threats, PKI also promotes growth of new services through increased confidence in online transactions. PKI has been based on fundamentally sound infrastructure that has been tested over many years. Yet even PKI has evolved and will continue to evolve. Some trends have developed to adapt PKI to various changes in technology, such as the emergence and popularity of mobile devices. Other trends include the advancement of security tools and increased compliance regulations.

Many of these trends have moved PKI vendors to develop seamless PKI solutions to accommodate the range of applications now relying on PKI. In the past, most PKIs required custom integration whether or not they were outsourced. Because most of the integration occurs on the application side, many application vendors are pushing back on PKI vendors for easier, simpler integration tools. We will look at integration in this chapter and the other key trends affecting PKI and its related components.

The Future of Mobile Security in PKI

In September 2000, Gartner Group claimed that by 2003 there would be more wireless devices than Internet-connected PCs (S. Hayward et al., "Beyond the Internet: The Supranet," Gartner Group, 11 September 2000). That has more or less become the case in certain key markets, especially in parts of Europe and Asia and to a lesser extent in the United States. Given that mobile devices are more accessible than desktop PCs, trust of transactions on those devices becomes increasingly important. For example, numerous services now exist to help aggregate a consumer's personal information, such as financial statements. In this manner, companies like Yodlee provide a single portal combining a person's financial information, such as bank statements, brokerage statements, and retirement statements, on a single site to give a real-time view of the individual's net worth. One aspect of this aggregation service is the ability to access this information from a mobile device, such as a mobile phone. Hence, with such services, it is critical to be able to provide a measure of security to increase the confidence and trust users have with the systems.

Currently mobile devices solve the problem of trust by implementing a wireless public key infrastructure (WPKI). In this manner, a CA can remain anywhere on the Internet, but the RA must communicate via this portal to issue certificates to the mobile device. (For more information on this topic, see *mCommerce Security: A Beginner's Guide,* Raina et al., McGraw-Hill, 2002).

There are numerous challenges to WPKI, including the difficulty in managing revocation and the problem of translation between the wired Internet CA and the WAP client through the WPKI portal. This translation creates a temporary security risk (because data must be unencrypted for a short period of time at the portal) called the Gap in WAP, as shown in Figure 11.1. As a result, adoption of PKI in the mobile space will remain relatively low.

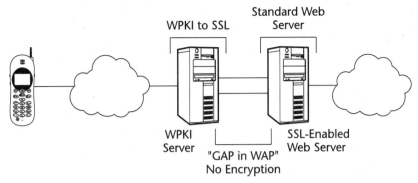

Figure 11.1 Gap in WAP security risk.

Trends in this area include the use of new cryptography to resolve some of the issues of the standard 3DES or the new AES on mobile devices. Generally, mobile devices have much less memory and computing power than standard computers; as a result, a more efficient and smaller footprint algorithm is required. We are beginning to see an uptake in the use of elliptical curve cryptography (ECC), which has been designed specifically for low-footprint devices such as mobile devices. Through ECC, small devices can generate and request certificates directly. This will spur increased adoption of PKI in mobile devices, especially for client certificates.

Mobile VPNs

Just as VPNs have become essential for most organizations' remote access purposes, the need is similar for mobile devices because VPNs are becoming increasingly important for the wireless world. Back in 2000, solutions for mobile devices were beginning to hit the market. Most of the solutions still do not use digital certificates. Many use cryptography to create an encrypted tunnel, but without the use of certificates. Encrypted tunnels can be thought of as point-to-point, encrypted data streams. Without the use of certificates, these tunnels use a symmetric key to create the encrypted tunnel. If mobile devices will exist in greater numbers than desktop PCs, then it will be very difficult to manage such numbers of mobile devices for an organization's VPN. Most likely, trends will lean toward incorporating digital certificates and PKI as part of a standard VPN deployment, regardless of whether the clients are desktop PCs or mobile devices such as PDAs. In addition, as mobile devices become more powerful and memory becomes cheaper, issues with PKI on mobile platforms will ease.

Other trends, perhaps in the more distant future, are always-on mobile devices, as might be envisioned for Third-Generation (3G) networks, or even wearable computing devices. Much like the situation with broadband and desktop PCs, 3G and wearable devices will become a convenience and result in increased security risks. We will also see the emergence of micro-VPNs, with clients designed for very small devices protecting them from the always-on exposure to the Internet or other networks. PKI, though, may take a back seat in this evolution and perhaps give way to simple symmetric encryption to provide point-to-point encryption. Eventually, mobile devices will be able to handle the requirements of PKI on such platforms, but until then the adoption of PKI in these micro devices will remain a distant future.

Lessening the Pain

We have seen throughout this book that solutions integrated with and built on PKI are very efficient. This concept of solutions building is an increasingly popular trend that has required many companies to build strong partnerships and indirect channels for distribution.

Trends in Integration

From a technical perspective, integration for trust solutions with PKI has been very difficult and painful. Propriety and costly tool kits, intricate specifications, and varying quality of SDK tool kits from vendor to vendor have made integration with PKI very difficult. Newer technologies and trends are making this process much simpler. Figure 11.2 shows a functional diagram of PKI integration.

One casualty of recent economic turmoil has been the reduction of strong developer programs. Currently, many developer programs have been cut back or are charging hefty royalty or support fees for tool kit integration. Developer programs, when implemented effectively, provide efficient methods of support for developers who are tasked with integration efforts. Most vendors provide free tool kits that allow application developers to leverage the PKI and build PKI functionality into the application. Because infrastructure vendors rely on applications to sell the need for the infrastructure, developer programs are needed to support and grow the number of applications.

In order to remove the complexity of PKI from the application and solution vendors as well as the customers, one key technology, XKMS (as discussed in previous chapters), has emerged to ease the pain of PKI integration. XKMS reduces the effort for application vendors and thus, in theory, accelerates the number of PKI-enabled applications available.

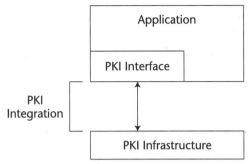

Figure 11.2   Functional diagram of PKI integration.

Solution Building

A direct sales model in which a company is sold various security technologies and services is becoming a less common sales approach. Due to reduced budgets and other economic realities, customers want streamlined, integrated solutions. These types of solutions help reduce consulting and other deployment costs. In addition, the more integrated an application with PKI, the better the rate of return.

Examples of this solution-building concept can be seen in applications such as form signing and VPNs. Form-signing applications are increasingly being created to be compatible with PKI out of the box. In addition, VPN vendors are looking to bundle certificates with their solutions.

One of the challenges with solution building is the need for all the various bundled components to be pretested before being delivered to the customer. As a result, certification and similar interoperability programs are required for all PKI-related trust solutions. Increasingly, companies are relying on these certifications as a way to reassure the customer that the solution bundle, in fact, works as claimed.

Consolidation of the Security Market

Given that the security market is still relatively nascent, most analysts fully expect the market to consolidate into a few strong vendors. One line of thinking is that all security vendors will eventually roll into a few large vendors, such as IBM. Another line of thinking is that given the complexity of the various security technologies, each niche area of technology will retain a few market leaders. The challenge in either market scenario is that security is a technology that, by definition, must change and grow rapidly to react to or proactively prevent security breaches. Given the rate of change in the security market, it is not possible to compare it with other established industries to gauge how the market might evolve.

Survey of the Security Market

To better understand how the trends may lead technology companies, it is important to understand the various types of security companies. We can divide security companies into two main groups:

- Operational security companies
- Functional security companies

Operational security refers to those security solutions that are required for organizations to function by defending against debilitating attacks. These solutions are for immediate and usually short-term tactical purposes. Functional security refers to those security solutions that are designed for defense in the longer term as well as to help advance functionality. The following sections go into the major security categories in which PKI is generally employed:

- Encryption
- Authentication
- Authorization
- Administration
- Firewalls and VPNs
- Operational integrity

Encryption

Companies in this space deal with the protection of data in storage or in transit. Some solutions are meant for easy setup and deployment through the use of appliances. Other solutions provide secure transmission links between sites.

Trends in encryption technology are very slow to appear. Recently the introduction and acceptance of Advanced Encryption Standard (AES) by the National Institute of Standards and Technology (NIST) has proven to be one of the few major changes in cryptography in a number of years. Currently, some vendors are utilizing this change-over from 3DES to AES as a competitive offering. Because vendors must redesign their products to take advantage of this new cryptography standard, it takes quite some time.

More and more products are building in encryption as a standard feature. For example, Microsoft has come a long way by including more robust capability for managing PKI and utilizing it for encryption. In fact, most of the PKI vendors have built encryption into applications to enhance their offerings.

Other trends include the dominance of the x.509 v3 standard. In 2002, Network Associates dropped support for the PGP encryption technology, which competed with traditional PKI vendors. PGP essentially used the concept of a web of trust, which worked well for smaller groups but not for large audiences. The primary uses of PGP have been secure email and file encryption (for local file storage). Although PGP, in its later stages, did have the concept of a certificate, it never gained popularity in the corporate sector. There are still a large number of PGP users in the market, but the future of PGP as an accepted corporate solution remains in doubt.

Authentication

This security niche can be broken down into several categories including the following:

- PKI vendors
- Smart cards
- Biometrics
- Tokens

PKI vendors have already dwindled to a few companies. This space will almost certainly be dominated by only one or two main competitors. One note is that depending on the geography, PKI vendors have different strengths. Very few players in this space have managed to gain a worldwide dominance. It is critical to watch developments on a macro level and may require some organizations to use different PKI vendors across their departments around the globe.

Eventually authentication will become an integral component of most services. Does this mean PKI vendors will become a commodity? As long as the chain of trust in a transaction requires identity vetting, probably not. Certain aspects, such as device authentication or Web server authentication, will become increasingly commoditized.

Trends in this space include a breaking of branding. That is to say that trust, while important, seems to be less important in more mature areas like the SSL certificates. In addition, as legal recourses catch up with evolving technologies, standard laws can assist in defense of fraudulent cases and, thus, not rely solely on technology. Currently, CAs and related trust brokers provide much of the protection against fraud and theft. Other trends include the increased use of appliances and pre-integrated solutions. Examples include an eroding market share for the SSL certificate leader, VeriSign, Inc. VeriSign, through its acquisitions, at one point commanded more than 95 percent of the SSL certificate market. By mid 2002, its share had eroded to about 85 percent. Its primary competitor that led to its share erosion was Geotrust. Essentially, Geotrust realized that not all consumers value the model of trust built into the SSL

certificate issuance process, which VeriSign had developed. As a result, cost-
(and time-) conscious consumers fled to cheaper alternatives like Geotrust. On
the other hand, VeriSign has developed a high-quality vetting process that
provides a strong amount of trust in the issuance process. The "trust" in
branding, though, has definitely given rise to cost efficiencies.

Biometrics, another space within authentication, has quickly heated up with
recent geo-political events, leaning toward tighter security and more individual profiling and tracking. For example, in London, cameras observe almost
every person and vehicle that travels in and out of the city. Some of these cameras are tied to crime databases that flag suspects or stolen vehicles through
the use of computer and biometric technology known as face recognition.
Other examples include the use of face recognition software in U.S. casinos to
scan for known cheats who try to re-enter the casinos. Facial recognition software compares every casino guest to a known database of suspects and alerts
security immediately when a suspect is identified.

The most common trend in biometrics is the decrease in the value of the
device as the most important component to the database. There is an increasing value being put on the authentication and authorization software suite.
Biometric devices are becoming commodities, and prices have been driven
down significantly. Integrated devices, such as fingerprint scanners in keyboards, have made the devices extremely useful. By the ease and cheapness of
such devices, we have a good fit to protect the private key in PKI and increase
the utility and security of PKI.

Smart cards as a security space have proven overall to be relatively weak,
especially in North American markets. The need for the cards to be physically
generated, the storage of certificates, and the device readers all produce significant obstacles for smart cards. Although the market is becoming more open
to smart cards, the relatively high cost of their use management makes them
still a niche product. In European markets, smart cards have been much more
successful. Although the use of PKI and smart cards in Europe is still only in
the beginning phases, national ID projects involving smart cards issued to citizens and digital certificates are definitely on the rise in Asia.

Finally, the last area of authentication security vendors is the token market.
Tokens are essentially single-purpose devices used for either authentication or
very small amounts of storage. Tokens can provide simple and cheap roaming
solutions by allowing the user to carry the token around and use it at whatever
terminal he or she is able to access. Tokens, like biometric devices, have
increasingly become commodities. Like biometric devices, the increasingly
valuable area is the management software for tokens. As a separate industry,
tokens will eventually fade. Tokens will become a standard offering as part of
larger company offerings.

Authorization

PKI provides a good platform for making policy decisions for the roles of users and devices on particular resources. Can organizations make these decisions without PKI? Yes, by the use of alternative authentication methods, including user names and passwords. Given the poor security that user names and passwords provide, PKI is clearly a strong choice for the protection of digital credentials. As a result, many vendors in the authorization space have integration or hooks to allow PKI vendors to interoperate with the authorization vendor products.

The authorization market, due to the large number of choices, has become saturated. Numerous companies from IBM to smaller companies like Netegrity have large, established product offerings. The challenge in this space is that most of these authorization systems tend to require large deployments and cost hundreds of thousands of dollars or more. As a result, authorization system sales are much slower than many other security technologies. PKI can use Lightweight Directory Access Protocol (LDAP) systems for the setup of authorization with that technology. Although LDAP does not provide the robustness of a full-featured authorization system, it is a good, cheaper alternative.

Eventually, the number of players in the authorization space will most likely dwindle to a handful of key market drivers. Most PKI vendors are getting directly into this game through their mergers and acquisitions or partnership strategies. After all, if a PKI is being deployed for a large corporation, authorization and access control will be a major aspect of the project. For example, Entrust purchased enCommerce for increased authentication offerings. VeriSign created a specific, integration solution with IBM's access management technology called Tivoli.

Administration

Given the complexity and management issues of dealing with various network devices as well as various security components, a market for security administration software remains strong. Like authorization software vendors, this market is dominated by a few large players, such as BMC Software and Computer Associates. An aspect of this area includes the concept of provisioning, which is simply the ability to add (or delete, as in the case of deprovisioning) users to various, disparate systems. Examples include adding new employees in Human Resources, badging (in other words, the issuance of physical credentials that identify employees visually and electronically), and network access systems. PKI is simply an aspect of that provisioning process. In the case of a new employee, the provisioning system would add that employee's information to a trusted database that the PKI system would use to determine the eligibility and level of certificate that employee should be given.

Again, it would be possible for an organization to provision or deprovision users manually. In tight budgets, a provisioning system would most likely be passed over for more pressing IT expenditures. Relying on LDAP, for example, PKI systems would need to have their entries updated via other trusted databases, such as the Human Resources database, or perhaps even manually updated. Most middleware software is being built out-of-the-box with hooks for integration with various administration software, such as entitlement software. Players in this space include Netegrity, Oblix, and IBM (Tivoli).

Firewalls and VPNs

Of all the security technologies, firewalls and VPNs are perhaps the most mature. Margins on pure firewall software can be as low as 10 percent for some resellers because of competition and market saturation. As a result, many companies treat firewalls as a commodity, or loss leader, that triggers increased revenue from consulting and training services associated with those firewall and VPN sales. Advances and trends in firewalls tend to lean toward multifunctional purposes, such as firewalls combined with virus scanners at the server level. Checkpoint Technologies, Inc., for example, has leveraged its desktop client to provide local PC protection through server-forced policies that protect the desktop from outsiders (for example, other computers connecting to other computers on the same network without specific authorization).

VPNs have taken the route of developing server appliances to keep deployment time and costs to a minimum. As a result, numerous players in this space have driven down the cost of VPNs dramatically. Although costs can still be high as a result of configurations, such as high availability, VPNs have become well understood, and the skill sets for VPN architecture and deployment have become readily available. VPN vendors have become increasingly sophisticated about technologies like PKI. Given the large acceptance and deployment of VPNs, vendors realize that management of VPNs is dependent on PKI. As a result, many vendors offer IPSec certificates with the VPN products.

Another upcoming trend is the area called Instant Virtual Extranets (IVEs). IVEs are positioned to replace VPNs by providing reduced functionality in exchange for reduced costs. IVEs are preconfigured, customized software systems built on hardened (usually) Linux machines that allow access to email, network file systems, and secure terminal access. The end user uses his or her browser to connect to the IVE hardware and through the browser conducts all his or her activities. IVEs will most likely be a transitional technology, giving organizations that may suffer during the economic downturn a cheaper alternative to VPNs. Because IVEs do not allow full VPN/IP-level functionality, they will not serve the need of very large organizations.

IVEs use PKI in two main ways:

- To ensure that a secure channel is created between the client and IVE Web server using SSL certificates.

- To authenticate the user to the IVE using client certificates (as opposed to using user names and passwords).

Operational Integrity

Operational integrity components include devices such as intrusion detection systems (IDS), distributed denial of service (DDOS) protection, and anti-virus software. DDOS is still a relatively new area for the security market because an increase in DDOS attacks has occurred only within the last few years. As a result, emerging companies have begun to produce solutions for this very specific problem.

Related to DDOS is the maturing IDS market. IDSs have been developed to detect and counter intrusions from hackers. Earlier versions of IDSs simply detected attacks. More recent IDS technologies provide counterattack capability. Due to legal implications, counterattack capability will most often be used in military applications.

One challenge that remains in almost all devices, but especially in IDS and DOS/DDOS devices, is the huge quantity of log files that can be generated. One of the weakest areas in operational integrity is the ability to sort and understand log files. Network management of various security devices that are able to quickly understand and report patterns and help make decisions is the area in which we will most likely see large gains in the near future.

OPERATIONAL INTEGRITY TOOLS: TRENDY SOLUTIONS

There is quite a bit of buzz about some new tools to help companies combat security risks. Some of the newer technologies in this area include defenses against DDOS and more advanced viruses. Some newer companies to watch for in the DOS/DDOS space include Arbor Networks, Asta Networks, Captus, Deep Nines, Forescout, Gillian, Mazu Networks, Niksun, and TopLayer. Also watch for a consolidation in the firewall/VPN arena, with an increased focus on performance, especially in the high-end bandwidth sector. Cisco, for example, came out with high-performance IDS solutions as early as mid-2002.

Companies will also be attempting to address the wireless space and create operational integrity tools for that space. Checkpoint, for example, launched its OPSEC wireless initiative in 2002. Other emerging companies are developing their own specific wireless defense tools.

Other trends include the development of chips and chip sets to increase performance for IDS, DOS, and DDOS systems. Moving from software-based solutions to hardware-based solutions will move these security components into, essentially, plug-and-play appliances in every organization's network data center.

Only the Strong Will Survive

In an extended economic downturn, many organizations will prioritize spending based on need. This naturally favors operational security because that is the bare minimum necessary to sustain operations. The challenge is that most security companies that focus on operational security tend to be relatively small.

As security technologies mature, most technologies will move from software to hardware. Because technologies such as firewalls, VPNs, and IDS are part of wireline aspects of a network (that is, monitoring all traffic coming across a network line), speed is very important. As a result, hardware will perform these tasks more cost-effectively and more securely.

One-Stop Shopping

Some security industry analysts have observed that customers are increasingly leaning toward a one-stop shopping concept for security services. This is backed by a host of merger and acquistion activities from 2000 to 2002 of smaller security companies by larger industry leaders, as shown in Figure 11.3. The nature of the security services demands stable, trustworthy companies. In addition, the complexity and integration required for effective security planning requires many different areas of security technology. As a result, an organization would have to interface with many different, specialty security companies to complete a thorough security plan.

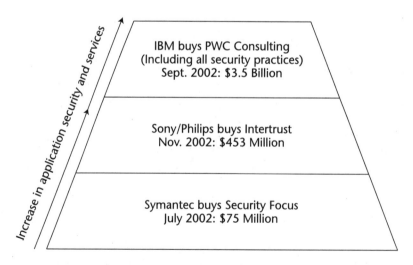

Figure 11.3   Examples of security acquisitions.

Is it advisable to choose best-of-breed solution vendors and assemble a portfolio of solutions? Or is it advisable to simplify the process with a single company? Companies must consider several factors before choosing a vendor:

- Does your organization have IT project management staff? (If you are using multiple security vendors, then it is important to coordinate various activities.)

- Does your organization have access to research or analyst reports about security companies? (Without impartial, expert information, it will be difficult to determine which companies are best of breed and, more importantly, stable and reliable.)

- Does your organization have the skills to understand and filter through the various RFPs and the claims that vendors make? (Without proper skills, it will be difficult to determine good vendors from bad vendors until after an implementation has occurred.)

- Can your organization quickly adapt if a vendor goes out of business or is otherwise merged or acquired by another company? (Because the security field is still relatively new and emerging, constant changes in the landscape will affect how technology develops.)

One emerging trend with the development of one-stop shopping is the decrease in choices of solutions. Given that security technologies are fairly complex to integrate, combining all components under fewer vendors simplifies interoperability. Although the market is not quite at a stage where a single company can possibly dominate the space in a Microsoft-esque monopoly, companies like IBM are developing the sheer size to corner the security market. An example of IBM's growth is its partnership with VeriSign in 2002, which created an interesting development in the PKI market. IBM essentially dropped its PKI line and gave its customers to VeriSign. IBM realized it could not easily retain its dominance in such a complex area. In exchange, VeriSign gave up significant consulting revenue to IBM. In this manner, IBM remained the lead firm that gathered clients and projects, and it subcontracted to VeriSign for PKI projects.

Another related example was IBM's acquisition of PriceWaterhouse's (PWC) consulting group in August 2002. This allowed IBM to gain several thousand security consultants who focused on various aspects of the security life cycle, including design, implementation, and crisis management (for example, incident response to a security breach). Even though IBM could have easily pushed its own PKI solution just because of its sheer size, it chose another (relatively) smaller, focused vendor (VeriSign) to manage this service. Furthermore, it put the PWC's beTrusted PKI service into decline after the acquisition because IBM had already decided to exit the core PKI market.

SURVIVAL STATS

IDC, a leading technology analysis firm, expects the network security market to grow to about $8 billion by the end of 2003. Investment firm 3i and the Economist Intelligence Unit give a more controversial perspective ("e-security — 2002 and beyond," a 3i white paper in association with the Economist Intelligence Unit, , January 2002). They suggested that 80 percent of the security market will be owned by about five or fewer known brands by 2005. The same study showed that about 47 percent of the survey respondents felt that security complexity and interoperability will be the biggest issues facing corporate customers by 2005.

These study results indicate a consolidation of point solutions into either managed service providers or one-stop shop companies. Initially many top brands will not be able to achieve efficient acquisition strategies because the security market is still relatively nascent. As deployment and experience increase, we most likely will see the previously mentioned statistics come to fruition. In addition, the skill set required in the computer security field is still scarce. Over time, however, network security skills will become less of a requirement as computer and network vendors improve their built-in security (or develop a prevalence of security skills among their network administrators).

Given that most security technologies need to work together (for example, firewalls and DDOS systems), a clearly growing trend is for the deployment of security management consoles. Security management systems will evolve in a similar fashion as network management systems, which now allow networks to scale and yet retain high levels of reliability and flexibility. We will see emerging companies with security management software; at the same time, traditional network management software companies will add security monitoring capability.

PKI Is Only Part of the Solution

As we have seen throughout this book, PKI is only one aspect of a secure and efficient infrastructure. Emerging trends in PKI will not change the need for strong defensive and proactive security measures. To enhance the security of PKI solutions, some outsourced PKI vendors will most likely develop security appliance approaches to PKI deployment. Because the security appliance would be hardened, it would also simplify the process of securing the platform on which the PKI would be hosted. An appliance model for a PKI solution would take one of two forms: either a gateway appliance that would provide the customization options necessary for an outsourced model or an insourced option that would include the entire PKI software and hardware suite.

The challenge for PKI vendors in producing an appliance is more of a business rather than a technical issue. Insourced PKI vendors create substantial revenues from deployment, consulting, and training of their solutions. Outsourced PKI vendors gain from complex customizations and training. An appliance model would essentially remove a number of these revenue streams. Appliances would greatly benefit the customer because the PKI vendor could configure the device before shipping it or configure the device remotely as per security policies. In addition, deployment would be simplified due to the fact that the appliance would be interoperable and tested.

Need for Good Security Policies

Another recurring theme we have seen throughout this book has been the need for good security policies. Good security policies provide the communication and legal strength to ensure that PKI can be implemented and legally enforced. Although security policies have been developed over time and tried and tested, policies must change with the times.

Some emerging trends we will see in security policies include the following:

Dynamic policy deployment. This forces policies onto desktops or portable devices from a central policy server. Many network systems already have procssess for delivering policies for access control. In the future, we will see many more policies focused on security at the desktop. An example is Checkpoint's NG VPN client, which forces the security policy from a central policy server onto the desktop.

Policy compliance systems. These are systems that monitor, enforce, and report compliance. For example, a centrally managed system would check all major applications, such as the HR system, to ensure that certain privacy laws, for example, were followed in the collection of resumes for job openings.

Liability shifts in policy to end users. With the advance of technology to protect private keys for certificates and other systems like biometrics that uniquely identify a user, we will see an increase in liability for the end user. Liability in the form of usage policies, for example, would put the burden of lost or stolen identities on the end user.

How do good auto-compliance solutions leverage PKI? Clearly, during the audit and compliance monitoring process, a great deal of sensitive data gets passed between compliance modules and a central storage database. In general, compliance systems will require specific application plug-ins or adaptors. These adaptors will be able to translate the defined policy into technical requirements that need to be followed. Most organizations have their applications on various systems and, perhaps, even in different geographic locations.

As a result, the transmission of data between adaptors and a central storage system will require encryption. In addition, to prevent spoofing from a rogue adaptor, authentication for each adaptor will be required to ensure that data does not get passed to an imposter.

The key success criteria for these auto-compliance solutions will be the initial definition of the compliance rules. Generally, we will see subscription-based services that provide for a basic set of compliance rules that are localized based on regional variations. Corporations can then add their own sets of compliance information.

Strong Audit Capability

Related to the strong compliance systems mentioned previously, increased audit capability will improve legal and technical analysis for compliance with corporate and governmental guidelines. In areas like IDS and firewalls, we will see an increase in management tools to help combine network and security logs for auditing purposes. In addition, new notarization services for transactions, such as digital notarization services from VeriSign, will allow more secure audit trails to be created, enhancing confidence in online transactions.

PKI will take a key role in helping develop legally binding audit trails. With a digital certificate, audit records can automatically be digitally signed and, therefore, treated as legal evidence. Audits can be used for consumer applications, such as digital receipts in online transactions. Audits can also be used for internal audit records, such as system logs or administrator access logs. Eventually insurance and liability companies will rely on strong audits to decrease the costs associated with fraud and hacking incidents. With PKI, an unalterable log file could be produced to resolve internal breaches or consumer disputes for online commerce.

Good Physical Security

Due to the threat of increased terrorism, physical security has taken on a new meaning. Trends in physical security include tying personal information to logical information (as in biometrics). Given the decreasing cost of security devices and cheap communication through the Internet, trends such as Internet-capable cameras have become increasingly common. The challenge that has arisen is how to secure communication between these devices and the Internet clients. For example, some baby-sitting services have Internet-capable cameras and a Web site where parents can go to see their children. Most of these services use user names and passwords, which could be easily guessed or otherwise stolen. Such a breach would compromise the privacy of the parents and their children and possibly put them at risk. The use of device authentication to tie that specific camera with encrypted images to a back-end service would provide increased security. In addition, greater security to identify the end user will be required in the future as the need for security becomes recognized.

The outsourcing trend seems to be declining. Most vendors with an out-sourced version of a product now also have a stand-alone, in-house version. The shift in thinking has partly to do with the reliability and security of the outsourced vendors. Over the past few years we have seen large providers such as WorldCom, Exodus, and others simply collapse. This uncertainty around core, critical business infrastructure has forced companies to absorb the additional costs of developing in-house solutions and maintaining their own systems. This will, of course, result in a trend for even outsourced PKI vendors to offer in-house equivalents of their products and services. Some may offer a service model to begin, with the ability to move that service to an in-house model at any time.

Summary: The Growth of PKI

With the rise of security awareness and spending, PKI will clearly benefit. Ven-dors will increase interoperability and embed PKI functionality into various business applications. In addition, as the government catches up with various technology areas, regulations will increase as technology becomes more mature and becomes an increasingly fundamental aspect of daily life. The future looks bright for PKI, and although the "year of PKI" may never arrive, the "decade of PKI" has already begun.

Appendix

The appendix has been designed to give you a quick overview of the range of information mentioned but not covered in detail throughout the book. This guide gives you more sources to further your knowledge and understanding of how PKI can help solve your security and compliance needs. Additional sources can be found on my updated site at www.securitypundit.com.

PKI International Projects

This section gives a brief overview of the efforts around the world to implement PKI and the relevant laws that help bolster its use. Please refer to other sources, including ones listed in this appendix, for further details. Many of these laws change rapidly through amendments and reactions to changes in technology. It is important to note that many of these laws have not been extensively tested in contested digital signature cases as they are still relatively new. Expect that in two to three years, after wider use, these laws will be challenged in transactions that will further shape the digital signatures laws.

Australia

November 25, 2000: Approved electronic signature bill law with action to take place from July 2001.

Gatekeeper model set up and designed to guide development of PKI infrastructure.

Australian Customs has developed a system called the Cargo Management Re-Engineering Project (CMR). CMR was designed to leverage PKI for improving Customs paperwork for import and export of goods.

Austria

Digital signature legislation provides full recognition of secure digital signatures with less (but some) support for insecure digital signature methods.

Bermuda

July 1999: Enacted Electronic Transactions Act of 1999, which provides legal recognition of electronic signatures.

Brazil

Superior Court of Justice will now publish its decisions online with a digital signature affixed to the decision to vouch for its authenticity.

Canada

The city of Toronto provides for the land (in other words, deed) registration documents that can be submitted and maintained electronically with digital signatures. More than 50 percent of the city's land documents have been implemented through this system.

Finland

January 2000: Act on Electronic Service in the Administration. This act defines the scope and structure of the elements of a PKI for digital signatures. Specific exclusions of the act are listed; unlike in other countries, this law excludes the use of digital certificates for the application to administrative judicial procedures.

France

March 13, 2000: Electronic signature law implemented.
July 16, 2002: A decree was issued that required cryptographic service providers to provide authorized (government-recognized) agents the ability to decrypt data on demand. Effectively, this required either an escrow ability for private keys in PKI or a cryptographic system that allowed for a "back-door."

Hong Kong

Hong Kong's government is offering free digital certificates for the first year of its Smart ID card program. The program was designed to build a system that can provide smart cards for all electronic activities requiring authentication for digital transactions.

Italy

The government has passed a regulation that provides for digital signatures in support of the relevant EU directive (93/99/EC). The regulation identifies two types of signatures: a light signature for person identification and access to general public administration services and a more secure signature for digital signatures of electronic documents.

Korea

The Ministry of Information and Communication requires Internet-based banking organizations to use government-issued banking digital certificates. Organizations already using nongovernment-issued certificates will be required to go to government-issued certificates by May 2003.

Malaysia

One of the earlier legislations on digital signatures, Malaysia passed its Digital Signature Act in 1997.

New Zealand

October 2002: Electronic Transactions Bill passed that provides electronic documents and digital signatures on par with physical contracts and signatures.

Singapore

June 1998: Singapore passed its digital signature act called the Electronic Transactions Act 1998 that provides for the legal recognition of digital signatures.

Web Site Sources of PKI Information

This section lists a very brief set of resources for you to continue your exploration of PKI-related technology and news. Nearly all these sites change on a regular basis, so it is important to monitor and update your set of resources continually.

- The PKI Page: www.pki-page.org/

  Although not very descriptive, this Web page does provide a quick scan of major links and vendors in the PKI space. Some of the material is outdated, but it serves as a good jumping point for research.

- PKI Forum: www.pkiforum.org

  Created by an organization designed to foster standards in PKI, this site provides good research on a range of PKI topics. A number of resources are meant for advanced topics and standards and do assume a certain level of knowledge in the world of PKI.

- ABA (American Bar Assocation) Information Security Committee: www.abanet.org/scitech/ec/isc/

  This site provides an excellent resource for legal research for digital signatures for American-based queries. This research can also be used as a basis for understanding non-U.S. legal systems as there are many assessment guidelines that can be generalized and applied with variations to various legal systems.

- PKIX (PKI Working Group committee): www.ietf.org/html.charters/pkix-charter.html

  This is a jump point for understanding and learning more about the PKIX, the group that helps define the technology standards that affect PKI initiatives worldwide.

- HIPAA Information: www.hipaadvisory.com/sitemap/

  This is a good overview site for all aspects of the HIPAA regulations and related technologies. There are many such sites, although this one appears to have a layout that is easy to use and follow. There are some sites, usually affiliated with law firms that deal with HIPAA, that actually do near real-time updates. To ensure that you have the latest information on HIPAA always check various sources, given the regular updates to the HIPAA guidelines by the U.S. government agencies.

- MISMO Information: www.mismo.org/

  This Web site contains information about digital signatures in the mortgage business. Although this site is focused on mortgages, the concepts and challenges discussed here can be applied to other transactions that deal with two parties involved in infrequent transactions (such as a B2B exchange or auction).

- Security Focus: www.securityfocus.com

  Before the buyout of Security Focus by Symantec, this site was a good general resource for security information and tools (it is unclear how the site will develop given the ownership by Symantec). The site tends to be anti-PKI based on articles over the years, but it is good to have all perspectives, whether or not they are accurate.

Definitions of Key Security Terms

This section contains a brief glossary of some terms discussed in this book. This is only a cross section of all the terms you need to understand to grasp all of the technical aspects of PKI. Nonetheless this section will be a good jumpstart.

Asymmetric cryptography   Algorithm that uses different keys for encryption and decryption, and where the decryption key cannot be derived from the encryption key. Public keys are also known as asymmetric cryptography.

Authentication   Verifying the identity of a person or entity.

Biometrics   Technology for measuring and analyzing human body characteristics, such as fingerprints, eye retinas and irises, voice, and hand measurements for human user authentication.

Certificate Authority (CA)   Authority in a network (PKI) that issues and manages digital credentials and public keys.

Certificate Practice Statement (CPS)   A detailed roadmap of how the certificate authority manages the certificates it issues and related services such as key management. The CPS acts as a written understanding between the CA and users, describing the obligations and legal limitations and setting the foundation for future audits.

Certificate Revocation List (CRL)   A list of revoked certificates and the reason for the revocation.

Certification path   Also called the certificate chain. The particular CAs in a PKI that make up the path of trusted signers of the certificates.

Cryptography   The science of creating methods of keeping information protected from unintended recipients.

Data Encryption Standard (DES)   Also called digital certificate. A specially formatted block of data that contains a public key and the name of its owner. The certificate carries the digital signature of a trusted third party in order to authenticate it. The format is most commonly defined by ITU/T X.509.

Digital certificate   A digital credential that is stored and administered in a directory. Although the information in a digital certificate may vary, usually the most basic information includes the identity of the certificate holder and the associated public key.

Digital signature   An electronic signature that authenticates the identity of the holder of the certificate, ensures the original content of the message is unchanged, is easily transportable, cannot be easily repudiated, cannot be imitated, and can be automatically time stamped.

Encryption   Process of enciphering or encoding data so that it is inaccessible to unauthorized users.

Hash   A mathematical summary that can be used to provide message integrity. Due to their fixed, small size, hash functions can be very good checks for message integrity.

Integrity   The preservation of a communication from sender to recipient without alteration of the message.

Internet Protocol Security (IPSec)   A developing standard for security at the network or packet processing layer of network communication. Is especially useful for implementing virtual private networks and remote user access through dial-up connections.

Lightweight Directory Access Protocol (LDAP)   A standard method for accessing and modifying directory information. LDAP is a common standard that is associated with the storage and retrieval of digital certificates.

Nonrepudiation   The basis of insisting that the document signed by a particular private key represents acknowledgment by the private key owner. Depends on the security of the private key.

Online Certificate Status Protocol (OCSP)   Standard for checking, in real time, the validity of digital certificates.

Private key   The private part of a two-part, public key asymmetric cryptography system. The private key is kept secret and known only to the key holder.

Public key   The public part of a two-part, public key asymmetric cryptography system. The public key is provided by a certificate authority and can be retrieved over a network.

Public Key Infrastructure (PKI)   A system that enables users of a public network to exchange data securely and privately through the use of a public and private cryptographic key pair that is obtained and shared through a trusted authority. The architecture includes key management, the registration authority, certificate authority, and various administrative tools.

Public Key Cryptography Standards (PKCS)   Set of standard protocols for allowing secure information exchange on the Internet using a PKI. Standards include RSA encryption, password-based encryption, extended certificate syntax, and cryptographic message syntax for S/MIME.

Registration Authority   The authority in a Public Key Infrastructure that verifies user requests for a digital certificate and tells the certificate authority it is all right to issue a certificate.

Rivest-Shamir-Adleman (RSA)   An algorithm used for key pairs for authentication, encryption, and decryption.

Secret key   Also known as a private key. Is an encryption/decryption key known only to the party or parties that exchange secret messages.

Secure Multipurpose Internet Mail Extensions (S/MIME)   Secure method of sending email that uses the RSA encryption system.

Secure Socket Layer (SSL)   Commonly used protocol for managing the security of a message transmission on the Internet by using a program layer located between the Internet's Hypertext Transfer Protocol (HTTP) and Transport Control Protocol (TCP) layers.

Symmetric cryptography   Uses algorithms that use the same key for encryption and decryption.

Virtual Private Network (VPN)   Private data network that makes use of the public telecommunication infrastructure, maintaining privacy through the use of a tunneling protocol and security procedures.

X.509   Certificate authority standard for the format and content of digital certificates.

Index